The Dalhousie Journals

Edited by Marjory Whitelaw

ISBN 0 88750 290 3

Design by Michael Macklem

Printed in Canada

PUBLISHED IN CANADA BY OBERON PRESS

555 MAPLE LANE,
OTTAWA,
ONT.
KIM ONY

George Ramsay, ninth Earl of Dalhousie, came to Nova Scotia as Lieutenant-Governor in 1816, after a distinguished military career, with honours gained in battle and with the army rank of Lieutenant-General. He was 46.

He was a year younger than both Wellington and Napoleon. The French Revolution broke out in 1789, the year after he joined the army; the long succession of wars with France began in 1793. He commanded his regiment in the West Indies, in Ireland, in Holland, in the 1801 expedition to Egypt. He was on Wellington's staff in the Peninsular Wars and at Waterloo.

In 1820, on the death of the Duke of Richmond, he succeeded Richmond as Governor-General of the Canadas, and retained this position until 1828, when he was appointed Commander-in-Chief in India.

He kept a journal from 1800. At the beginning of his Nova Scotian years he notes in his journal, with practical candour, that one reason for his taking the job was his need of money, after the heavy building expenses he had incurred at Dalhousie Castle. The castle in fact says much about the Ramsays. It still exists, near Edinburgh, in the county of East Lothian. Sir Walter Scott believed it to be the oldest inhabited house in Scotland, certainly the oldest used by one family. It was built early in the fourteenth century, when the Ramsays had already been living in East Lothian for some 200 years; the first Ramsay of whom there is record appears in the East Lothian registers in 1140.

The ninth Earl succeeded his father at seventeen and entered the army when he was eighteen, in 1788. He was educated at Edinburgh High School, along with many eminent Scotsmen of his time, Sir Walter Scott among them. Scott, in his own journal, gives an interesting account of meeting his old schoolmate in 1829, after the Dalhousies' return from Canada: "He has served his country in every quarter of the world and in every climate, yet, though my contemporary, looks ten years my junior.... In all incidents of life he has been the same steady, honest, true-hearted Lord Dalhousie that Lordie Ramsay promised to be when at the High School."

He married at 35 Miss Christina Broun, an heiress – which was useful, for the Ramsay family was not rich. The Brouns were also long established in East Lothian. Lady Dalhousie was an exceptional woman and it seems to have been a remarkably happy marriage. There were three children, all boys – Ramsay and Charles, whom they left behind in England in 1816, and little Jim, who came to Halifax with his parents.

Very little has been written about Lord Dalhousie's years in Nova Scotia; even contemporary comments are scanty. No biography exists; he has perhaps been overshadowed by his more famous son, for little Jim grew up to become, eventually, the tenth Earl and Governor-General of India in a time of violence and turbulence in that country.

But there is in fact surprisingly little material on early nineteenth-century Nova Scotia. So we are fortunate to have Lord Dalhousie's journal, for he gives us much valuable detail about the province during his time here.

He kept his journal partly as an *aide-mémoire* for his official correspondence, and much of it could be fairly described as a record of his official duties. There are gaps, sometimes of weeks, and many of the issues of the day are not mentioned at all – the controversy between King's College and Pictou Academy, for example.

However, a happy part of his official duty was to familiarize himself with conditions in the province, and in the accounts of his journeys around Nova Scotia it is clear that nothing gives His Lordship more pleasure than to climb upon his horse or take to sea with the Admiral and go exploring this new countryside, stopping everywhere there are people, talking to everyone. He not only wrote good vigorous English but was a good reporter, a man with seasoned judgment and an eye for the practical detail. He asks questions. He's out at midnight watching fires, down on the Halifax wharf in the morning talking to the captains of newly arrived vessels.

And always the private man comes through – in his pleasure in the countryside, in pithy comments on Nova Scotian life, in private heartbreak or wounded pride, in exasperation at government or Assembly, in affection for his staff and love for his wife and children.

He does not in fact write much about his family, but we are given glimpses, vivid and often delightful, of lively little boys and a wife and mother who was not only loving but merry as well, and ready for adventure in a way that must have endeared her to her children.

Sir Walter Scott describes her as "amiable, intelligent and lively." Joseph Howe, the journalist and politician, says that "without being handsome, [she] was remarkable for the plainness of her dress and the elegant simplicity of her manners." We discover from other sources that Lady Dalhousie was a patroness of literature and the arts; in 1824 Julia Beckwith, the first Canadian-born novelist, dedicated her first novel, *St. Ursula's Convent,* to her.

It is no surprise to find a well-educated Scotswoman of the time with such tastes, but Lady Dalhousie's interests ranged far beyond the merely conventional. She was a good botanist; in 1827 she presented to the Literary and Historical Society of Quebec a catalogue of Canadian plants that she had herself gathered and classified. And on a holiday at Mahone Bay in Nova Scotia she became a passionate rock hound and could hardly be dragged away, so involved was she in chemistry and mineralogy.

They both had the utterly attractive quality of finding life in Nova Scotia interesting. Between spells of army duty Dalhousie had spent his time on his estate in Scotland, with several farms to be worked, and he obviously has considerable knowledge of good farming practice, especially of animal husbandry. Then, too, as a countryman he is much aware of weather, and particularly in his early months in Nova Scotia he keeps careful records of daily temperatures and barometric pressures, and is obviously fascinated by the variable pattern of Halifax weather. These must be the earliest meteorological records now available.

Dalhousie gives as his second reason for accepting the Nova Scotian command that it was important to reach the rank of Command-in-Chief before he became a full general and retired (presumably on half-pay). At that time colonial administrative appointments were made from among the senior army officers, and Dalhousie's appointment to Nova Scotia was a useful step upward in his army career.

He left a Britain that had for years been in turmoil. The wars had been endless. George III had been on the throne since 1760, and since 1788 intermittently insane. The Prince of Wales, officially Prince Regent since 1811, was spending several fortunes on his mistresses and his houses, while hunger was prevalent in town and country. In 1812 the Prime Minister, Spencer Perceval, was assassinated in the House of Commons, and the roar of gratification from hungry workers alarmed the country. The routing of Napoleon at Waterloo was a great boost to morale, but it was followed by a terrifying economic depression and, in 1816, the worst summer on record. Everywhere people were crying democracy and revolution, and dying of hunger. Mass risings turned into tragedies. The crowd at the Spa Field meeting in London was reported to be as large as Napoleon's army at Waterloo; it was so again at Peterloo in Manchester, where a riot broke out in which eleven people were killed and several hundred wounded. The French Revolution was all too recent; democracy was a frightening word, a synonym for violence. If Dalhousie seems at times scornful of democracy and democrats, from Thomas Jefferson to Robert Gourlay, it is important to remember the events that shaped the opinions of his time.

In Nova Scotia he took his orders directly from Earl Bathurst, Secretary of War and the Colonies, and any communication from the Prince Regent came through Bathurst. It's interesting to observe that Dalhousie never mentions the Prime Minister, Lord Liverpool. He seems very much a King's man, his loyalty at the service of King and Country rather than the government; in fact he is frequently highly critical of government policy for Nova Scotia.

His sense of loyalty extends to the Prince Regent, and he writes affectionately of "the good old King" and "the good old Queen," though when Queen Charlotte is dying he does not seem to understand the painful nature of her illness, and writes of her deathbed with sentimental piety. He is angry, too, with Mr. Speaker Robie in Halifax, who refers to the King as a "bedlamite," though Dalhousie must have been aware the old man's mind had been disturbed for many years. Perhaps he considered Mr. Robie guilty of *lèse-majesté*.

The Nova Scotia to which he came had also felt the wars, and indeed the war with the Americans had not long ended. But there were all kinds of immediate practical problems to be faced in this new country struggling to get on its feet: roads to be built, land to be cleared, immigrant settlers to be encouraged. Particularly roads and bridges still to be built. The two main roads (to Truro and to

Windsor and the Annapolis Valley) were good. But new settlers were coming to areas without roads, and many communities were more accessible by boat. Much had been done since 1800 or so, but the hazards of travel at the turn of the century were still very considerable. In the older areas trails had been blazed through the woods, but blazes could be easily obscured in winter, when snow would drift and cover the marks on the trees. In new settlements men used pocket compasses to make their way through the woods, as sailors do at sea. They tried to keep tracks, even roads, to high ground, for low ground meant swamps or rain-swollen rivers.

Halifax, founded within living memory, in 1749, had some fine buildings and a population of about 12,000; there were some 80,000 people in the province, many descendants of United Empire Loyalists who had come from New England in the mass Loyalist migration of 1783. Many Maritimers today like to think of their Loyalist ancestors as having come ashore to a man with Harvard degrees in their pockets. The current trend among historians, however, is to give emphasis to statistics, which indicate that the great majority of Loyalists were butchers, bakers, carpenters and cabinet-makers, and that a very small group, perhaps no more than three or four percent, were educated men. It is interesting, therefore, to discover how many of the leading men of the province among Dalhousie's acquaintance were from Loyalist stock (or, which was considered even more desirable, descended from the pre-revolutionary Loyalists).

There were Loyalist farmers too, some of them notably unsuccessful. But Dalhousie's strictures on agriculture and its mismanagement probably refer more often to the experience of disbanded soldiers who had obtained grants of land and were attempting to clear land and hack out some sort of living on it. His own interest in farming, and his friendship with the agricultural reformer John Young (the famous "Agricola"), must have done something to advance agriculture in the province, but Joseph Howe in later years suggested that the improvement had been only temporary: "His Lordship's example," he wrote, "set all the Councillors and officials and fashionable mad about farming and political economy. They went to ploughing matches, got up Fairs, made composts and bought cattle and pigs. Every fellow who wanted office or wished to get an invitation to Government House read Sir John Sinclair [a Scottish proponent of advanced farming methods, and the first president of the British Board of Agriculture], talked of Adam Smith, bought a South Down [sheep] or hired an acre of land and planted mangel wurzels. But no two Governors think alike or patronize the same. When Sir James Kempt came he had a passion for road making and pretty women, and the agricultural mania died away."

It was 1824, when they had been in Canada for four years, before the Dalhousies got home leave. In their four years in Nova Scotia they seem to have taken only one holiday away from the province—to gaze in awe at the Falls of Niagara. In his delightful account of this early venture, Dalhousie gives us much detail on other subjects: on steamboats on the St. Lawrence River, on the boundary commission that was settling the boundary between Canada and the United States, on the War of 1812 and the hated Yankees, so recently the enemy.

By some historians Dalhousie is seen as authoritarian, by others as liberal, and he seems in fact to have moved back and forth between the two. On the question of marriage licences he was certainly not liberal, given the frontier conditions in Nova Scotia. Generally marriages were performed after calling banns in the church, but Anglican clergymen had the right to perform marriages by special licence. The dissenting ministers wished to have the same right. But Dalhousie felt (as did the Presbyterian Church in Scotland) that there were already too many irregularities in the system (some Anglicans were obtaining licences and then turning them over to dissenters), and he wished to see licences restricted to the Anglican Church. He thought the matter settled as he wished by the time he left Halifax, but the dissenting churches proved to be stubborn, and the question dragged on until the eighteen-thirties, when the final decision went against him.

Dalhousie is very much a Scot. He is a friendly man; in his unofficial relationships he altogether lacks the kind of *hauteur* which at that time might have characterized an Englishman of equal rank. Scots phrases creep into his writing; he goes to the Scots kirk once a month (in Scotland, the Presbyterian Church was, as it still is, the established church). But he is nowhere more a Scot than on the question of education, King's College and Dalhousie College. In Scotland since the time of John Knox an education had been considered the right of every man, and the Scottish universities were by express policy non-sectarian, open to all. Whatever Dalhousie's political affiliation, he was a Scot from the Age of Enlightenment in Scotland, at a time when Oxford and Cambridge accepted only Anglicans and seemed (to outsiders) little more than clubs for sporting parsons, a time when the Scottish universities were bending their talents to develop scientists and philosophers and political economists.

He arrived in Nova Scotia to find that there was only one college, and that one lamentably inadequate, attempting to model itself on Oxford and exclude non-Anglicans, in a province where Anglicans numbered only a fifth of the population. King's College was the pet project of Dr. Charles Inglis, a Loyalist from New York and first Bishop of Nova Scotia; to do him justice he was not happy about the requirement that students accept the Thirty-Nine Articles of the Church of England, but he had been over-ruled by the Board.

As Lieutenant-Governor, Dalhousie's official duty was to the state church – so it is rather interesting that his immediate reaction was that of a Scot, that King's was an unsuitable institution for the colony. It was not long before he was writing to the University of Edinburgh for advice on how to set up the right kind of university for Nova Scotia.

At about the same time, another institution was being established in Pictou by the exceptionally gifted Thomas McCulloch. One of the intentions at King's had been to train ministers for the Church of England in Nova Scotia, and McCulloch's purpose in launching Pictou Academy had been similar – to train Presbyterian ministers. McCulloch, however, did not belong to the Church of Scotland but to a branch of the Presbyterian Church known as the Secessionists. Perhaps because of this, or perhaps because they were personally incompatible, McCulloch and Dalhousie did not get on very well. But it is curious that McCulloch is never mentioned in the journal, because by the time Dalhousie left Halifax he had had a major confrontation with McCulloch, and Pictou Academy (which by 1830 became one of the hottest political issues of the day) was already offering a good liberal education to highly promising students.

Dalhousie laid the foundation of "his" college before he left Halifax, and in his speech he expressed a vision of education that was, for the time, both very liberal and very Scottish: "This College of Halifax is founded for the instruction of youth in the higher classicks, & in all Philosophical studies. It is formed in imitation of the University of Edinburgh. Its doors will be open to all who profess the Christian religion, to the youth of His Majesty's North American Provinces, to strangers residing here, to Gentlemen of the Military as well as the learned professions, to all in short who may be disposed to devote a small part of their time to study." In the legacy which he thus left to Nova Scotia he could not have had a better memorial.

But is was to be some time before it actually came into being. In the end, the money available to him for the College (the Castine fund, collected as customs duties at the Fort of Castine in Main during the 1812 war) was quite inadequate. It was 1838 before it opened its doors to students, and, ironically enough, it was Thomas McCulloch who was its first president.

It must often have been very difficult for men of Dalhousie's stamp, army officers accustomed to issuing commands and to being obeyed, to have to wait for the elected Assembly to decide in its own good time to do the things that needed to be done. Certainly Dalhousie, so liberal in matters of education, was less than diplomatic at times with the elected Assembly, particularly when it seemed to him that they were failing to give proper respect to the symbolic position of a Governor as the representative of the Crown.

But the years in Nova Scotia must have come to seem an idyllic interlude after he became immersed in the tangled affairs of Lower and Upper Canada. Dalhousie had the warmest admiration for French Canadians, but he had to cope at a constitutional level with the rising tide of French Canadian nationalism, led by Louis-Joseph Papineau. Between the policy of the Colonial Office and the demands of French Canada, he was placed in an impossible position, and he was recalled in 1828, and sent to India in 1829.

His administration was considered to be unsuccessful, but few men could have handled the situation as well as he did, and with a weaker man it could well have ended in violence.

The portrait of Lord Dalhousie on the jacket and title-page has been taken from the original in the National Gallery of Scotland. Plate 1 is an early map of Nova Scotia; the other seven Plates are reproduced from sketches by Major John Elliot Woolford, who had been in Dalhousie's regiment through a number of his campaigns. Plate 2 is a view of Zwicker's Inn at Mahone Bay, Plate 3 a sketch of Mount Uniacke, Plate 4 a drawing of Cook's Mills on the La Have River; Plate 5 shows the ruins of the Fortress of Louisbourg as they looked from the glacis; Plate 6 is a scene on the road between Chester and Mahone Bay, Plate 7 a scene on the River Roseway, with a sawmill in the foreground; Plate 8 gives an idea of what the Saint John River looked like from the deck of a steamboat. Woolford spent several years in Edinburgh as a successful landscape painter, and then returned to Dalhousie's service when he came to Nova Scotia. He accompanied Dalhousie to Canada, and on a tour to the Great Lakes as far as Lake Superior, sketching as he went. He spent his later years in Fredericton, where he designed the old Arts Building at the University of New Brunswick, as well as the fine structure which has in recent years been the headquarters of the R.C.M.P. but which in Woolford's day was Government House, overlooking the Saint John River. For both of these buildings people thank him today. Woolford is thought to have been an apprentice in the Drawing Room of the Board of Ordnance in the Tower of London, and it is also likely that he studied under Paul Sandby, professor of drawing at the Royal Military Academy at Woolwich. Those were the days when artillery and other army officers studied the principles of watercolour sketching; before the invention of the camera it was the best method of studying the terrain.

My thanks are due to the present Earl of Dalhousie for giving me permission to publish this portion of the diaries of the ninth Earl. My thanks are due also to the Department of Special Collections in the Killam Library at Dalhousie University in Halifax for giving me permission to have some of the Woolford sketches in the Morse Collection photographed, to the North British Society of Halifax for giving me permission to photograph Woolford sketches in their possession, and to Mr. Ferenc Stefani of Dalhousie University, and his staff, who made the photographs. I am grateful also to the staff of the Scottish Record Office for much willing and expert help and to the staff of the Public Archives of Nova Scotia for answering a thousand questions and for giving me much sound advice. To the Ontario Arts Council, I am deeply grateful for the generous grant that made work on this book possible. And, as I finish the book, I find I would also like to express thanks to the ninth Earl of Dalhousie, for his keen enjoyment of Nova Scotia, for being such a good writer and such a sound reporter that he stirred me into undertaking what has proved to be a labour of love for the two countries I regard as my own—Scotland and Canada.

MARJORY WHITELAW

The Journal of George Ramsay, Ninth Earl of Dalhousie, during his years as Lieutenant-Governor of Nova Scotia, 1816-20

MAY 1816. In the spring of this year I carried Lady D. to London with Ramsay and Charles, for the purpose of fixing them at Dr. Pearson's school at East Sheen; while in town I heard that the Lt. Government and command in Nova Scotia was likely to be soon vacant. I made an offer of my services to go there, & my offer was received with great civility by the Duke of York and Earl Bathurst.

The situation however had then been offered to Sir Gordon Drummond in Canada, and nothing could be done further until his answer was received.

JUNE. Early in June I returned to D. Castle; it was not till the 18th July that I received intimation from Lord Bathurst that he had submitted my name to the Prince Regent, who had been graciously pleased to appoint me to the Lieut. Govt. of Nova Scotia, & requiring me to press my departure—Lord Melville being then at Ormiston assured me that the *Forth* frigate of 40 Guns was to convey me out. I therefore set about my preparations to leave home for a period of 5 years at the least.

My motives in accepting command abroad in time of Peace were chiefly – that it was of the highest importance to me to reach the situation of a Command in Chief, before I attained the rank of full General in the Army and consequently placed out of further Service. I had in view the Chief Command in Canada which Sir John Sherbrooke is not supposed to retain more than two years from this time. I look to be full General in 5 years—and having placed my two elder boys at an excellent school, my mind is at ease on their account for that time.

My 2nd object in accepting command, was to retrieve my private financial concerns in these times of general distress, & after my heavy building expences. Leaving my home property untouched after 5 years, I should return home in times improved, & with elbows free from debt. Under such impressions, & Lady D. cheerfully agreeing to go abroad, I had little difficulty in putting all my affairs under the care of John Smith, and by the 20th August I was resolved to start.

On that day accordingly we set off for London, taking my 3rd boy James with us, and sending our servants & baggage by sea.

We had considerable arrangements to make in London, & large supplies of house stores to provide for our first winter; these however were all accomplished by the 3rd Sept. when we left town for Portsmouth.

8TH SEPTEMBER. We took Ramsay & Charles down with us that they might see us embark in the *Forth* frigate, & long impress it on their memory. My sister Mary & Hay met us at Portsmouth from Collipriest & remained with us till we embarked on the 8th. They went on board, dined with us, & took, with a long farewell, the two boys on shore with them.

It came on to blow very hard next day from the Westward, & we thought it more prudent to remain at Spithead than to begin our voyage by fighting against a gale in the Channel.

11TH SEPTEMBER. The wind moderate this morning, got up our anchor at daylight & put to sea. Wind S.W.

12TH SEPTEMBER. Off Portland wind dead foul.

13TH SEPTEMBER. Anchored in Torbay to put Lady Louis on shore.

14TH SEPTEMBER. Again weighed, wind at S.S.W. gave us a good slant down Channel.

15TH SEPTEMBER. A thick fog & very little wind, we tumbled about, doing no good.

16TH SEPTEMBER. At 12 o'clock supposed ourselves off Ushant bearing S.W.40 miles. Calm & Heavy swell.

17TH SEPTEMBER. Last night a breeze sprung up at East & today at 12 we have run 100 miles. Wind S.E....

20TH SEPTEMBER. During the night very tremendous lightning with Thunder, about 4 o'clock Lieut. Hume's watch – a very vivid flash was instantly succeeded by an awful clap of thunder, which knocked down a number of men then hawling on the mainbrace – one of them close to Lt. Hume fell as if shot, the others were severely scorched but were sensible after it. The mainmast was splintered in several places all round, & the sails a good deal burnt in the top. To us below, the shock was not felt otherwise than by the noise it made, exactly as if a very heavy gun had been overloaded & fired. I heard it distinctly, but thinking it only a signal Gun I paid no attention to it, & only learned what had happened when I went on deck at 8

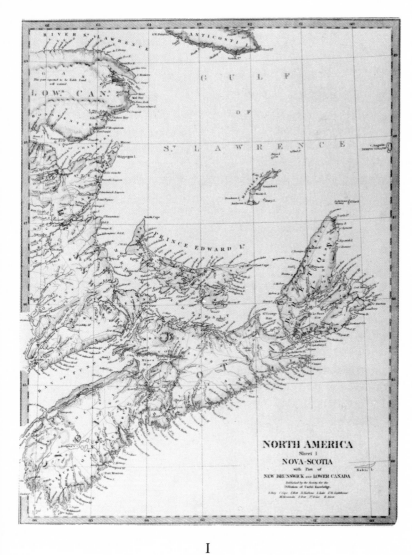

NORTH AMERICA
Sheet 1
NOVA-SCOTIA
with Part of
NEW BRUNSWICK AND LOWER CANADA
Published by the Society for the
Diffusion of Useful Knowledge.

I

o'clock. I then saw several men laying on deck under the surgeon's care. Immediately after the ship was struck by the lightning, it fell dead calm for several hours.

About 10 o'clock saw a ship of war under a press of sail before the wind then at S.W. On nearing her a little, she appeared under jury masts above, and thinking we might hear something from Algiers, we ran down towards her, & telegraphed. She proved to be the *Leander,* Admiral Milne's ship going home to repair damages she had sustained in action with the batteries. Milne had gone before with dispatches in the *Glasgow.* We were delighted in thus accidentally getting authentic information of these events.

It blowing fresh, she soon left us, & we stood in to make the land off Cape Ortigal, which we did about 3 o'clock P.M., blowing hard, dead foul....

24TH SEPTEMBER. It blew this morning in strong squalls with rain – nearly 12 o'clock I was on deck with Sir John Louis, when a heavy shower induced us to go below. I was scarcely in the Cabin, & reported that it was blowing very hard & wet, when the tiller rope went round with prodigious force & the ship was struck by a sea nearly astern. We thought we had carried away our rudder, but going on deck I found that the wind had suddenly chopped round in the squall, took us all aback & caused that violent run of the wheel. In a few minutes the sky cleared up, the sun shone; from a melancholy south-wester we had a most delightful change to a fair wind at N.W.

The decks were soon cleared & swabbed, and every appearance of a gale that had blown these last 4 days was removed. This afternoon was occupied in getting up our rigging which being all new had yielded & got slack in the gale....

26TH SEPTEMBER. A delightful breeze at N.E., all studding sails set and now talking of Madeira in three days....

28TH SEPTEMBER. Today 207 miles without a shift of sail. We expected to have made the land today, but find ourselves drawn 60 miles in towards the Gut of Gibraltar, so strong is the current that sets in that direction. At noon hauled up due west & run with a press of sail till dark but no land.

29TH SEPTEMBER. At daybreak close on board the island of Porto Santo, & by breakfast were in with the headland of Funchal bay, expecting to anchor in an hour. But the land is so high that we entirely lost the wind under it, and lay all day becalmed. In the Evening we drifted off with the falling tide, and during the night picking up a light seabreeze anchored very early close in.

30TH SEPTEMBER. I sent Major Couper on shore with letters we had for Mr. Gordon, wine merchant, & went up to breakfast with him. Lady D. had a sort of Lapanquin sent to the landing place for her. The weather is excessively hot, but not to prevent us going out at midday.

We visited the Portuguese Governor, an old General Officer worn out & severely wounded in his early day—then the Consul, and after paying a short visit at the Convent of Nuns, we went 3 miles up the hill, to see the country house of Senor Carvayhal, a very rich Portuguese—a very nice house with gardens & rides on a great scale; it is quite a show place & well worth the trouble of going up to it. We dined with Mr. Gordon & about 10 o'clock went on board. It is impossible to express the kindness of Mr. G., who did all in his power to keep us on shore. However, we had seen as much as gave us a good idea of Madeira. We got some Pipes of wine on board, & as the wind still held fresh at N.E. I felt very anxious to proceed on our voyage.

1ST OCTOBER. After breakfast, weighed anchor, & with a fresh breeze stood right away to the South to secure the trade winds. By 2 o'clock P.M. we had lost sight of land....

14TH OCTOBER. These two days past we have had squally & blowing weather, in consequence of having hauled so high to the Northward as to leave the trade winds. In the 13 days prior to this we hardly shifted a sail, tho' we had everything set, were studding sail on both sides. The moon was at full, & bright almost as noonday, so smooth the sea that altho' we were usually at 8 or 9 knots an hour, the midshipmen were dancing on deck to the Bank till 11 o'clock at night, not feeling that the ship was moving.

Enquiring for the people who had been struck by lightning on the 20th September I find they are all returned to their duty except the man who fell near Hume. There is a round spot as large as a dollar quite burnt on his head, which the surgeon thinks must be trepanned, and doubts that he ever can recover—his nerves & frame are constantly trembling....

19TH OCTOBER. One day more and we hoped to have made land near Sambro' head, but the wind now headed us, & we lay North, making 128 miles in Lat. 41. [Long.] 58.30. We still hoped to get so much of northing as to enable us to lay into Halifax with a N. Easter, which prevails on this coast.

20TH OCTOBER. Today nearly calm in Lat. 40.50, [Long.] 59.40. We put about and stood to the southward. Very fine weather however. Saw some Dolphins playing about the ship, which went off on the appearance of a large shark under the stern, attended by two pilot fish, his constant companions. All hands and hooks were in a few minutes at work to catch him, and Yates actually had him half out of the water, strongly hooked in the mouth; he got it out however, & we lost all hope of seeing him again. In less than an hour he was playing under the bows, & was again very soon hooked, brought on board, cut up & divided among the crew, who really scrambled for their shares as a pack of hounds devour their fox.

This caused considerable sensation in the ship, as it is a received maxim among sailors that a shark always follows a vessel where there is a dead man. Now it so happened with us that yesterday a man died, & was to be buried today. The shark was therefore a sort of apparition in waiting, and everyone was highly pleased in having caught him before the hour of burial at 4 o'clock P.M....

22ND OCTOBER. Tried to make land today, but could not altho' at 11 P.M. the master assured us he saw the Sambro light. We fired several guns, but no answer made, altho' the orders require Gun for Gun.

23RD OCTOBER. Very thick fog today, could not see a mile ahead. Stood off shore, spoke an American schooner fishing – her latitude exactly the same as ours. In the evening spoke a schooner from Cape Breton bound to Halifax, but knew nothing of his latitude. He was waiting for a clear day, & would then know the coast he made. All this we thought very tantalising, & of course we were not in the best humour.

24TH OCTOBER. An hour before daylight again stood in shore; the sun rising clear & beautiful, we found ourselves within 12 miles of the Light House on Sambro. We were soon all on deck, and with inexpressible delight we sailed up the harbour with light but fair winds, saluted the Admiral's flag when close in, with George's island on starboard, & the town of Halifax on larboard side – dropt anchor near Dartmouth & the navy yard & then breakfasted.

My old friend Major St. Clair of Artillery first came off to me, & then Col. Darling, whom I had appointed my Military Secretary. The former acting as Dy. Q.M. General came off from General Smyth, Administrator, & commanding the Garrison, to receive my orders as to my landing, at same time informing me that the troops were under arms already & the Council assembled to receive me and administer the oaths to be taken. All this appeared to me extremely expeditious, and rather hurrying, but I did not like to make any difficulties, nor to lose the advantage of going thro' the shew on a most delightful fine day. I therefore fixed 2 o'clock to land, & at the King's wharf I found General Smyth with the staff & a number of Officers. The troops lined the streets. I went direct to the Council room & took the same Oaths as are at all times administered in taking my seat in Parliament. I was then introduced to the 12 Members of Council, the Chief Justice Blowers the only one absent by illness. I then rode up thro' the streets to Government House, where the Military were introduced to me, & the Civilians also came to make their bows. I remained on shore about an hour with Sir John Louis, & then went on board to dinner, intending to land for good next day.

25TH OCTOBER. The weather was still as fine as summer & at 11 o'clock Lady D. with James accompanied me & Sir John Louis in his barge & under salute, the yards manned, we took leave of the *Forth*. It is impossible to express, & certainly I shall never forget, the kind & constant attentions paid to us by Sir John, & by every individual in the ship.

During the six weeks we were on board, from the first moment to the last, there never passed an angry word, nor I do believe, an angry thought among us. Our voyage altogether passed like a party of pleasure, & on looking back to the time, we could scarcely persuade ourselves how it had escaped us....

31ST OCTOBER. We have now been here a week, chiefly occupied in arranging our family & unpacking our baggage and stores from England. It is singularly fortunate that all my wines & supplies from Dalhousie Castle shipped at Greenock in August, had arrived some days before us, and also a ship from London bringing our goods from thence, so that we are already completely & comfortably settled. The wines had a narrow escape, as the ship from Greenock, having run ashore in a fog about 30 leagues East of this, was for a day deserted by the Capt. & crew, but next day being fine & a fair wind, they returned on board and got her off & safely into this harbour. I have been also most fortunate in picking up at once a pair of carriage horses, and 3 sadell horses, all very good. My carriage had been very well packed, & has arrived without a hurt or scratch. We have been very kindly received by everybody; Capt. Wodehouse of the Navy now here Commissioner & Admiral Griffiths, have both been extremely attentive.

Yesterday I had my first Levee to receive both Civil & Military. Mr. Jeffery, Collector of the Customs, & Mr. Rupert George, Secretary of the Province, having been appointed my Civilian Aide de Camps, introduced the civil class by name, and Major St. Clair did so as to military. I made however short work of it by walking round the room, & moving on without much stop, except with those with whom I had already been made a little acquainted. In half an hour my Levee was over, but at 2 o'clock Lady D. held her drawing room, which was more fully attended than mine – the day being very fine, and according to etiquette in morning dress, all the Ladies had turned out, & completely filled both our dining & drawing room. I took Lady D. in, & just walked round the Company, occasionally stopping one moment where she had also made some slight acquaintance, and in half an hour this ceremony was also got rid of.

I then went out a-riding with Sir John Louis, who has for the present taken his quarters with us.

The Admiral has issued his orders that the squadron shall sail on the 7th Nov. for the Bermudas to winter, and as his own flag ship the *Akbar* is ordered to England to be paid off, the *Forth* has received him.

11TH NOVEMBER.... I ordered the *Forth* to be saluted by all the Batteries as she passed in succession, and I rode out to Point Pleasant to see it. The scene was very beautiful – the Grand Battery, George's Island, Fort Clarence, Point Pleasant, followed each other. The *Forth* then abreast of the North point of McNab's island, hove to & backed her topsails, so as to lay herself right across the stream, returned the salute, in the most magnificent style, & then filling handsomely stood down to York Redoubt where the Battery again saluted her— and we took our leave with sincere regret of the friends on board her who had been so kind to us on our passage out.

Among many acts of goodness, Sir John Louis left us a Piano Forte, which was a thing not to be got here.

16TH NOVEMBER. The Society of this place has for some time past been very dull. In order to start it a little we have got up an Amateur Theatre, very well indeed. All Naval & Military Officers. Last night Lady D. gave a Ball to the better class of the society. About 200 people came to it, not powerful in either beauty or good dancing, but on the whole it showed a very good set of people, very much inclined to be pleased, at same time extremely civil & attentive.

18TH NOVEMBER. I rode this morning to breakfast at the Fultz Inn, about 14 miles on Windsor road, just to see the Country. The day was soft & warm as a day in April. We walked out after breakfast for a couple of hours to look at the awful ruin of the woods by fire & strong winds. All the large wood is laying black & tore up by the roots, in masses of confusion. Others remain erect but dead and rotting, to fall by next blast. There is however some fields cultivated....

23RD NOVEMBER.... Took a long walk today (with Couper, Henry Dundas, Mid. of the *Niger* here, & the spaniels) round by Point Pleasant and the woods, skirting the Northwest Arm. No game or living thing to be seen except 4 old Indian native women, sitting like savages round a bit of fire, pictures of misery.

24TH NOVEMBER.... Went to St. Paul's Church, Dr. Inglis preached his first sermon as Rector of the Parish, an excellent discourse.

26TH NOVEMBER. Bright sunny day & hard frost, sleighs going, & everyone shod in mocassins or cloth shoes. We last night patronised a set of Players just arrived; they got thro' the Road to Ruin & Mayor of Sarratt extremely well, & had an overflowing house – we felt no inconvenience whatever from cold....

29TH NOVEMBER.... The *Hydra,* 32 guns, Capt. Roberts, arrived today from Newfoundland, 11 days, brought accounts of the total loss of the *Harpooner,* transport from Quebec to England, 300 men of reduced 4th Regt. & other corps, of whom 200 souls perished – on Cape Pine, nearly the same spot where the *Comus* frigate was lost a month ago. Capt. Roberts speaks of the truly melancholy state of the survivors, but particularly of two young ladies who were by miracle cast ashore, their father (surgeon of the Regiment), Mother & several other children of the same family having sunk before they quitted the wreck. This being St. Andrew's Day, there was as usual a Levee at Govt. House, but very thinly attended from the wetness of the day.

1ST DECEMBER. A Publick dinner was given yesterday at Mason's Hall in honour of St. Andrew's Day. I went to it by invitation. About 150 sat down and spent a most excellent day, Mr. Wallace in the chair. Some excellent Scotch songs were sung....

2ND DECEMBER. The transport Brig *Prince of Orange* sailed today for England. Lt. Col. Henderson, Late Inspecting Field Officer here, took charge of invalids & a Bag of dispatch for Earl Bathurst....

6TH DECEMBER. Lady D. gave her 2nd Ball tonight at Government House....

15TH DECEMBER. Sunday. Went to the Scotch Kirk today where a seat had been provided for us by the Elders & Session. Dr. Gray is clergyman of it, a poor preacher rather....

The *Hydra* troopship sailed this forenoon for Bermudas & Barbados. Capt. Roberts commands her; tho' in appearance a gentlemanlike young man, has got into several scrapes here, behaving very ill indeed....

18TH DECEMBER. A dreadful fire broke out last night in the lower part of town, in a spirit store of a Mr. Grassie, which raged with great fury till 2 o'clock this morning, and all this forenoon it continued to burn in the lower cellars of the houses that fell last night. I went out to it & returned about 12 o'clock, when it was evidently got under. The night fortunately was calm but the cold very severe, the therm. at 2 degrees above zero....

22ND DECEMBER. Sunday. At 9 o'clock this morning the glass in the Ball room was at 0, & continues now at 5 with a bright sun at 2 o'clock. The wind however is most intensely cold & penetrating. On returning from Church, Lady D. drove to the Commissioners in the Dockyard, not more than half a mile distance; on reaching it the Coachman was frostbit all over, had no power whatever, & quite delirious, or rather insensible of what he said. With the utmost difficulty they got him from his box, stripped off his boots, & rubbed him with snow; gave him a glass of brandy & recovered him a little, but he was not able to drive home. From the fineness of the day he had neglected to put on his great coat, & waiting a quarter of an hour at Church, the piercing wind had quite frozen him.

23RD DECEMBER. The glass today is at 37 degrees, mild & delightful. The Coachman is considerably better, but his legs & feet much swelled, & feels bruised all over.

26TH DECEMBER.... Mr. Head, a junior Officer of the Commissariat, has at present a tame otter that follows him like a dog. He purchased it some days ago & in 24 hours the animal became quite attached to him, distinguishing him among a crowd of others. He puts him into the sea, into rivulets, where the animal hunts for fish & comes out when called as readily as a spaniel.

28TH DECEMBER.... An Amateur theatre opened with *the Comedy of John Bull,* extremely well got up.

1ST JANUARY 1817.... Held a Levee as is usual on New Year's Day. A most ridiculous ceremony, & troublesome from the frequency of them. I have been a good deal occupied lately in framing a report to Lord Bathurst on the measures advisable towards encouraging the further settlement & population of this Province. It is to be found in my publick letter book.

7TH JANUARY. Sent large dispatches today to England by the *Victory,* merchant ship for Liverpool, destined to return early in the spring.... Dr. Inglis, our Parish Rector, tells me that the Barometer is not formed to answer correctly on any part of the continent of America, but can give no reason for it. I watch my Barometer carefully, & do find it very often incorrect.

15TH JANUARY. Last night late the November mail from England arrived via New York, a sad roundabout way. Brings papers to the 8th Nov. This last week the weather has been severe frost with snow laying, & very clear & steady winter weather, sleighing in the best style. There is no sort of exercise in it, & I therefore prefer a daily long walk. But it is a gay scene, from the numbers & society it creates, & the bells with which all horses are obliged by law to be ornamented.... Another fire happened in town, broke out about 6 o'clock in the morning & consumed the whole chocolate manufactory of a Mr. Fergusson. It was however soon got under.

24TH JANUARY. These last 10 days have been hard w. severe cold, except on 18th when it blew very hard from S.E. with rain. The snow melted in rivers in town; during the night the wind suddenly shifted to the opposite point of the Compass N.W. & froze extremely hard; in consequence the streets are a most dangerous sheet of ice, carriages & sleighs swinging at every turn so as almost to pull the horses down. On the 19th the surf on the shoal called the Thrum Cap, and on Mauger's Beach, was very tremendous. The latter is a small outport of 6 men to take care of materials deposited there for the building of a mertello tower & light house. Two of the poor fellows crossing from one hut to another were caught by the surf & carried off.

26TH JANUARY.... Sparrow is gone in sleigh with Judge Wilkins to Windsor for a few days. I have some idea of fitting the Barrack there for me the next summer as a centrical situation from which I may make excursions into the different corners of the Country.

Closed today for the dispatches to England & sent them by the *Earl Bathurst,* cutter, to New York, in hopes of overtaking the Packet homebound, & to sail 5th February. I scarcely however can expect she will....

31ST JANUARY. The Harbour today is frozen over very far out. In my walk which in spite of the cold was quite delightful, I see two small vessels off Point Pleasant caught in the ice; one of them appears deserted, the other has 3 men on board labouring to break around them but without doing any good. Two nights ago a small boat with the mate and one sailor going to their vessel near the shore, has drifted to sea; it is supposed they were drunk, and in that state they are the more easily nipped by the frost—that they had lain down in their boat and were frozen to death, but neither they nor the boat have been heard of.

1ST FEBRUARY. One of the small vessels in the Ice have got out today, with the assistance that a boat from York Redoubt gave them; the other with the 3 men is still fast & labouring hard. The poor devils must be suffering most severely....

3RD FEBRUARY.... Mr. Black & Mr. Hill, two of the oldest & most respectable inhabitants here, who have for 30 years kept a Register of the weather, say that this is the most severe they ever remember.

Mr. Hill states that his Therm. at daybreak on 30th was 10 below zero.

5TH FEBRUARY. Very cold today, wind at N. west and the Barber on the water. This Barber is a very curious thing. It has the appearance as if the surface of the Sea was covered in loose snow, & the only account I can get of it is that it is the exhalation rising to the effect of the Sun, & frozen as it were in the air; it hangs in the air a little above the horizon & drifts away before the breeze. The name is a vulgar common Phrase, but there is none other except that sometimes it is said "the harbour is smoking"; in this state of very severe cold the wind is always at Northwest.

Some days ago a Brig arrived from the West Indies; almost all hands had suffered most severely from cold. A brig sailed today for the West Indies. We now look for the December Packet every day from New York and count upon its arrival by the 10th.

7TH FEBRUARY. A little more snow today but the weather is still so fine as to tempt me to go up to Windsor tomorrow, stay Sunday and return on Monday, for no purpose but to see the Country just now in its complete winter, and to try the travelling in sleighs. Judge Wilkins, Sparrow and myself go in one sleigh, Col. Duke sets off today in his own, and will reach Windsor early in the morning, to make preparation for us.

11TH FEBRUARY. We returned late last night, having made a most pleasant excursion indeed, leaving this at 10 o'clock, & with a pair of fresh horses at the halfway house, we reached Windsor by 4 o'clock with great ease – 45 miles. The roads were well beat & smooth as ice the whole way. At times the sun was quite at summer heat.

Mount Uniacke is the only Gentleman's seat on the road, finished last year, has a very comfortable neat appearance, but tho' called is not a Mount, but situated in a bottom between two very pretty and extensive lakes, surrounded with wood, Pine & hard. From Halifax to the top of Ardoise Lake 30 miles, the soil is rocky & extremely bad in general—a great quantity of wood, but from wild fires & sweeping hurricanes of wind, half of it is erect but burnt, while the rest is blown down, uprooted, being now decayed. The habitations however—little Inns & cottages—are very thickly set.

12TH FEBRUARY. There are some very pretty spots & lakes which in summer must be beautiful; one I remarked particularly belonging to Mr. Morris, the Surveyor General. He has just begun on it, by building a small hut and a barn.

The moment we begin to descend towards Windsor, the country assumes a new and better appearance. The Ardoise is a ridge of high land rather than hill, extending a considerable distance East & West. On the Windsor side no fires appear; a great number of fine trees are laying blown down or leaning over dead on their adjoining, which gives a wildness to the scene very striking. The woods are perfectly thick & impenetrable, unless to an Indian—mixture of spruce, fir & hemlock, with hardwood of Oak, Birch, Beech and Maple, very lofty, but not large dimension, from being so thickly set. Some few larch, here called the Hacmetac. Numbers of very small cottages with a few acres cleared around them, and another piece in process of clearing, shews the manner in which this Province is increasing, both in numbers of Cultivators and in quantities of arable land.

There is nothing romantic on all this road, and when the wood is cut down, which is at present the grand object of every new settler, there will be little to interest the traveller's eye.

The day being very clear, we had an extensive view from Ardoise Hill of Windsor, Horton, Cornwallis, Cape Blowmedown, & the Bason of Minas towards the Cumberland district.

On Sunday I went to Church, after having walked early thro' the old Fort and Barracks; the former has disappeared, the latter are ruined and useless.

The Church is about a mile out of town in the Halifax road, & opposite to where the King's College is placed on the summit of a hill—a building very ill adapted to the purpose, & altho' only erected about 15 years ago, is already falling down. I visited Dr. Porter and Dr. Cochran, President & Vice, but I am sorry to learn at variance with one another. Of course the affairs of the College must suffer. There are only now 12 students & these dissatisfied & doing little good.

In the evening it began to snow and yesterday morning the roads were pronounced impassable, however I had no choice left me; it was necessary I should return without delay, and accordingly we started at 8 o'clock. We soon found the road a smooth surface of snow, about 10 inches deep, not a soul had gone before us. Of course we were obliged to be very cautious how we advanced. However, about 3 miles out of Windsor we passed the house of Mr. Smith, the Sherriff of the County, and he immediately fancied we might find difficulty & mounted all his servants and horses—three pair of them—overtook us, offered his services to open the road; we readily accepted & he conducted us safe to Mount Uniacke on the border of his County. I never met with a more civil & kind mark of attention. He went full 17 miles in deep snow, and having landed us safe, turned about & went home again.

We stopped a little while at a small miserable publick house, kept by a man Spencer, whose only recommendation is his wife, a very pretty woman who supports a large family by her industry alone. Her story I don't yet know, but she is the daughter of a clergyman, near Falkirk in Scotland, & ran away from her parents with this man. She spoke of them with tears overflowing. They were alive last spring. Hereafter I shall endeavour to learn her story more fully. We stopped two hours at Mount Uniacke to refresh our horses, & then changed them at the Halfway House, between Windsor & Halifax. With much difficulty we got home at 7 o'clock.

The travelling in sleigh is the easiest mode certainly in this climate, and facilitates the communication in the country. It is also remarkably quick & the whole day in deep snow & open air, none of us felt any cold.

13TH FEBRUARY. The Legislature met today for the dispatch of business. I went to the Council & opened the Sessions in the same manner as Parliament is opened by a Speech, & sitting with my hat on, I felt it both awkward and unpleasant. I was told that my appearing in coloured cloaths was taken as a compliment; I therefore did so. A great additional fall of snow took place yesterday, which has impeded the arrival of the distant Members, and makes it very uncomfortable to walk the streets at present.

15TH FEBRUARY. The late Speaker of the Assembly, Judge Wilkins, having vacated that Chair, a competition took place between Mr. Robie & Mr. Ritchie; the former was chosen.

Today I received the Addresses from the Council & House of Assembly. The cold is more severe today than I have ever yet felt it. My therm. is 4 degrees below zero only, & has stood so notwithstanding the Sun is bright all forenoon.

17TH FEBRUARY.... The harbour has been frozen completely over these two days, and for the first time for a great many years people have walked over from Dartmouth to Halifax. The ice extends down to the point called Mauger's Beach. On enquiring today on the wharf how the tide made under the circumstances of being strongly frozen, I find that the whole great surface rises & falls in one unbroken body, except at the edges where it gives way.

19TH FEBRUARY.... The harbour entirely frozen over, has been walked across by many people, and now exhibits a smooth surface of snow.

21ST FEBRUARY. Continues very fine with bright sun, but today tho' the wind is at north, it feels quite a thaw, & the ice on the harbour is giving way & dissolving as if from the power of the Sun. Several people walking on the harbour today have fallen in, but no fatal accident has happened....

24TH FEBRUARY.... Three vessels from the West Indies arrived within these two days, come for cargoes of Ice which sells at Jamaica at a dollar per 1000 lbs.

People consider the winter now broke up and in two or three weeks we shall have arrivals of shipping from every part of the world.

27TH FEBRUARY. It did blow a strong gale from W. and S.W. two days ago, and the old inhabitants say that it never fails to be so, the gale at S.E. being invariably succeeded immediately by another from the directly opposite point of the Compass. The North West still holds with hard frost, Therm. at 15 degrees or 20. The streets in town are in a dreadful state from masses of melted snow and ice, with deep cuts made to let off the torrents that in the thaw were rushing down every street. We look impatiently now for the mail from New York-Falmouth of December....

4TH MARCH.... 3 Brigs arrived today, one from Sicily, out 80 days. She has been 18 days off the mouth of this harbour, not daring to come near the Coast.

I had last night letters from General Ainslie at Sydney, Cape Breton, via Antigonish of 5th February, and also letters from Sir. J. Sherbrooke at Quebec of 12th Feby. We consider both of these quick communications at this season.

From Fredericton the post at present is brought on a small sleigh by dogs to Fort Cumberland. The postman runs, pushing behind on snow shoes.

9TH MARCH.... We have had this week daily arrivals of small craft from the States and from the West Indies – great mortality it appears at Barbados, among the military & also natives. Nothing material going on here; the Assembly attends to their business with a degree of assiduity & undisturbed tranquillity that does it great honour & is most pleasing & comfortable to me....

12TH MARCH.... Yesterday, notwithstanding the thickness of the weather & strong gale, our long expected *Bathurst* returned from New York & brought our mail of December – most acceptable when bringing good news, which thank god it did to us of all our own immediate relations and concerns, but Sparrow, poor fellow, took up a newspaper and first learnt of the sudden death of his father, a most highly respected clergyman at Walthamstow in Essex.

Couper also was mortified by the suppression of his sinecure as Secretary to the Govr. of Annapolis; this to him is a serious loss as out of his military pay he has long contrived to add essentially to the support of his old father and 3 sisters very poorly off in pecuniary circumstances.

14TH MARCH.... The ice is breaking up in Bedford Bason and floating down into this harbour, impelled by the northerly winds; it appears to incommode very much the shipping & intercourse with the Dartmouth side.

21ST MARCH.... Two Brigs arrived yesterday but when as high as Mauger's beach both were surrounded in ice & stuck fast. One from Newfoundland got up today, the other has been drifted on shore & is in danger. She is from Antigua – 36 days....

27TH MARCH. The *Queensberry* sailed this morning for England full of passengers. A Mr. Elwyn, an Englishman on board her, dined with me two days ago, a very intelligent Merchant of Bristol. The Brig on shore in ice has been emptied of her Cargo and ballast, & the harbour quite clear of ice, she has got safe up and hauled along the wharf....

2ND APRIL. The House of Assembly having finished their business I prorogued it today at 2 o'clock, and it is really with great pleasure I have noticed the quiet, peaceable and diligent manner in which they have applied to publick business. It is very natural that a little self interest and private friendship should have a place in the distribution of money granted from the publick purse to the repair of roads and bridges already made, and to the opening of new roads thro' the wilderness & forest lands. £25,000 is annually apppopriated from the Province's Revenue to that purpose and it is the most difficult of their labour to mete it out in small sums & satisfy all the Members in their publick capacity and their private views.

£8,000 to purchase seed Corn for the relief of the distress experienced this year in certain districts. Bounties to Agriculture, Fisheries and Commerce, drawbacks on Exportation & the Civil Establishment of the Province, very moderate in its salaries, make up the Publick disbursement this year—£62,000.

The Treasurer Mr. Wallace tells me this is improvidently large, but I differ from him; the Province is rapidly increasing in resources — it has not a shilling of debt, & the only tax is the support of the Poor. If the Assembly has overstept the amount of the Revenue a little, it is in giving a circulation of money in the Province, chiefly in roads and seed Corn, which cannot fail to be of great service to the Country, and it is always in their power to check the issue next year for the relief of any debt they may contract in these times of distress among the lower orders.

Mr. Robie was Speaker this session, & has conducted it to the great satisfaction of the House, and equally so of the Council as "Lords House."

3RD APRIL. Another fall of snow all this forenoon, wind at S.E. blowing hard. An old Gentleman, Dr. Cochrane, Vice President of the College at Windsor in this Province, dining with me today, says he has kept a regular Journal of the weather and observations on it since 1774, and he finds nothing equal to this season, but the years 1780 and 1798. In both these the fall of snow was very deep and did immense damage in its thaw, by carrying off bridges, mills, and every building near to rivers. This season has the advantage of its thaw being so singularly gradual; so much is already gone, that no damage can be done.

10TH APRIL.... Impatiently looking for the January Packet for many weeks past; we have been disappointed in the arrival of two ships of war, both from the West Indies & bringing no news. The *Hydra,* Capt. Robert, has brought up 300 men of the 15th Regt.

from Grenada, and the *Fly,* Brig of 18 Guns, Capt. Baldwin, from England via Barbados, & bound to her station at Newfoundland.

15TH APRIL.... At last our January packet is coming up the harbour 4 days from New York.

18TH APRIL.... The Merchant ship *Northumberland,* 1st ship of the season from Europe is arrived today from London, brings Papers of 4th March; very late news & very important to us, in detailing the insult offered the Regent in going down to open the Session of Parliament, and the measures adopted in consequence. We cannot help thinking the report of the Secret Committee exaggerates the dangers in the country, but yet we consider that exaggeration justified by the policy of rousing the nation to adopt effectual & immediate measures of safety.

22ND APRIL. Arrived the March Packet in 28 days from Falmouth bringing papers & dispatches of 21st March from London. This is considered as the opening of our Spring & new Season. Accounts of the state of England are highly satisfactory, tumult has subsided, stocks have risen to 70 and wheat & grain, as well as Money very plenty.

Immense reductions in the Military & Departments, some of them here create most severe and cruel hardships on many very old and meritorious Servants of the Public; some of them 30 years' standing in the Commissariat as Clerks are dismissed without any provision but one year's pay as a Gratuity.

23RD APRIL.... I began on the 18th to dig some shrubbery by a dozen men, but the garden is yet too full of snow & too wet to meddle with. At this season the quantity of Robins here is quite astonishing, a bird as large as a thrush, breast & black head like a bull-finch & thousands of them are shot about the town & carried to market every day by idle shop boys, Blacks and other unemployed or unindustrious vagabonds. Not a bird of any description except a croaking raven, has been seen during the winter, and now all in a week Robins & many other small birds like linnets are innumerable....

27TH APRIL. Our shipping from England now pours in upon us. The *Egeria,* Sloop of war, has just anchored, 36 days from Portsmouth, the *Louisa* Brig & another from Aberdeen 38 days; it is singular that these Brigs left Aberdeen within an hour of one

II

another, had never seen one another on the voyage, & coming in today in very heavy rain & thick weather, they dropt their anchors within half an hour of each other. They are both fine brigs, & the masters had laid a bet on the race, who should reach Halifax first.

29TH APRIL. Quite warm Summer these two days, and the grass now pushing quite green.

Arrived this morning the *Protector* from Greenock 39 days, & a Brig from London – two more now standing in.

Major Couper left me a few days ago on an excursion to New York & Washington to see some relations, and Sparrow is about to sail for Jamaica being appointed Dy. Adj. Genl. there with the rank of Lt. Colonel – a great step to him. I shall deeply regret his loss in my family as a most gentlemanlike & pleasant young man and very smart officer.

1ST MAY. May day is most delightful; by 6 o'clock the whole town almost was out walking towards Point Pleasant gathering the Mayflower all cheerful & gay. Welcome Spring with all its charms!

3RD MAY. Every succeeding day continues still finer than the former. Ploughs and all hands are at work as busy as ants. The oldest inhabitants now foretell that after a most severe & long winter, we have every prospect of a fine spring & seed time.

10TH MAY. Constant southerly winds this last week (with thick fog which however generally cleared away in the forenoon), has brought forward everything that feels the influence of spring; the grass pushes up almost visibly, potatoes & corn putting into the ground & the little cottage gardens assuming an air of neatness & comfort all round this neighbourhood.

The April Packet 20 days from Falmouth, 10 or a dozen ships from London 23 days, and several from Leith & Aberdeen also in 23-28 days, have been daily crowding into this Port, a very cheering & delightful sight. I have received by them considerable quantities of seed wheat, oats & Potatoes, which come most opportunely in these times of distress among the poor. I have distributed the whole of them & find them almost a blessing to them, besides obtaining my first object I had thought of, the introducing a new seed Potato into the Province, a thing much called for.

The Assembly had voted a Sum of £1500 in 1816 to purchase seed grain for the poor but being too late last year has been imported now from Liverpool. In 1817 it voted £8000 also to purchase seed grain, but this to be sold at low price to such as wanted, this has been imported from the States, & arriving just now for distribution, will brighten our prospects & with the blessing of God will restore plenty & comfort to this land. Government has also given its powerful aid by authorising me to distribute seed potatoes to the Refugee Negroes, to the amount I dare say of 800 families.

In spite of the known distress that has existed, and the many difficulties & hardships to which new settlers are exposed on their arrival in these Provinces, I find these last ships from Scotland are full of emigrants to us. The labourers are almost immediately engaged, but carpenters, masons & other superior workmen are sadly put to it. Provisions at this season extremely dear, & house rent or lodgings most extravagant.

18TH MAY. This last week I have been almost constantly occupied in Official correspondence to England as the Packet from New York homeward bound takes our accumulated business in answer to the Dispatches of January Feby. March and April. It is now done and I only wait the arrival of the Admiral, Sir David Milne, to set me free to begin my excursions into the Country. The delay of his arrival surprises us all. All the Merchant fleets of the season have reached us from England, but not one of our own Squadron has seen this [place] from Bermudas since November last. Their only duty is to check smuggling & they ought to have been at their post two months ago.

In weather, this week has been equally fine; a day or two of rain or fog has done no damage; the accounts from the country are very cheering, but not a plant nor leaf has yet burst out, except the little Mayflower, very pretty & sweet, putting out its flower in the woods & by the little streamlets, so concealed that it is very difficult to find them & is now the occupation of all the little children, bringing them in large posies.

24TH MAY. The *Pactolus* frigate, Capt. Dobie, has at last brought us some account of the Admiral at Bermuda; he will be detained there on publick business till towards the end of this month, & expects to be here the 1st June. The *Pactolus* is found to be in the same rapid state of decay as the *Niger* and is in consequence ordered to Quebec to take home the seamen discharged on the Lakes. The *Niger* is too bad to leave this harbour. All those fir frigates built 3 years ago have gone to dry rot in a most extraordinary manner. The wind has been almost steady about south this week bringing in fog & raw atmosphere from the sea – nothing however to do any damage – the grass grows most rapidly, but no trees yet in leaf, nor flowers except daffodils & rananculus.

1ST JUNE. Early last week on Monday I went to Windsor, stopping at Mount Uniacke to dine; next day 27th rode up to breakfast with the Chief Justice and look about a small place I have taken for summer residence near him, & returned again to dine with Uniacke. Next morning walked about his place & farm, and then returned to dinner at Halifax. Weather delightful all the time we were absent. The Commissioner Wodehouse, Duke & Sparrow went with me, the party altogether most pleasant.

Mount Uniacke, situated on the margin of a fine Lake & surrounded by the woody wilderness mixed up with great granite rocks, is a very gentlemanlike, & may in time be a pretty place, but at present has little to recommend it, except the new comfortable house and the cordial hospitality of its Proprietor.

Small patches of grass park already show a great deal of industry, & very great expense of money, which I could not have understood had I not had this opportunity of witnessing the progressive steps in the clearing of land in this Province. Mr. Uniacke had this winter cut down some 100 acres of wood; he was now burning them in some places; in others this had been done; the great logs dragged off, and he was planting potatoes in hills (like the molehills) or sowing oats with grass seed (the sweeping of his hay loft); this last was the most clumsy & strange performance I ever saw, by a sort of harrow, a log cut in the woods with some iron spikes driven into it just to scratch the ground over the seed. A pair of bullocks drag it among the stumps & roots, & when it catches at anything, a labourer going behind lifts it up & shakes it free. This done, the ground is left for 10 years to what little grass may grow, & while the stems & trunks of the large wood rot & become more easy to take out.

As no manure is given, nor a ploughing practicable, I shall be hereafter much astonished if either Potatoes or oats come to maturity upon it.

The seat of the Chief Justice is a small Box in the worst possible order; he lives at it in Summer and shuts it up all winter without even a Servant to keep a fire in it. Nothing could be more uncomfortable to all appearance....

8TH JUNE. Fine Summer set in, and every tree now bursting into leaf. The Poplars may be said full out. The *Hydra* returned some days ago from West Indies with the remains of 15th Regt. and today we have the pleasure to see the Admiral now beating up the harbour against a fresh Northerly wind. So large a ship in so narrow a Bason, & saluting the forts after being saluted, & weather beautiful, makes altogether a fine sight....

16TH JUNE. At 2 o'clock A.M. a fire broke out this morning in the range of Officers' Barracks, & raged with awful violence, but was fortunately got under before 6 o'clock. Our half of the building is burnt, the other has been gutted to stop the flames.

19TH JUNE.... As is generally the case, the cause of the fire cannot be ascertained, but I do not think it any way surprising that such an accident should happen in a large wooden building, 3 stories high, & full of officers lodged in pigeon holes with their swords near them. All descriptions of ill behaved people going in & out. The morning scene I am told was most ludicrous. Gentlemen & Ladies bolting in the utmost consternation, little or no cloaths on them, one saving a box of money, another a bundle of cloaths, Ladies flying but blushing at their dilemma, trying still to hide, rain pouring fortunately in torrents, & affording abundant supply for the Pipes, helped at once to check the flames & start the flying from their lurking places, not unlike rabbits in a warren when a ferret is first in among them. With such a swarm within I am not surprised at the accident.

23RD JUNE. For some days past I have been engaged in the half-yearly Inspection of the Battalion in Garrison. The 15th is much the finest Regt. here.... 7th Btn. 60th ordered to be drafted into 2nd and 3rd, but chusing generally 2nd. I have allowed them to volunteer, discharging a great number as totally unfit for the service, indeed the whole Battn. is unfit in one respect, that it is composed of French conscripts who entered our Army from our Prisons, & expecting their discharge at the end of the War are now discontented, & desert on every opportunity they can get....

30RD JUNE. We have been most impatiently looking for the May Packet from Falmouth; it is now coming in after a tedious passage of

46 days. For some time past we have had constant westerly winds, which bringing the finest weather imaginable for us on shore, have been directly contrary to all arrivals from Europe.

In this respect we have witnessed several large ships arriving with great numbers of passengers (300 in one vessel) in a state of starvation after 60 days passage.

On the other hand however & happily it is so, a finer season for seed time and crops generally never was known. All Canada, as well as this Province, rejoices in the prospect we have at present.

10TH JULY. We had nothing of any importance from England by this last Packet, and as the Admiral had proposed to me a short cruize on board the *Leander,* I made arrangements to go with him to Moose Island, visiting Shelburne & our near harbours as we returned. Today I was requested by Mr. Wallace, Mr. Hartshorne and other respectable inhabitants of Dartmouth to lay the foundation stone of a church to be immediately built there. The Admiral attended with me, but no uncommon shew or assemblage was invited & it passed very privately.

14TH JULY. The Admiral has now required me on board, a fine Northerly breeze promising a good run along the coast, & take Lady D. & Jim, Colonel Wright, my Chief Engineer, and Couper. This last week the weather has been very warm, the Therm. from 65 to 72. No interruptions of rain or fog or blowing weather, quite delightful summer.

15TH JULY. It fell nearly calm yesterday about 4 P.M. when off the Sambro' Light House. *Earl Bathurst* and *Iona* tenders with us. At 8 A.M. this morning we are close in with Cape Le Have; the 7 hills or rather knolls over it, are the only remarkable feature to be distinguished by a strange vessel along the whole southern coast of this Province. A fine fresh breeze at S.W. heading us all day, we beat down, and left the small craft very far astern.

16TH JULY. Same wind & same delightful weather beating down along the coast, till about 3 P.M. We anchored in Shelburne harbour, running in beautiful style at 9 knots; in the Evening landed to take a walk, when we were received by Colonel Buskirk, Mr. Campbell & Mr. Barry from Liverpool.

In former times, that is, soon after 1783, an emigration of Loyalists from America came here & settled under Lord Shelburne's

37

administration & Patronage, to the number of 12,000 people, and in imitation of Lord Halifax in 1749 gave his name to this intended rival capital of Nova Scotia. Bringing with them very large property in money they built fine houses, neglected the more immediate objects of new settlers, the clearing of land for food, or the establishment of fisheries, for which the situation of the settlement was admirably adapted, and having very soon wasted & squandered their funds were obliged to fly back to America leaving large grants of land untouched to this day, but laying still as the property of these individuals. Now, Shelburne is the picture of despair and wretchedness. The population does not exceed 90 families, perhaps in all 400 people. The large homes, rotten & tumbling into the once fine & broad streets, the inhabitants crawling about idle and careworn in appearance, sunk in poverty and dejected in spirit.

The fishing trade so totally extinct that not even a fishing boat brings a supply to market for daily use, altho' in a few houses off the Light House they might load vessels with fine cod, as fast as the people can haul them up. An English church, the clergyman Mr. Rowland, a very good man, a Scotch Kirk, but so poorly appointed in Salary that the old Preacher threatens to leave it; and a very neat Methodist Chapel, are each of them fully attended.

A grist mill about a mile out of town very prettily situated, but apparently falling to ruin. I saw a poke net laying on a rock near it, by which, I was told, the miller made a better livelihood than by his mill, catching prodigious quantities of gaspereaux, or large herring, that shoal up the streams of this Province at this season, and are cured for winter use and exportation.

A miserable decayed battery close to town, six guns mounted, & one Artilleryman in charge. We called him "the Commander of the Forces," as he talked & moved with a consequence as if commanding all that part of the Province.

17TH JULY. We landed early this morning and first I looked over the maps & Surveyor General's Plans of the County of Shelburne at Mr. Campbell's but from the confusion and tattered state of these papers, it was utterly impossible to investigate them. Scarcely any property marked as originally granted, now is found under the same name. Almost all the proprietors of the first day have returned to the

United States, most of them leaving their land in charge of Agents. Many new people, old soldiers, sailors, Black & Colour people from New York have seated themselves on parts of these properties, & not being disturbed, have cultivated for 25 or 30 years small farms on which these Agents now claim & enforce rents.

I received today a great many Memorials from that description of people claiming the protection of Government, and licences of occupation to sit free on these deserted lands. Also from a small tribe of Indians that is said to be settled and industriously fixed on Long Island in the Roseway River.

We then got some horses & buggies & drove a short distance into the Country. Nothing worth notice. The Barracks on the sloping side of a hill on the opposite of the harbour, are falling in utter ruin. They are too far from the town to be of any use. I shall therefore recommend them to be condemned & sold or grant away the land. A Mr. Guest, a shopkeeper in Shelburne, has been Barrack Master for many years on 3 /6 a day, a very improper appointment by Sir Geo. Prevost, in this that Mr. Guest never did serve his King or Country in any manner whatever, & I do consider these little situations as belonging exclusively to old soldiers or publick retired servants.

18TH JULY. I addressed a letter this morning to Mr. Buskirk & Mr. Campbell, jointly as Members of town & County of Shelburne, requesting they would obtain or make up for me a Report of all lands in this county liable to Escheat, in order that I may adopt some steps to give new life to this miserable place.

We had intended to have sailed today but the wind was blowing right into the harbour & not sufficient for the large ship to beat down a narrow passage, we again landed. I walked with Mr. Rowland to the Church, very neat & clean indeed, inside; in the Churchyard is a handsome stone erected to the Memory of Patrick Maxwell, brother of Jack Maxwell of Springhill, an Ensign in 6th Regt. and my schoolfellow at Edinburgh High School—he was drowned here about 1791, sailing in the Bay with another officer & his servant. The people yet speak of that accident with great regret.

From a black moss of considerable extent behind the town quantities of excellent peat are dug & used as fire.

19TH JULY. Wind still light & right in. We went down to Sandy

Point to hawl the seines & did catch loads of fine flounders, with a variety of Scalpins & other fish not eatable, extremely disgusting in appearance.

Here I found an old German Soldier Andrew Gothack, settled & very well off, having brought up a family of 10 children on this spot, but he is in similar case with those already noted who are plagued and oppressed by Agents who demand rent of him, altho' I find his little domain of perhaps 10 acres is a reserve of Govt. for the purpose of establishing a battery at this point to command the entrance to the harbour. He also complained that no money circulated in this neighbourhood—for butter, eggs or whatever they had to sell, they got a barter of Sugar, Tea or Rum, & all these of the worst quality, smuggled by the American fishermen who infest this Coast.

It is really to me quite inexplicable that these complaints of the people, & this state of things, should have remained so long neglected by the Governors & Government of this Province.

Quitting our fishing sport, we rowed across to Gunning Cove; on the rising ground here, another battery had been projected & 19 heavy guns 24 lbs. are laying ranged on the point as preparatory— certainly this cross fire would most completely secure the harbour against shipping attack....

21ST JULY. At daylight the wind having veered round to Northwest, we got up anchor, and with a fine fresh breeze leaving the Light House about 9 A.M., we dropped anchor in Liverpool Bay before 3 P.M.

Mr. Newton the Collector of the Customs, Col. Tupper and a Mr. Parker immediately came off to us and invited us to land in the Evening which we accordingly did & drank tea at Mr. Newton's, returning on board early.

We gave up our plan to visit Moose Island on the assurance of our Pilot that tho' we did beat up to it in a couple of days, we might not get out again for a month, shut up in constant and impenetrable fogs, & deferred it till October, when the Bay of Fundy is clear. We then agreed to visit Liverpool & Lunenburg on our way back to meet the Packet at Halifax.

23RD JULY. Yesterday we breakfasted with Mr. Parker, walked all about town, visiting Capt. Gorehan, Mr. Barss, and inspecting a very fine Bridge just now finished by private subscription. It is 1100 feet long with a drawbridge in the middle of the stream to allow vessels to pass up the river. It is a work in the highest degree creditable to the inhabitants of Queen's County, whether it be considered as marking the publick spirit, or the private liberality of this part of the Province. Rode out to Col. Tupper's sawmills, about 3 miles up the river, a very busy & thriving establishment. All the work done being paid in hard money, every individual I saw wore the appearance of prosperity and contentment.

Liverpool is in all respects a most striking contrast to Shelburne. The houses large, clean & handsome, many new ones building, the streets broad, gay & bustling in work, the people wealthy and confessing themselves to be so. Their concerns are mercantile & in the Labrador fisheries. They do trade to the West Indies but on a small scale. They were fortunate in Privateering speculations during the war with America, & are keenly bent on that pursuit against the States. Agriculture is not attempted here; Mr. Parker alone has just begun to clear a very rough & stony field of 10 acres over the town, which I have no doubt will amply repay the heavy expenses of the work.

We dined with Mr. Newton, but it set in a very wet night, blowing hard and thick fog. Having some doubt of reaching the ship, we persuaded Lady D. to remain on shore, & fortunately we did so, for tho' we did get on board, it was with difficulty, and after a long row, & firing pistols as signal, which at last the ship heard & returned us a gun.

This morning we went for her, & after breakfast weighed anchor, having a fine breeze & weather. At 12 passed the Light House, and at 4 dropt anchor in Lunenburg, 5 miles below the town & like Liverpool also an open Bay, having a large island in the entrance to afford shelter for shipping in it — it has deep water very far in, but a sunk rock & shoal exactly in the middle of it greatly injures the harbour. After a hasty dinner on board, we landed on a point called the Drum Head, from the beating of the waves into hollow caverns along the west shore. We found a very comfortable farm of one Neisner a German, well cultivated by him & his brother, both young men with large families. His father had purchased this land for him, & has occupied it more than 40 years, but he complains that new people & new surveyors threaten to deprive him of a considerable portion of his farm. We found a very clean house, & a large folio family Bible in German on the table.

24TH JULY. I sent up Major Couper early this morning to find a magistrate, & procure gigs or horses to visit the neighbourhood of Lunenburg. Col. Creighton, & Rudolf of the Militia, were both in town, & received us on landing. The fort saluted, & a Captain's Militia Guard attended, commanded by Major Ernst.

At Col. Rudolf's we were visited by all the respectable people of the place—Dr. Bollman, a Mr. James, Capt. Oxner, Mr. Aiken the clergyman, Mr. Jacobs, Mr. Macara, two young men surgeons just established, the former a remarkably fine young man.

This again is totally different from Liverpool. All here is German, scarcely do they speak English intelligibly. Agriculture is their only pursuit, they are not wealthy, but live very frugally, & are all comfortable, a singular circumstance that there never has yet been a Pauper, maintained by the Parish.

We rode out 7 miles, returning another road by Zwicker's tavern at the head of Mahone Bay. It is a rich & beautifully diversified county but yet miserable farms, all in patches, raising potatoes & hay for Halifax market.

On a rising ground at the farm of one Smeltzer we stopt to admire a most commanding and extensive view of the Mahone Bay or Archipelago, studded with upwards of 300 islands, wooded & some of them cultivated, shewing small white farm houses, Chester town & Church in the distance, the high rocky district of Aspotogon on the right covered with wood, & today a tremendous wild fire raging in them, added greatly to the grandeur and beauty of the Picture.

Having taken a cold dinner at Col. Rudolf's & visited Capt. & Mrs. Oxner, a rough, hearty and most kind couple, we returned on board at 5 o'clock.

I find this a very prosperous settlement, but as at Shelburne great complaints of want of fishing lots, proper grants of their land and of the too great extent of the common round the town. It was fixed at 3000 acres originally but by custom & common use has extended itself to more than 7000 acres.

I was much pressed to ride tomorrow to Le Have & Pleasant rivers, but am anxious now to reach Halifax.

Lord John Hay has just anchored along side of us, reports the Packet not arrived.

25TH JULY. Quite calm this morning but yet we weighed at 8 o'clock, & towed out till we found a light air from S.W. which soon freshened, & brought us into Halifax by 5 P.M. We rounded the Sambro Light House about 3 and run up so fast, at 9 knots, that we were anchored at the Dockyard before the proper Officers there were aware of our approach. The style in which we passed George's Island on our starboard side, the Fort on it saluting, & then the ship — shooting so quick, steady & close past the town wharfs, crowded with people, was altogether a most beautiful scene.

We did not land till the cool of the Evening about 7 o'clock, when Sir David again saluted us, manning the yards in the same style as when we embarked—thus closing a most delightful & most fortunate cruize. Delightful by the interesting & beautiful parts of the coast we have seen, but equally so by the unremitted kindness & attention of the Admiral & every individual on board. It was fortunate in the extreme in point of weather & winds daily favoring our intentions & exceeding our utmost expectations.

29TH JULY. At last our impatience is relieved. The Packet signal announces her 42 days from Falmouth. Yesterday we had a fine rain all day, which from a long spell of very dry & very hot weather is now much required for every kind of crop.

10TH AUGUST. Sunday. When all in joy and happiness we welcomed the arrival of the English Packet, little did I think that it brought us tidings of the deepest affliction—tidings that will be to us a source of lasting sorrow & grief in this world. A fortnight of calm & peaceful retirement at our little cottage here [at Windsor] has restored Lady D. to composure, and enabled me again to resume my little memos of our passtime in this distant corner of the world, separated from all relations & friends; but I resume it only to note the sad & distressing thoughts of the death of my poor & dear little boy Charles. So sudden a blow, so utterly unexpected and un-thought of in the state of comfort and really happiness in which our time had glided & was passing along, struck with electric force. Couper came hastily into my room and threw down two letters, rushing out in evident distress; the first idea struck me that he had himself received some melancholy news from home, as Sparrow lately had that of his father's death; I followed him & could not for some time comprehend the meaning of his actions untill he shook his head & said "Poor Ramsay." My blood ran cold; looking at my two letters I observed one was from Mary with a black seal & the other from Mr. Gordon, also black. I left Couper's room and immediately after met Lady D. flying down all joy for her letters—

A fortnight's retirement has now, thank God, restored us all to composure, and I trust to a sincere & humble resignation to the Allwise dispensations of the Almighty. Time alone & a proper sense of Religion, can afford us that comfort & balm to the mind which every thought of our loss will long call for.

I cannot however but consider it also a Mercy of Heaven, in thus conveying to us the death blow, instead of having heard of the dangerous illness of our boys by this Packet, & hanging on in anxious suspense untill the arrival of the next, which would bring the fatal end of our hopes & fears.

We have lost a most interesting, hopeful, & dear little boy. In looks, I thought, the image of his Mother, in disposition mild, quiet, kind & tractable, in ability slow, sensible, & retentive to an uncommon degree in memory, in principle, upright, honourable, & manly; an untruth or equivocation never passed his lips. His shrewd, dry remarks, or advice to his brother, often bespoke a character singular as a boy, but such as I have fondly flattered myself might have proved a sound & solid foundation of a distinguished after life.

Almighty God has taken my dear Charles to himself; his Will be done! Lady D. has today attended Church here, and meeting the public in this manner will now be inclined to see her friends, & receive that expression of consolation & sympathy which at first is always distressing, but at same time is customary & soothing. . . .

16TH AUGUST. Sunday. The expected arrival of the homeward bound Packet from New York, & the usual publick correspondence to go by it, tempted me to go down to Halifax on Tuesday last, & I returned last night. No Packet had arrived. The *Victory*—a fine ship trader to & from Halifax & Liverpool, sailed on Friday. I wrote several letters by her, and as she returns here early in November, I have given directions that my dear boy Ramsay shall come out in her to join us, or by the October Packet from Falmouth. A tutor will accompany him, and I trust in God that he may long be spared to us, a comfort and a happiness.

A good deal of rain in the course of the week and unusual heat (Therm. one day at 92 degrees) have not favoured the hay, but the grain crops already take a yellowish tinge. Altho' the farming classes do seem busy, yet it is nothing to the active industry at home at this season—the hay fields are all cut in little bits, which they toss one day and drive home the next, then turn to another little bit; seldom more than two men are mowing together. Great thirst for *rum*, and generally in the evening I observe the labour staggering along the roads, noisy & roaring like ill-doing blackguards.

21ST AUGUST. Day before yesterday being fine and cool, we took an early dinner and drove over the hills to see the township of Horton—a beautiful tho' very hilly road, 17 miles in which are 3 distinct ranges of hills, the first rising from Avon bridge & descending to Halfway river, next rising very steep & descending to Gaspereaux River, then rising & descending extremely steep on Horton—the Bason of Minas, Blowmidon & the coast from Partridge Island Eastward closing in a fine expansive Bay. There is no town of Horton; it is a scattered settlement of neat common houses, small farmers, but rich in their way of life. A considerable exent of salt meadow dyked in, produces a great stock of hay, in which their chief wealth seems to consist. We put up at Graham's tavern, the other Fowler's, also good but very small indeed.

Yesterday we intended going on to Cornwallis, but a heavy rain set in; we waited 12 o'clock; it did not promise to mend, & we resolved on returning home. Horton has a handsome Anabaptist Church, & an English Established Church is building on a much smaller scale. In winter they declare it quite a common thing to baptize in deep water, breaking the ice for the purpose; & that men & women come in their best cloaths to be thrown headlong into it— they go directly to some neighbours near, where they had sent dry cloaths to shift. By their way of talking there is not much reverence of Religion among them—they are not active or industrious, lounging idly about their doors; they could give no satisfactory account of any roads distant 4 miles from them.

On my return I found the English mail arrived & waiting us.

With trembling I flew to the Bag, but happily received accounts that Ramsay was perfectly recovered & at Dalhousie Castle. Dreading any continued bad accounts of the weakness or dregs attending Measles, this was a comfort & relief almost inexpressible, & far beyond our hopes. Today Lady D. feels as if a heavy load & oppression had been removed from her mind & thoughts; she feels herself a different being.

I cannot but be deeply impressed with gratitude and thankfulness that a Merciful God has supported her with so much fortitude under her affliction and sorrow. The worst is now over, and the comfort this Packet brings will help her to go forward. Time alone, with a well regulated mind & just confidence in the Almighty, will support her, and remove all our sorrows. But we may, & shall long, long lament the loss of our dear Charles.

Anxious to see as much of the Province this summer as I can well reach, I feel I can now leave Lady D. for a few weeks with her friend & kind companion Miss Cochrane at this retired cottage, and again proceed with the Admiral on a cruize on the Coast. We intend this time to visit the harbours Eastward, the Gut of Canso & Pictou. There my horses shall meet me and I'll ride home by Truro, laying out my time so as to be at Halifax on or about the 21st of next month.

25TH AUGUST. I left Windsor on 22nd, in gig with Couper, & having a fresh horse at Lacey's, reached Halifax early to dinner. Two days of heavy rain have enabled me to close my dispatches in answer of this Packet and now wait a fair wind to proceed with Sir David.

27TH AUGUST. We embarked yesterday in *Leander* under the usual salute and sailed with a fine breeze at N.W. At sunset we were close in with Liscomb harbour but did not venture it till this morning at daylight, dropping anchor round the first head on West shore & opposite a bar passage leading around a large island to the East. We lost no time after breakfast, a very fine day, in proceeding up the harbour in the *Jane* tender & our rowboats. The Jane took the ground about 5 miles up, & we then got into the boats, landing occasionally to shoot; but a solitary Gull or woodpecker were the only living creatures seen. I observed the footmark of a large deer, probably Moose, but soon lost it in the thick wood. The harbour, about 8 miles from our Anchorage, branched off right & left, ending on the

West or left hand in a very small rivulet; to the East it runs up in deep still water about 200 yards broad, finely wooded on both sides for a mile, when we were stopt by a considerable cataract tumbling thro' & over broken crags, extremely romantic, and wild as if no human being had ever been there before. When we returned however some miserably poor fisherman living near the anchorage told us that above that cataract the river became quiet, still & navigable by canoes 12 miles up the Country.

28TH AUGUST. This morning we took some cold meat and supplies for a few days in the *Bathurst* and *Jane* tenders with our boats, and by the bar passage rounded the headlands of East Liscomb, or Jejoggan, the Indian name, into St. Mary's river; another very fine harbour but dangerous of access from sea. About 6 o'clock P.M. we had stood near 14 miles inland; the *Jane* took the ground, and after some difficulty getting her off, we dropt anchor for the night. The Admiral & I had early in the day got into his gig, and shot small curlew & gulls all the way up the river. As this is subject to tides, very broad & very flat mud banks at low water, the birds kept shy of us, and our tenders were obliged to wait the flowing tide to come up. The course of the river is closely settled, but the utmost poverty appears in every hut; they subsist entirely by fishing and their small potatoe gardens.

29TH AUGUST. On anchoring last night I sent up a letter to Mr. Wentworth Taylor, the chief magistrate residing in this district, desiring to see him, but he is absent just now; but learning that a new settlement called Sherbrooke lay at the top of tide within two miles of us, we went up this morning with our Guns and fishing tackle. I got one Partridge, the Admiral, Capt. Chambers, Col. Duke & Lord Schomberg Kerr killed a load of very fine silvery sea trout, generally of 1 to 2 lbs. each.

The greater part of my time I walked with a Mr. Archibald, the Chief Proprietor of this neighbourhood, & now forming this settlement in the shape of a town. He has already laid it off in broad streets, a dozen houses built, a saw & grist mill, carpenter & blacksmith's shop, & an Inn nearly finished. A neat schoolhouse where 25 children attend daily; the master officiates in reading prayers on Sunday. The soil is a dry sandy loam, very fine woods of lofty Beech & Maple, with thick undergrowth mixed up with natural spruce &

hemlock. A broad black river, sometimes broken, sometimes a long stretch of still water & winding beautifully for some miles I walked above the village, strongly recalled to my thoughts the situation of Dunkeld.

We spent a very delightful forenoon and returned on board at 4 o'clock, intending to have gone down the river with the tide, but we find the *Bathurst* now on shore & dry. We must therefore wait daylight tomorrow.

30TH AUGUST. At midnight the flood tide set us allright again, & this morning dawning with a nice breeze at North, we got away and rounding the headlands of Jegoggan, reached the ship today at 11 o'clock. We expected to have got up anchor & been off directly, but as noon approached the wind veered to East & we were obliged to keep fast in Liscomb.

This Evening one of the poor fishers here came on board to petition for a grant of a point of land he had settled upon. His history is curious. His name is Drayton, an Irishman of good family, but in early life he had run from them, and enlisted during the American war. He had been educated at Trinity College, Dublin, & still retained a perfect knowledge of Greek & Latin, speaking the latter fluently. Mr. Brown, the Admiral's Chaplain & tutor to his two boys, examined the old fellow, & found him quite a Master in Latin, altho' he asured him he had not seen a book for many years.

He mentioned the names of several gentlemen in Ireland who had been his intimates at College, particularly a Mr. Nixon, and it singularly happened, that a very fine young man of the *Leander,* a midshipman, standing by at the moment, was a son of that very Mr. Nixon, & by many questions from the old man corroborated his story.

He said, he had in his day spent a great deal of money. He had sown a plentiful store of wild oats, & reaped his crop of Misery. He had served the whole American war, & then come to this Province, pitched himself on the point of land he now asked for, had married a neighbour's daughter, had now 11 Children, 8 of them girls, mostly yet young, & found it hard indeed to feed them all.

His appearance is quite original, long, lanky white hair hanging over a very old & wrinkled head, a hat in rags, & often sewed together with rope yarns, a shirt of flannel, red & yellow pieces patched – a pair of soldier's old pantaloons & no shoes – a most miserable figure altogether. He had a very fine smart boy in his boat, about 14 much better dressed. The Admiral gave him a Bag of Biscuit, the sailors loaded him with cloaths, & he went away as drunk as he well could be.

I could give him no promise of the land untill I made enquiries about it, and he has promised to be at Halifax about the 20th Sept. to meet me, or to send his wife in his stead.

31ST AUGUST. Sunday. Last night at 10 o'clock Mr. Wentworth Taylor and Mr. Archibald came on board from the St. Mary's River, & brought us a few sheep we had bespoke while there. We had a good deal of conversation about the state of their new settlement, & roads into the Country, of which they gave us a most miserable account, shewing that district of the Province utterly neglected in the House of Assembly, as there was no Member residing near them nor connected with them. After supper, we sent them to sleep in the *Bathurst,* under promise that they would return on board to break-fast & go round with us today into Country Harbour, but at day dawn, they were seen go into their own boat, & have returned to St. Mary's.

We weighed at daylight, wind at East, but as it is only 7 Leagues distant, we thought we would easily beat up. It came however to blow fresh, & we have only now got in, about 2 o'clock. The *Jane* has made it out with us but *Bathurst,* a very bad sailor, could not do it, & we suppose she has bore up for Liscomb again.

Country Harbour is another very fine anchorage; tho' narrow it is deep & capacious, but like all other parts of this south coast of Nova Scotia, it is guarded by small detached islands & rocks near the entrance, & which at present being little known are dangerous. One of these rocks with breakers is called in old charts the Bassoon, & it appears Des Barres had been induced to name several other rocks he surveyed there, in similar fancy. There are now the Bassoon, the Fiddle, the Flute, & a large black rock inshore he has named the Orpheus, as Presiding over the band.

Sir David Milne has a complete set of Des Barres' charts of the American Coast which he has as yet found most accurate – they are very difficult to be got now.

2ND SEPTEMBER. We have anchored about 5 miles up this harbour within the round hill forming Cochran's Creek. Yesterday it continued stormy & raining hard all day, which prevented any of us going on shore. This morning breakfasted early & went up the river as far as the tide permitted our small boats, in a large fishing party. About 7 miles from the ship anchorage we entered the fresh water river, & proceeded 5 miles farther up it – not so large as St. Mary's, shallow, rocky & full of stumps of large trees floated down.

The harbour has detached settlements along its banks. On East side is Capt. Leggett's large property in ruin, then a Mr. Archibald who has an Inn, a Saw & Grist Mill, an active industrious young man – then a Capt. Cameron, a Magistrate; after entering the fresh water we came to the schoolmaster's, Johnstone, an intelligent fellow; Hudson & Mason, farmers, well doing men with large families. The latter has been both soldier & Sailor, settled 35 years here, has 14 children & another, he says, just coming. He petitioned for 200 acres adjoining his land for his son, which I promised to enquire into.

The Admiral staid till almost dark, killing a great quantity of the same kind of white silvery sea trout he met with at St. Mary's, red flesh, excellent to eat. On our return down the stream, our host struck on a sharp point of a large tree, which run quite thro', so that the water filled us instantly, & we just could get her safe to land; fortunately the Barge was near us, took us up & we got on board very late. The schoolmaster & natives, all carpenters & handy fellows, soon put in a new plank & sent our boat after us.

At Mason's the valley opens a little, perhaps to a mile broad, is pretty, with very fine woods, but not nearly so romantic as St. Mary's.

I found great complaints of the state of the settlement in this remote corner. Only one Magistrate, & he not active. No Clergyman within 40 miles. The population increasing fast, & the young people growing up in very riotous & dissolute habits. It is a very extensive tract granted in 1783 to a Major Wright in the 82nd Regt; the men very soon left their lots, selling them to their Officers for a dollar. Thus Capt. Leggett has acquired a very large property in land; he is dead, the children idle, & the widow a poor indigent person in Halifax, of ladylike manners, & with a most pitiful story comes frequently to me an urgent beggar. The large tract of land lays useless & derelict, subject to an escheat to the Crown, were I so to order the Process; Mr. Cameron & all in that corner strongly advise that step, but I still feel it would add accumulation to the distress of that family.

3RD SEPTEMBER. Again the Admiral went up to the fishing stream. I went with the Commissioner & Archibald Maclean of the *Leander* to call on Capt. Cameron—he had observed the Admiral go up, & fancying I should be with him, had followed the boat. I did not see him, but his wife received us, very well bred & very civil—a nice young woman and three beautiful little children. The spot on which they have placed their miserable small house is extremely pretty, a round promontory having a long view down the harbour (or rather lake it appears), but not so far as our Ship. On our return we landed at different points & hauled the seine, without any success. Maclean quitted us with my gun & dog, & walked 5 miles along shore, till he came opposite the anchorage—saw nothing whatever to shoot. The weather today excessively hot.

On reaching the ship I found *Bathurst* arrived & having Wentworth Taylor and a Mr. McKeen in her. Taylor is the Deputy Surveyor in that district; he had prepared for me a plan of that part of the Coast with all the existing roads, & a proposal for the formation of a township at St. Mary's River, a measure certainly of importance, & shall be done if possible. After dinner they started on a new road towards Antigonish, and seemed delighted to get their Congé. They had both proved very bad sailors in *Bathurst*.

4TH SEPTEMBER. Early this morning Capt. Cameron came on board—a tall rawbone Highlander, a very rough countenance, pitted severely by the smallpox, lost one eye – has been 35 years here without almost ever having been absent – his present cottage is his first house, built by himself, but is now able & preparing one more comfortable. He is a sensible man, served the whole American war, and is the only Officer remaining who settled in this part of the Country. He seems to know nobody in Scotland now & cares for no one; he is happy in his family and contented with his lot. Verging on 60, he is becoming indolent, and dislikes the duties he is obliged to perform as the only Magistrate.

5TH SEPTEMBER. Thick fog outside, we still have stood fast, hauled the seine near the mouth of the harbour, caught only lobsters in cart loads.

I observed while walking along the shore a kind of Pea or vetch, uncommonly pretty in flower & very luxurious, growing among the seawashed pebble stones. I made the sailors gather me a bag of the pods now ripe, which I think may be useful at home as food for cattle & horses....

6TH SEPTEMBER. Calm today we durst not move – the ship's company was exercised at the great Guns, shotted & made excellent practice; the broadside was brought to bear on a point on Cochran Head. Sir David shewed me that the long heavy 24 pounder will throw 3 shot at once with prodigious effect and to a great distance not diverging or scattering from the right line at all. Congreve's short & light 24 pounder will not do it, too thin at breach, & apt to burst, & therefore Sir David condemns them most decidedly & severely.

9TH SEPTEMBER. On Sunday (day before yesterday) we got under weigh at dawn of day, but soon found that the wind at sea was very different from that within the narrow harbour – it blew however fresh, and enabled us in this fine ship to beat up round Cape Canso before Evening. Sir David intended to have dropt anchor under Cape Argos, but it was a very moderate & fine clear night, we lay off and on till morning. All anxious to see the beauties of this Passage (vilely called the Gut of Canso) and the entrance into the St. Lawrence, we were up before day. It dawned most beautifully; the moon in her last quarter was still up, & the crescent tho' small was more clear & bright than I ever saw it. A star also near it singularly brilliant. The Sun rose deep red, & in magnificent splendor some streaming black clouds hanging over it like a drapery fitted to the picture. The land below it was Richmond Island on the Cape Breton shore, broken into innumerable points and head lands covered with wood. The wind very light, heading us now & then, created great fears that we should be obliged to drop anchor, however about 8 o'clock at breakfast it again favored us as we neared the narrow opening of the Gut of Canso, and at 10 o'clock we could lay with nice steerage right up, the wind on our larboard quarter. We went very slow & majestically – the forward & the lower sails clewed up, the top gallant sails & Royals alone full – the weather bright & hot sunshine on deck could not have been more fine & favorable for our purpose.

About 12 o'clock the wind died away, & the ebb tide taking us, when abreast of the Plaster Cove on the Breton shore we drifted back a mile and dropt anchor in Ship harbour.

We had dined, got out boats to visit the shore, guns & fishing tackle all prepared, when near 3 o'clock a fine breeze sprung up, & the tide now making in our favour Sir David got under weigh, & passed up in grand style quite clear of the narrows before sunset. While at anchor we observed many of the people on the Breton shore gathering about their houses, as if expecting a visit from us; when we suddenly departed, they crowded to the doors as if expressing regret – in our party particularly an old Highlander tuned his pipes, & played to us as long as we could hear him.

The scenery altogether is most picturesque, both sides finely covered with woods, and thickly settled by fishermen – small squares of perhaps 4 acres at each house, just sufficient to raise them potatoes, & some coarse grass cut for the little cows' hay for the winter. The houses appear comfortable, & all of them full of children in nests of six or eight – very well cloathed, and no symptoms of poverty such as we saw at Country Harbour or St. Mary's. The hay harvest is now making everywhere. The Plaster also is working but it does not look so valuable as the quarries near Windsor. 11 Schooners are laying in the cove waiting cargo. Just opposite this Cove is Cape Porcupine, a very fine headland covered with noble woods but not the smallest attempt at settlement upon it. It is the property of Sir John Borlase Warren, granted to him while he was Admiral on this station; it certainly ought to be escheated.

Having cleared the narrows, we found it blew very fresh from West. We could not easily fetch into George's or Antigonish Bay, & it being very bad anchorage we stood across to Cape George (called by the French Cape Louis) & at midnight anchored to the northward of it; today it is fine weather but the wind light & heading us, we are beating into Pictou with little speed.

10TH SEPTEMBER. It was 5 o'clock last night before we got to our anchorage off the mouth of Pictou harbor, and we therefore did not land until this morning. We breakfasted with Mr. Mortimer, who has kindly provided quarters for all our large party.

We had imagined this a considerable town, but find it a very small village, & as the Judges are now here on their Circuit, the accommodation for travellers, bad as it is in general, is at this time infinitely worse, but Mr. Mortimer's attentions have removed all wants in that way.

We paid our respects in full uniform to the Judges (Halliburton & Wiswall) in Court, & sat awhile to hear the case in discussion. The subject was a trespass in cutting a neighbour's wood, the value of which was stated at half a dollar per ton, cut in the woods—the whole damage at present sued for might amount to £3.10 sterling; the expense of process could not be under £20. But the bodies are here extremely fond of law – the whole district is settled by Highland emigrants. The Court house is poorly but sufficiently fitted.

In the course of the day took a short ride with Mr. Mortimer—our horses having met us here from Halifax—nothing worth seeing but the situation of the village, which is pretty, on a fine merchant harbour, branching into 3 distinct considerable rivers, East, Middle and West. They are subject to the tides, and at low water have a great extent of flat mud bank. A very large party dined at Mortimer's and danced reels in the Evening.

11TH SEPTEMBER. I had given up all thought of visiting at Antigonish, but Major Cunningham of that place being here on business of circuit has pressed me so hard, I have agreed to try it tomorrow, & he has set off to procure horses for us at Arisaig; a small landing place on the south side of this bay near to Cape George.

Sir David, Mr. Mortimer and I tried today to get up the East River to the Coal Mines, but were too late, & with considerable difficulty came off to *Leander* just as it grew dark and began to blow. We were on the Admiral's gig, a dangerous little boat & hard to pull 10 miles off to the ship, the Bay being flat & only 7 fathoms, Sir David would not venture nearer shore; he was uneasy about this trip, as his boat was not fit for any swell, nor for so heavy people as himself & Mortimer.

It is now fixed that if the wind serves, the ship will drop tomorrow to Arisaig; if not we shall give up Antigonish.

14TH SEPTEMBER. Sunday. We landed again today at Pictou, highly delighted with our excursions. On Friday while at breakfast we run down with a fine & fresh breeze & landed at Arisaig Pier for about 11 o'clock; the Admiral did not like a long ride & preferred going to fish at a small river near there at Malignant Cove, a name given to it from the *Malignant* sloop of war having been wrecked there some time ago.

Major Cunningham was waiting us with plenty of horses, and at least a dozen of the proprietors of Antigonish with the sheriff of the County at their head – a young active fellow of the name of Macqueen from Ayrshire. We started immediately; the day being hot we rode very slow, & reached Antigonish (18 miles) about 4 o'clock. Among several Gentlemen who came out of the village to meet us were an old man, a Capt. Hierlihy who had settled there in 1783, & was the first who cut a tree as fixing this settlement. He is proud of it, has acquired a considerable property, & is much respected. Another was a Mr. Symonds, who keeps the tavern in the village, an excellent house, the best I have met with. He is a most enormous fellow, lately from the United States (Massachusetts)–little less than the monstrous man exhibited in England; on horseback, he wore a girth double breadth to support & keep his belly quiet. He has all the style of American speaking – as "I vow, I guess now" – so disgusting to our ears, & tho' a good natured & well behaved man, he seems from that idea of his being a Yankee, much disliked & laughed at by the Highlanders.

On our arrival we were received by a Company of militia drawn up, & by a salute from 2 rusty old iron nine pounders, propped up with stones & quite dangerous to fire from; the Sheriff, however, a Militia Officer, seemed to value them so highly, that I promised I would send them two light field pieces, on condition that they formed a Volunteer Artillery Company of 100 men to take charge of them. This was instantly agreed to.

The road from Antigonish to Guysbro' is said to be better than that which we have come, good to ride but not better than to call possible for a light Gig. The coast all round Cape George is thickly settled, but not further deep than 2 miles, the interior of this country being granted to individuals who have not yet made any improvement.

I made particular enquiry into this fact and the cause of its continuing, as the King's instructions declare that if a man obtaining land shall not cultivate & improve he shall forfeit it by Escheat to the Crown. I find that the process is difficult to carry thro' the Escheat Court at Halifax; a great Proportion of the large proprietors in this Province are liable to this penalty and therefore not willing to encourage it. For instance, in the immediate neighbourhood of Antigonish is a property of 6000 acres in the name of a man Boylston, who came to this Province a Loyal Emigrant in 1783, but soon changing his sentiments returned to the States, & has never cut a tree on the property.

Another adjoining it, is a property of 23,000 acres, belonging to a Mr. Hartshorne, a wealthy merchant in Halifax, who has acquired immense tracts of land, but of which he makes no use. I am told he is laying it off in lots of 200 acres each which he sells at one pound per acre, thus obtaining £23,000 without laying out a shilling.

The only remedy I can see to these evils, is the establishing by Government of a Land Office of persons from England; unconnected with the individuals of this country, & having no interest themselves, they might under the Lt. Governor take special cognisance of all lands granted or ungranted.

While lamenting the state in which these lands lay, we could not help admiring the magnificence of the woods thro' which we passed, and the extreme rich sward of which clover thick as a carpet grew up on every little spot cleared enough to admit the sun to it. The soil is almost uniformly a red loam, light, sandy & gravel with now & then a tract of red clay. The trees are Beech & Maple, fir, Spruce & Hemlock of very large size, not however exceeding the common run of good trees of the same kind in Scotland.

When about six miles from Antigonish Mr. Cunningham stopped me to notice a very singular character settled there in the heart of the woods. He was standing close by the road waiting for us; his little hut of logs placed about 200 yards back in the centre of 10 or 12 acres of felled wood, his own individual work without assistance during this last winter. About a couple of acres were dug and planted with all sorts of vegetables round the hut. On conversing with him in bad French I saw in his countenance a picture of good nature & contentment. He is an Italian, has had a good education, served as Lieut. in the Army in Italy during the greater part of the war, & was employed as an Engineer in Bonaparte's Army in the campaign of Moscow. Under the Viceroy Eugene, he was present in all the battles of that Division, & sustained the severity of the whole of that dreadful retreat on foot. With the remembrance of that winter he seemed to scorn the cold of this climate & hard life he now leads.

The Catholic Priest at Halifax, Father Burke, met him in 1814 at Rome, brought him to Paris as a servant, was kind to him, and Antonio in gratitude & attachment accompanied the Father to this country, & now is working on Burke's land with only a trifling allowance of food for the labour.

Antonio I presume is a feigned name; he speaks a few words of English only, and very bad French. He is solitary in that wood without a neighbour within several miles; no companion to speak with, except as he said, "trois petits pies" — 3 small blue jays of this Country that he had fed & tamed in winter. He had seen, he said, "20 ans de tapage & de misère," and his "retraite aux bois" was perfect happiness to him. At dinner Antonio again made his appearance as our waiter, & served 16 people at table as well as if we had had half a dozen servants. At a dance in the Evening Antonio requested permission to sing a song of his own country, which he executed in the Italian style very well indeed, with a fine voice & knowledge of musick. I could not well understand the words, but it was evidently a composition of his own, & probably his own personal history; lamenting the loss of a country & friends; a wanderer in foreign lands where he has found protection & kindness, but still thinking of the fond hope of his return to Italy. This interlude of the Italian Song was a very ludicrous contrast to our dancing musick, a Highland piper, occasionally relieved by a very wretched fiddler; still to that our reels were kept up with great Glee, snapping of fingers & all the wildest, rudest & joyous expression of the Highland fling; our ladies were neither formal nor shy with us, nor were the Gentlemen too sober for the occasion. We spent a very happy day. Macqueen the Sheriff had the village splendidly illuminated, and as I was the first Governor who had reached Antigonish, it was quite a Fete.

Yesterday morning before I left them I was waited upon by Capt. Hierlihy & Mr. Symonds, as a deputation to request I would allow that the village, which had never yet been named, might take my name; this I declined, but on conversing with them I strongly advised them to adhere to the name by which this harbour & bay was known on all maps & charts, & which naturally led a stranger at once to find them, an advantage which no new name could acquire in less than centuries. They were quite satisfied, & adopted my advice.

After breakfast we started again, & reached Arisaig about 2 o'clock; it had poured rain on us the whole way, & when we arrived we found it blew very fresh and a heavy sea broke on the shore; a new pier building there at the public expence under a Mr. Lowdon enabled us to get into our boats, & we got on board *Leander* very well. Sir David weighed immediately, & before 6 o'clock we had again anchored off this harbour but 4 miles nearer shore.

15TH SEPTEMBER. This morning we went in the Barge to visit the Coal Mines on the East river of Pictou. Sir David having some knowledge of mineralogy, & of the working of Coal in England and Scotland, I was anxious to know his opinion of those here, as I have lately received orders to lease them in behalf of the Crown. He was astonished on seeing them. The thickest Seam in England, & there is only one of that dimension, is 30 feet of solid coal, the common run is 3 to 7 feet thick; here they have bored 47 feet & did not get thro' the pure seam. Sir David on considering the rising ground on which we stood, & the height above the river, calculated that the coal must be considerably more than 60 feet thick. The mine now working is let right into the side of a hill, & carts drive in & bring the coal from the chambers, carrying it at once about half a mile to the flat barges on the river, & these carry down about 5 miles to load vessels of 200 tons. With these advantages of so easy access & a navigable river, these coal mines promise to be highly valuable, both to the Crown and to the Province.

Three rivers, or rather three branches of the same, empty into Pictou harbour, East, Middle and West, each of them navigable for several miles inland, and certainly coal is to be found on each of them. Coal is also found near Chignecto in Cumberland, near to Truro in Cobequid, & on the Lake Mauger on St. John River, New Brunswick, all laying in vast solid bodies, but yet unexamined by any scientific person....

This morning I sent Woolford away to travel the road from this to Antigonish, Country Harbour, St. Mary's, Musquodoboit to Halifax, & to take sketches of the country as he went along.

17TH SEPTEMBER. Yesterday we parted company with Sir David, he going on to Prince Edward Island & Cape Breton, we proceeding direct to Halifax, the Commissioner Wodehouse, Col. Dick, Couper & myself on horseback. The first 10 miles from Pictou to Blanchard's tavern is quite a clear cultivated country, thickly settled; next 7 miles to Mount Thom (whch by the bye is much miscalled, for it is scarcely a sloping hill) is less settled, & thinly populous; next 8 to Archibald's, not at all settled, woods are beautiful; and then 14 miles to Truro, the far greater part without a hut, laying an entire wilderness, & yet the road is a delightful ride—dry light sandy soil, thro' lofty & magnificent wood of spruce, Beech, Birch & Maple.

The cause of this sad state is, that this tract was granted in 1783, several hundred thousand acres to Loyalists from Philadelphia & is now called the Philadelphia Grant. Some years ago it was escheated to Government but strong claims of remuneration from families who had suffered, being yet undecided & unsatisfied, it still remains waiting that decision, particularly in respect to one family of the name of Pagan, whose case I understand is hard. However, I am determined this shall not long remain so, and I shall before spring spread upon it the superabundant population of Scotch now gathered into that corner of the Province.

A description of this road from Truro to Pictou, Mr. Uniacke the Attorney General gave me lately, strongly shews the gradual improvement of that part of the Country, but as his stories generally incline to the wonderful, I don't give it full belief.

He says, he remembers going to Pictou in 1775. At that time there was no road formed, not even blazed out; that is, marking by a broad hatchet slice on the North or South side of the trees as a direction point to the traveller.

He and his companions travelled on foot with their knapsack & cooking kettle. The moose deer were in those days so plenty, that they daily shot what they wanted to carry with them as next day's provision. Only three persons were then settled on that spot where Pictou village now stands, a Mr. McCabe, & a Mr. Robt. Patterson, a very hospitable old man whose niece Mortimer married, & got large landed property there with her.

Now a carriage with 4 horses may travel to Pictou.

Mr. Archibald of Truro, a Lawyer & one of the leading members at the Bar, at whose house I am most hospitably lodged, came out to meet us about 9 miles yesterday afternoon. It had just begun to rain, & it poured the rest of the day. We lost the view of this cheerful settlement reckoned the garden of Nova Scotia, but still we were delighted with our day's ride of 39 miles.

This morning I got up early & took a long walk on the rising grounds over this village, placed at the top of tide of the Bason of Minas, which is seen in the distance in front across the flat; on my right lay the townships of Onslow & Londonderry, which appeared as if one continued village, laying for 10 or 12 miles around the Bay, & in a circular amphitheatre; on my left again a similar view of Truro township stretching to the mouth of the Shubenacadie river, the whole forming a gay lively picture. The soil as in Pictou a red light loam most inviting to cultivation, but it is melancholy to remark how strongly the Rum prevails among the lower class here, & paralises all industry.

19TH SEPTEMBER. Two days ago we left Truro & came 30 miles on our way homeward, stopping that night at Key's tavern – I had intended to make a rapid ride into Cumberland, but the late heavy rains, our time being limited to the 21st and the knowledge that the country is very similar to that in Pictou, induced us to abandon that plan & get home with all haste. At a mile from Truro Court House we struck to the left as if into the woods. Then we had 8 miles of new, well shaped but soft road, the hanging woods its only beauty – no settlers on it – the cause I found was, that the whole township of Truro was in one grant to certain trustees for the general benefit. These trustees are now dead; their individual heirs and successors filling their place, are now all quarrelling, maintaining a right to grant the lands to themselves in lots as original settlers, & thus disputed the country lays a wild but beautiful wilderness. A man named Gibbons on the Souiac river has a fine clear farm, & a large sheep walk, the only park I have seen in the Province. About 12 miles from Truro, on the right of this road is a fine Lake three miles long, laying parallel with the Shubenacadie. On this I understand Sir Alexander Cochrane has a large estate, on which he has laid out large sums of money, fixed several Scotch farmers, but all to no good

—they have turned out Rum drinkers & Rogues, absconding with all their stock.

It is yet I may say universally the case in this country, from its infant state: no man derives any advantage from the property of land unless he lives upon it & cultivates it himself.

At 26 miles from Truro on crossing the Gay's river, the soil instantly changes to a cold whitish clay, with ridges of granite rock quite forbidding to agriculture.

The Souiac and Gay's rivers run a considerable distance from the East to the Shubenacadie, & on each of them are thriving new settlements, but I was obliged to pass on, leaving my visit to that interior till a future opportunity.

Yesterday morning we left our miserable quarters at Key's at daybreak. I must however say that we had a very good supper, & that the people, very poor, did everything in their power to accommodate us. We rode 20 miles to breakfast at Fultz' tavern at the junction of the Windsor & Truro roads from Halifax. The ride is rough & rocky indeed, nothing interesting but the wild aspect of the country covered with very inferior fir wood, thro' which fire had raged, leaving everything dead & black. A low brushwood is now pushing up, intermixed with quantities of a pale pink flower, very appropriately called the Fireweed. In winter the strong N.W. gales have torn up from the roots the greater proportion of the taller burnt wood, and in this dreadful state of devastation the whole of these 20 miles are laying. We reached Halifax early to dinner.

Upon the whole I have been highly delighted with this tour round the Eastern part of the country. There is a great deal of very fine land indeed, capable of any culture, and I am sure there can be but one feeling by those who may see it, that of deep regret that Government does not apply some extension Plan for the immediate settlement of the interior parts of this Province. I shall stop at present with a note I took of a conversation with Judge Stewart this morning, one of the most sensible & intelligent men here.

I was suggesting to Judge Stewart the advantages that appeared to me would result from a system of Proprietors of extensive tracts granting to new settlers long leases, or life rents, allowing 5 years to clear the land before any rent was paid, & then to commence at a trifle only, & increasing periodically; he said that he himself was willing to adopt that plan, but in this Province it would not do. Settle a man in that way, he soon asks his neighbour whose land he works upon. "My own," is the answer; & further tells him it is folly to clear land for another; the children of the present Proprietor at the end of your lease of 20 or 30 years will turn you and your children off this land, & what then have you done? Nothing, you still have another beginning to make. The new settler turns himself instantly to obtain a grant for himself, & no longer will rest satisfied on the farm. This is certainly very true. A man emigrates to this Country on the information that he will get land for nothing—& he will not take a farm when he can get some hundred acres for £13, the fees of Office paid for it. Every man consequently is laird here, & the classes of the community known in England as Tenantry & peasantry do not exist in these Provinces & probably will not be formed untill a full stop is put to the system of granting lands.

24TH SEPTEMBER. Windsor. After staying a couple of days at Halifax to transact civil business, I came here to attend an Annual meeting of the Governors of King's College. The meeting is held for the purpose of examining into all its concerns. The institution is not a favorite with the public; the only two teachers or Professors in it are Dr. Porter, the President, and Dr. Cochrane the Vice President; they are at violent open war with each other, & in consequence of this, the proceedings are in general a discussion of complaints and recriminations, extremely indecorous and unpleasant.

The College is founded by Charter under the same rules as the Universities of Oxford & Cambridge. Students are required to subscribe their name to the 39 Articles. They must observe strictly regular term residence, and the Charter confers degrees. It is not suited to the state of this Society, where the Church of England, tho' the Established Church, is not the most numerous; the far greater part of the population being divided in sects, Methodists, Anabaptists, Church of Scotland, & dissenters from it; in Sydney County, the highlanders along the Gulf shore are all Catholicks, and in Halifax also there is a most respectable Catholick Congregation. All these classes are excluded from participation in the benefits of this College, & the House of Assembly for this reason refuses any aid from the public means. Its funds are about £1400 sterling to cover all expenses whatsoever. The number of Students at present is only 14. The state of the building is ruinous; extremely exposed by its situation, every wind blows thro' it. The passage doors are torn off, the rooms of the students are open & neglected. The expense of living is very heavy, as there is no butcher market or fish at Windsor. In short there are a thousand objections to it, & reasons why it should not prosper in its present situation, laws and conduct.

Dr. Porter is a strict disciplinarian & rather an ill-tempered man. Dr. Cochrane is the most perfect contrast, a man of singularly mild & amiable manner, with a talent for instructing & captivating the disposition of his pupils by easy & relaxed discipline. The students cling to him, are unruly & rebellious towards the President, riotous in their private College rooms, and galloping about the Country when not in class.

We have had laid before us a long statement by the President complaining of the behaviour of the students generally, but in particular of one young man whom we have severely reprimanded. Complaining also of want of support from the Vice President. This last is a dish annually served up, has been discussed with much violence and ill humour, and in that unpleasant manner the two last days have passed. My own decided opinion is that the state of this Institution in all its parts should be laid before the Archbishop of Canterbury as Patron, for revisal & correction.

As the Falmouth Packet has now been due a fortnight, it may be hourly expected. I shall go down to Halifax tomorrow to meet it, and in the meantime prepare for another tour, taking the direction of Annapolis & New Brunswick.

28TH SEPTEMBER. Sunday. Halifax. Yesterday I went to visit the Chesapeake blacks at the Preston settlement, & saw them busily employed in clearing road I laid out for them. They appear in the highest degree pleased & grateful for the little attention of my occasional visit.

29TH SEPTEMBER. At last the Packet is arrived, and brings me most comfortable accounts from home – that Ramsay has perfectly recovered from the measles and was in good health at Dalhousie Castle; this is unspeakable relief & comfort to us in our sorrow. I hope in God we shall now soon see him out here with us, to remove all our anxiety & fears which the arrival of a Packet now excites.

2ND OCTOBER. Windsor. Having answered all dispatches by this Packet I returned here today on horseback, having fixed with Sir David Milne, that he would join me here on the 5th and start on our travels on the 6th. I had ordered the *Bathurst* Sloop here to attend us in case we wanted her; I have today dispatched her to meet me at Annapolis, and Woolford is gone in her to take some sketches of Cape Blowmidown & Partridge Island on the Cumberland shore, nearly opposite to this. Our weather generally at present is delightful, tho' rather too hot to be quite pleasant. The crops of grain are all got in to the large barns, & the farmer is now getting up his potatoes. Everyone appears & speaks highly contented with the abundant crops of every kind.

4TH OCTOBER. I rode this morning to visit the township of Newport—crossed the ford of the St. Croix river at Winckworth—a deep mud bank on both sides but the bed of the stream hard & safe.

I visited old Mr. Allison and Dimock, members for this township to the Assembly. They are substantial farmers living very frugally on their industry. The former I met riding home, his saddle bags filled with nails he had been to purchase. The other I found at home without coat or waistcoat, just in the dress of a labouring man. We continued our ride to the bridge across the Kennetcook (commonly called Kenticook) river, & then returned by a circuitous road which falls into that from Windsor to Halifax about 10 miles from Windsor.

In this township the fields seem better cleared of stumps and the inhabitants very much more comfortable in their houses than other parts I have seen; but the soil is a white sandy clay—their roads are deep rutted & greasy, the woods small & stunted, altogether a district less desirable to live in than Windsor, Truro or Pictou. It has however considerable advantages which will lead to its prosperity— short communication to Halifax by an excellent road, the navigation of the Bason of Minas & Bay of Fundy by the Windsor river from which the Kenticook & Cockmegun rivers lead into the interior & navigable 10 or 11 miles. In the district are very fine quarries of free stone of excellent quality, quarries of Gypsum & lime & appearances of coal are seen which leave little doubt of finding that also.

6TH OCTOBER. This morning we left Windsor, Lady D. and Miss Cochrane in the Carriage, the Admiral, Col. Duke & Major Couper

III

in their gigs. I rode on horseback & left them going over the mountain road direct to Horton. I turned off to the right at Falmouth Church taking the lower or Mount Denson road which keeps by the river, & joins the other close to Horton. I passed the farms of Mr. Knowles and Rathbone, respectable proprietors, but did not stop; they lay on the flat near the river, a marsh of cold nasty soil, producing heavy crops of rank grass or rather weeds, which is cut in hay, and then large flocks of cattle & sheep are put on them by graziers & butchers for Halifax winter market. Immediately opposite to the village of Windsor a road & ferry passable only at low water, leads into the Mount Denison road which I was riding. After passing that, the country & soil changes to a light fine gravel, with good woods, & very pretty scenery, for 9 miles to the halfway river, then rising an extreme steep bank on the North side of a swampy valley, I rode full 6 miles to the Gaspereaux river. This distance is thickly & beautifully wooded, but only a spot here & there cleared, and that had the appearance of the utmost poverty; I was told a very large property of this trace belongs to Colonel Crane, a very harsh & illiberal landlord, and certainly the marks of that are evident.

From Gaspereaux bridge to Graham's tavern in Horton 8 or 9 miles is well cultivated and thickly settled. The Grand Prairie (or Gran Pray as the common people call it) lay on my right a considerable extent of flat land, dyked from the sea, the hay crop had been got off & the flocks of cattle & sheep were grazing on it in great numbers. This Mount Denison road is much longer than that over the mountain, is much neglected, & therefore much worse than the other.

7TH OCTOBER. We had intended to push on last night to Peck's & Dennison's at the turn into Cornwallis, but the County Magistrates being assembled there in Court for two days on the Summary Trial Act we could not be accommodated; we therefore stopt at Graham's & Fowler's & did very well. This morning we breakfasted at Peck's, a pretty spot called the Oaks, a grove of good trees but not at all remarkable in size; observing the acorns just dropping in great quantities, Lady D. and Sir David gathered a basket full, and I left orders to send me to Halifax a barrel of them which I shall send home. It is the Red Oak of America, fast growing, with long luxuriant smooth shoots, the leaves much cut or indented. After leaving Mrs. Peck's (a very civil little old woman) the country was thickly wooded, & a deep sandy uninteresting road. It came on to rain hard; I got into the carriage the rest of the day.

The Courthouse stands on the confines of the townships of Horton & Cornwallis & has gathered some houses together into a sort of village. We have tonight stopt at Crane's & Harris, this last a new house unfinished, yet we did very well. The Admiral & Duke killed a quantity of very small trout, which helped the dinner materially. The Annapolis river is here a still ditch rising out of the Caribou bog, in which also the Cornwallis river has its course, but running in a direction exactly opposite.

In this part quantities of potatoes, vegetables, Indian corn & pumkins are grown, & every house has a considerable orchard of extraordinary bad apples.

8TH OCTOBER. Last night it blew a hurricane from the South East & the rain beat in a manner that quite alarmed us for Mr. Harris' house, for tho' it is habitable the foundation is not yet built. It stands at present on 4 blocks of wood which are knocked away in succession as a wall is built on which the sills of the house rest. We feel also some anxiety for the *Bathurst,* for if she has not already reached the Annapolis Bason, she has had to sustain the gale without any harbour to shelter in. This morning was very fine and as our day's journey was to be 24 miles only we did not start untill we had breakfasted.

Early in my ride I met Judge Halliburton near to Mr. Buskirk's, & also to Clermont, the seat of the late Bishop of Nova Scotia. I dismounted & walked an hour with him. It is a nice small cottage going rapidly to decay—a small garden and a field sown out this year with grass seeds shew a most luxuriant produce. The soil in this part near the public road appears a dead poor sand, but the Bishop's field shews of what it is capable, and Halliburton tells me that the hill or high land on the right, & towards the sea all along this side of the province are a rich wheat soil producing very fine crops, & that the settlement & population is rapidly spreading on it. After 12 miles of this sandy road the soil changes to a red light mould; a road branches off to the left called the Nictau, and another at the house of a Capt. Ruggles on the right of the main leading up the hill; at the distance of 3 miles there is a fine view of the Bay of Fundy, but on attempting this road, I found it so ill made & so greasy wet by the rain of

66

yesterday that I quitted it & returned to the main.

The Annapolis river here at Lennard a fine broad stream for boats & barges in a valley which I think may be perhaps 6 miles broad from the range of hills on right to that on the left parallel both with the main road.

This is the township of Wilmot, considered a well doing & rich district, but I see no symptom of industry; extreme lazy & bad farming, & the lower orders ill cloathed, poor & have no idea of civility; they stood & stared at us as we passed with the utmost American impudence.

8TH OCTOBER. In Wilmot the grants of land are laid off on the south side of the river in 30 rods of front and 4 miles back from the river; on the North side they are 40 rods of front, and 2 miles back.

9TH OCTOBER. We left Mr. Lennard's, a miserable house, but most civil and obliging family, very early this morning and reached Annapolis after having breakfasted at Spurrs' tavern about halfway.

At 5 miles below Lennards' we crossed the river to the south side over a good wooden bridge, but there the river is sunk in deep mud banks subject to a tide which brings up vessels of 100 tons; I was told it rose 18 feet....

10TH OCTOBER. This morning I got an early walk thro' the fort and Barracks which are in tolerably good order; it was frosty and very cold; the wind was westerly & fresh, Sir David advised our taking advantage of it, and to defer the ride I intend in this part untill I returned from New Brunswick; accordingly we made arrangements to leave our horses, carriages & servants, and got on board *Bathurst* about 11 o'clock. After a very pleasant sail down the Bason, we dropt Anchor at 2, under the Granville shore near the Gut of Annapolis. It appeared to blow hard outside & threatened a stormy night. We got out boats and all landed to take a walk. A few fishermen & small farmers' huts are scattered along a very good road that leads from Digby along that side to Annapolis, but a low typhus fever prevailing we did not go into any of them. Sir David & I scarmbled up to the top of the steep ridge to try for a look into the Bay of Fundy, but after penetrating a full mile into the thick of the wood, we thought it prudent to retrace our steps while we could make them out; we got no View, nor could we find any game with our spaniels except one solitary snipe. We came on board to dinner.

67

12TH OCTOBER. Yesterday it continued to blow so hard out, that Captain Harper of the *Wye* who has been on this station for more than a year, advised us not to attempt St. John. We then sailed along the shore of Digby, and went up a creek near it to Mrs. Allison's Inn, a very retired sweet spot, where we have been most comfortably treated and lodged. As the party all went a-fishing, I took a walk alone, following a road that struck off from the main road S.W., directly into the woods. Sauntering on & looking with a small spy glass across a finely wooded valley, at some patches of corn in the wood which denoted new settlers, an old man came up to me carrying a very wretched gun. He was civil, & told me all about that settlement – he carried me about two miles forward to a hut where there was a very old Negro living with a prodigious swarm of children of all ages about him – he had the appearance of the utmost poverty, but yet he had upwards of 20 acres of cleared land, some sheep, cows & plenty of potatoes, he said. He was a Loyalist, settled there in 1783, and had I suppose 300 acres of which only 20 cleared in 30 years, but he was content.

My walking friend amused me by a great flow of sentimental conversation, leading me to suppose him a very sensible, religious and devout man, sinking under family misfortunes which he ascribed to several extravagant sons who had left him. When I was about to leave him, he begged I would tell him who I was. I plainly saw he suspected, & had been informed of the party at Mrs. Allison's. I had therefore no hesitation in complying, & I promised to visit him again today; however on enquiring about my friend Mr. Gyphon (for I also asked his name) I found he had been a worthless talkative fellow all his life, a perfect Atheist & outcast from society here – he completely deceived me yesterday.

The weather was still blowing early today but as the tide made, we thought it better to get the *Bathurst* out of this Creek where she lay aground and we anchored near the *Wye* off the town of Digby.

13TH OCTOBER. At daylight, Sir David made signal from the *Jane* to get under weigh, but soon after came on board to us to say that it would not do. The sky lowered & rapidly changed appearance in a most extraordinary & rather awful manner. At 9 o'clock while we were at breakfast, it blew in heavy squalls which broke up at last in a storm of tremendous thunder peals & very vivid flashes. At 10 it suddenly all cleared away, & the wind chopped round to East, bringing a beautiful blue sky—& we are again all in a bustle & going to cross in the *Wye* as the Bay of Fundy is generally a rough bubbling sea.

14TH OCTOBER. We had yesterday a very pleasant sail of 4 hours' passage after clearing the Gut, but then the tide run in like a sluice prodigiously strong, so that had not the wind favored us with a good breeze we must have put back, as did the small craft for some hours. We anchored in St. John about 4 o'clock, but did not land till 7, when we were received by General Smyth and Mr. Wright the Collector of the Customs, with an immense train of lanterns carried by soldiers & which had in a very dark night a very ridiculous effect....

After breakfast I rode with General Smyth round the posts, batteries & Barracks, all of which are ruinous except a stone Martello tower just built on Carlton heights, to which we walked with the Ladies, & where we had a very fine view of the town, anchorage and Partridge Island. The steam boat had sailed yesterday morning to Fredericton & could not return in less than her usual fixed day, 3 days' hence – our time hurrying us very much, we had almost resolved to give up our intention of seeing it, but yet I was very anxious, & it was agreed to start tomorrow for Moose Island, & return here so as to find the steam boat ready for us.

17TH OCTOBER. We have made the most rapid & fortunate excursion that we could possibly wish – on the 15th we sailed about 10 o'clock, with a light breeze in our favour & a delightful day, sea quite smooth, and at Sunset dropt anchor in the *Bathurst* in Bliss harbour completely locked in within innumerable islands, & just opening the narrow passage along shore to St. Andrews. The scene all around beautiful, but one miserable hut only shewed it to be an inhabited land. At daybreak yesterday some of us went to it, & got some milk for breakfast, others went a little way from the vessel & caught instantly quantity of very fine haddock & herring. When the tide served we started again, but had to beat thro' the narrows all the way up to St. Andrews; we had again a delightful day, reached it & landed at 2 o'clock, but it is a very small village, & strongly inclined to the Americans. I only inspected the block house & barrack, both of which are in good state. The Collector, Mr. Armstrong, a half pay

Captain, a young man, was extremely civil. The village is placed on a nice dry point of land & has beautiful wood & water scenery all around it. At 4 the tide again favoured us, & about 6 we dropt anchor at the town on Moose Island just at Sunset. An invitation came off from the inhabitants who had prepared a Ball & supper, but we declined; Major Couper went & apologised for us. He reports a sad mixture of all sorts, but extremely civil, a proof of which he feels in a headache from toasts in Champagne. Capt. Gibbons of 98th commanding here at present is a very smart Officer, & altho' under the unpleasant administration of martial law, has given great satisfaction to the Americans — at this moment the question is deciding by mutual commissioners to which Country these islands shall belong, & untill this is settled, martial law is continued.

At daybreak Sir David, Col. Duke & I went on shore, visited the forts & barracks, walked about for two hours, & came on board to breakfast. At 9 got up Anchor, the tide favored us to pass thro' the clusters of small islands, and a S.W. breeze in the Bay of Fundy brought us up to this before dinner. Having accomplished our plan, the pilot, old Reid, said, in the shortest time he had ever known it done. This old Reid is the chief Pilot in the Bay, has made a very large fortune by his own industry & the trade of St. John. He went with us as a volunteer, & claimed old acquaintance with Sir David from the circumstance that he had been impressed by Sir David 25 years ago. The Admiral perfectly recollected doing so. He was an excellent Seaman, & always well behaved. He is in affluent circumstances but still he & several sons continue the pilotage.

With respect to Moose Island, I think it is not of the smallest importance to Great Britain, & being a part of the American shore, for the neck or passage is dry at low water, certainly ought to be restored to them. Campo Bello & Deer Island are undisputed, are large fine islands & command the anchorage in that narrow passage just as much as Moose Island. Campo Bello is claimed as property by a Mr. Owen, brother of Sir Edward Owen — he is a perfect savage, detested & despised by Yankees as by the British.

1817 24TH OCTOBER. Windsor. On the 18th the steam boat offered a convenient and certain command of our time in our desire of visiting Fredericton, & we started that day about 12 o'clock, General Smyth going with us, & intending to remain there during the winter months. It was a disagreeable day blowing hard & right against us, extemely cold & cutting—notwithstanding we went steadily about 6 miles an hour. At first the scenery was romantic, but in less than 10 miles it began to open, & continued as we advanced. The river is magnificent, & branches off right & left into immense lakes, deep & navigable, into the very interior parts of the Province. Of these the Kennebecasis & Washadamoic, the Grand Lake & the Oromocto river higher up (in which last more than 200 sail of square rig vessels have been built within a very few years), are the largest, & give most important advantages to the rising agriculture & improvement of New Brunswick, but there industry is yet, as in Nova Scotia, in its infancy.

At Gagetown, we put Couper on shore to wait our return. Some years ago his younger brother, an Officer of Artillery, was upset & drowned near this. He had heard he had been buried here, & he was anxious to visit the spot & ascertain the fact, & he found it was done in a manner that pleased him very much.

We reached Fredericton about 4 A.M. next morning, having been detained some time by running aground on a shifting bank. We had most comfortable berths, & the ladies an elegant apartment separate.

At daybreak, Sir David & I went on shore & had a long walk before the Ladies came to the Inn to breakfast. We went to Church & visited a Judge Bliss, & a carriage being sent by a Col. Moodie, son-in-law of Mr. Sproule the Surveyor General, we rode about & saw the neighbourhood of this capital of N. Brunswick before dinner. It was hard frost but a fine day.

Fredericton can only yet be rated as a village, but it is laid off very well in large broad streets; the Assembly of the Legislature, the Courts of Justice, & the Head Quarters of the Military, have gathered here a very respectable community, and their dwellings neat & clean give to Fredericton an appearance of superiority & prosperity. It stands on a flat on the river, said to be 800 yards wide; a range of sloping hills on both sides at some little distance & yet covered in wood forms a fine valley. But it is insufferably hot in summer, & intensely cold in winter.

I can't think the river so wide, but it is fit for any commercial purpose, & continues so 50 miles higher. The Governor's house is beautifully situated on it about a mile from town with a good cleared farm of 40 acres for his use.

Next morning at 8 o'clock we re-embarked in the steam boat, with a fresh wind quite fair, but extremely cold, & we arrived at St. John at 1/2 past 6 P.M., running the 90 miles in 10 hours nearly.

Lady D. had a visit at Fredericton from an old man who many years ago had been much employed by her father about Coalstoun as a molecatcher. She recollectd him perfectly as soon as he had sent his name up. The old man was quite delighted to see her, making a thousand enquiries at once, about all the old people of Coalstoun. He had come out on chance to New Brunswick, &, a cunning Yorkshireman, had contrived to scrape together a little money; he had got a grant of 300 acres of good land immediately across the river at Fredericton, had built himself a farmhouse & barn, another house in Fredericton, a rum shop or tavern; he had purchased another farm of 150 acres with house & barn 50 miles up the river which was in lease; he had a wife & three children, & in every thing he said he was quite happy. On conversing with him, he ascribed all his present good fortune to predestination, & seems a very religious good man. His name is Christopher Brown.

Having ordered the *Bathurst* to move up to where the steam boat stopped, we went immediately on board, & there slept. Next day (21) the tide served about 11 o'clock, & we passed down the falls, then quite full, but the stupendous rocks on either hand were very romantic. On reaching the town Sir David came on board & we made sail immediately for Windsor in the wish of seeing the narrow pass into the Bason of Minas, Cape Blomidon & Partridge Island. Anchored that evening after an unpleasant tossing sail, under Cape Dore. The *Wye* had attended us but put about off the Isle Haute. At day dawn up anchor again with a wind quite fair, untill we rounded Blomidon where we found it directly contrary to us with heavy squalls & rain. We however succeeded in beating into Windsor river with that tide, & dropt anchor when it turned; we had 9 fathoms water in midstream; at lowest tide we found it had fallen 42 feet.

24TH OCTOBER. Windsor. About midday it cleared up so fine that we all went on shore & took a long walk on the Horton side, at the farm of a man who had been a drummer in the American War. He has a fine family around him of grownup sons. Some very good land apparently & tho' his house denotes poverty, he seems highly contented.

We waited the early tide of yesterday (23rd) morning & beat up the river in very pretty style, landed about 12, and walked home to the Grove.

On sailing from St. John we dispatched Col. Duke and Major Couper in the *Jane* to Annapolis to forward the carriages & horses with all possible haste, and they are just arrived.

26TH OCTOBER. Halifax, Sunday. Yesterday we left Windsor, & breakfasting at Mount Uniacke reached this in good time to dinner. This hasty run thro' different parts of the Province has at least given me a good idea of the state & appearance of the Country generally, & in a few words I may state it correctly.

It is a country in its infancy, shewing in every corner the promise of becoming one day a valuable & powerful state. But at present helpless & neglected by its Parent.

The people are very poor & indolent; fond of rum, they appear generally half drunk & wasting their time; they loiter about their houses & their field work, & seem content in raising a sufficiency of potatoes for winter. But the country is capable of great improvement, & were proper encouragement held out, much good might result. They are all lairds, they pay no rent & trifling local taxes. There is therefore no spur to industry, nor is there any example of gentlemen Proprietors of land to give instruction towards the improvement of agriculture.

The great roads are good, but the byeroads scarcely entitled to the name. The Acts of Statute Labour are not enforced, the grant of money much squandered from want of proper control or inspection, & what is repaired this year equally requires it the next.

The facilities of navigation & fishing are great advantages possessed by every part of the Province, but these also are neglected, & the fishers in small craft subsist chiefly by a smuggling trade with Americans on the shores of the Bay of Fundy, & by a miserable carrying of fuel wood on the South Shore, to the Halifax market.

I am convinced the Province will creep on in poverty, untill Government shall alter the present Colonial system of trade, & open ports to the flag of other nations.

The Eastern districts from Gay's river appear to me by far the finest & most beautiful part of Nova Scotia; having carried Woolford with me everywhere I have got a very large collection of sketches to keep me in better remembrance of this excursion.

10TH NOVEMBER. Since my return home I have been busily occupied in bringing up the civil business which had got in arrear, & which requires an almost constant attention, particularly that which regards the Petitions for and the Grants of land.

Towards the end of last month, before my return, the *Forth* frigate, Sir John Louis, arrived from England, my A.D.C William Hay of Spott came passenger in her. In coming into harbour she unfortunately struck on the S.E. Point of the Thrum cap, & considerably damaged her keel & rudder. I went this morning to see her hove down, and had great satisfaction in finding that her repair will be easily accomplished. But it is quite lamentable to see how she is pulled in pieces & dismantled in preparation for this; but a few days ago she was coming into harbour in the highest state of order, newly fitted in England, & newly painted, she was beautiful; when this trifling accident has torn every part of her out & made her a perfect wreck....

11TH NOVEMBER. The Packet of October from England was most unexpectedly announced at breakfast this morning by signal from the hill. I instantly dispatched Couper on board & by 12 o'clock we had Ramsay safely in possession at this house.

Tho' his arrival sadly renews the affliction we have suffered, yet the happiness of seeing him & the comfort of having him with us affords us every balm & consolation.

He has had a very fine passage as to weather of 35 days in the *Chichester,* Capt. Kirkup....

21ST NOVEMBER. It was so fine yesterday that I rode with Ramsay & his tutor Mr. Temple to see the black settlement at Preston, but about 2 o'clock it overcast, and in half an hour it lay deep snow. This morning hard frost, has all the appearance of set in winter.

Today old Drayton from Liscomb Harbour came to put me in mind of my promise to him of a Grant of his land to him, to which I found there was no objection to be found....

1ST DECEMBER.... I dined today with 120 Scotchmen in honor of St. Andrew—yesterday being Sunday. Old James Fraser, a Lovat, in the chair, a very well conducted & pleasant party.

6TH DECEMBER. Changeable weather this week past, but generally Easterly winds with snow showers; today it freezes hard, wind at North; the Admiral taking advantage of it, is now under weigh with the squadron, & saluting the Garrison while he passes George's Island.

I lately suggested to the Officers in this command the great comfort and advantages that might result from the establishment of a Garrison library; the idea has been discussed and every Officer has entered into it. We propose to follow exactly the plan of the Gibraltar Library as far as circumstances admit. We have already subscribed £400, and I have appropriated £1000 from a public fund at my disposal, the Castine duties, to aid its first attempt. Our half yearly subscription will be about £300, amply sufficient to cover ordinary expences when our first collection of books is purchased.

At present the young men in garrison are much at a loss to get any reading; there is not a Bookseller's shop in Halifax, nor is there an individual possessed of anything that can be called a Library.

13TH DECEMBER. In the early part of this week we had soft close weather, exceedingly dirty & disagreeable. Latterly it has frozen hard and skaiting the order of the day. I am astonished to observe how very few good skaiters there are in this severe winter climate—& these not to be compared to English skaiters. Wind at S.E. threatens fall of snow....

1ST JANUARY 1818. New Year's Day opened thick & misty calm, but the sun already powerful cleared all away and it is now a most delightful day. I held a Levee this forenoon, but have cut off this senseless formality as much as I can, by limiting them for this year to the Birthdays of the King, Queen & Prince Regent....

10TH JANUARY.... A brig from New York, the *Eagle*, Capt. Deane, brings a report of the death of the Princess Charlotte of Wales in childbed. I am most unwilling to believe it, and yet the circumstances are so detailed as to create the most serious apprehensions. I have just had an extraordinary meeting of the Council, to take Capt. D's deposition on oath; he states that he sailed from N. York 6 days ago; that on the Evening before he sailed, he read in a Liverpool paper of 12th November brought by an American ship 46 days from thence, a detailed account of the death of Her Royal Highness, just after being delivered of a male child still born; that the paper had broad black edging, as indicating mourning, & that no doubt was entertained of the truth of it at New York.

It is impossible to imagine an event of higher importance to the Empire, or one more dreadfully afflicting to the Royal Family & the Nation at large.

I feel deeply oppressed even by the Report, but yet it is made so sweepingly calamitous, and so notorious, so characteristic, & so habitual is it now become with the Americans to circulate false reports & idle lies of their own fabrication without ostensible motive, that I will still hope the whole story to be void of truth....

13TH JANUARY. Today I have received the London Gazette Extraordinary via Boston, confirming all this most melancholy & deplorable calamity. Most anxious now I am for our November Falmouth mail from Bermudas but I much fear it may be detained late in England....

18TH JANUARY. Sunday. Altho' no official intimation has been received of the sad Events at home, I have taken them on the Papers received to be undoubted. All classes of Society appeared this day in deep mourning. The Churches are hung in black, & Dr. Inglis, Rector of St. Paul's, preached a funeral Sermon on the mournful occasion. The whole was most solemn and affecting. The day being the Queen's Birthday, the Standard was hoisted half mast high, and the salute from the Batteries & shipping were omitted....

5TH FEBRUARY. In several days very boisterous stormy weather, with a great deal of snow. This being the day fixed for opening the General Assembly, I went down *in State,* in my sleigh with 4 horses as a Post chaise. Several Members had reached town only this morning with the utmost difficulty, the country roads being blown up extremely deep. The streets in town are in a dreadful state by mountains of snow & sheets of ice. Several vessels reached the Port today from the West Indies, describe the weather at sea lately as dreadful.

New York papers of 14th January are received, and a Star from London of 20th Nov. confirms all the mournful details we already have had.

8TH FEBRUARY. At daylight a Brig of war was signalled, having a Mail on board. At 10 A.M. the *Saracen* had anchored with the mails of November & December to 17th. Had terrible weather at sea. The *Vixen* (a Dockyard brig) from the Bermudas 17th January with the November mail, had been dispatched but had been obliged to put back in distress after being nearly lost. The *Saracen* threw six of her guns overboard & sheet anchor to lighten her....

[*For the remainder of February Lord Dalhousie noted little in his journal except the extraordinary weather; for two weeks the harbour was an unbroken sheet of ice, but a quick thaw along with the salt water and the action of the tide made the ice spongy and unsafe, and several people drowned crossing on the ice from Dartmouth at night.*]

5TH MARCH. A heavy gale last night at S.E. with some snow. This morning one of those extraordinary instances of the climate called by the natives a silver thaw; while it rains hard, it is also freezing & the trees are covered with a white coat, bowing down the twigs & branches in very elegant forms, and occasional gleams of the sun make the whole sparkle like crystal.

11TH MARCH. A week of the finest spring weather I ever saw. Wind at N.W. hard frost at night, and rapid thaw by day. Lady D. driving out daily, in an open Barouche as in summer.

Some days ago, I got a severe cold, after playing in the Fives' court, which has seized me all over with rheumatism, so much so that I have not been out of the house these 4 days.

17TH MARCH. My cold became feverish & pluratic, has laid me in bed for several days, & obliged me to be copiously bled. Most delightful weather continued till today, & fresh snow storm is falling all forenoon.

I received last night from Quebec a dispatch from Sir John Sherbrooke himself, announcing his having totally lost the use of his left side by a Paralytic stroke – he speaks of it in easy and unaffected language, & requests of me to make arrangements with Sir David Milne for his early return to England in a frigate. He expects me at Quebec as his successor by the 1st June. I am preparing to run down to Bermuda in the *Forth* frigate, as soon as the House of Assembly rises. I am pushing to obtain that by 24th & am anxious to lose no time that I may be returned here again by 20th April, when I shall expect the dispatches by the March Packet will decide whether I go to Canada or not....

28TH MARCH. The General Assembly having brought their business to a finish yesterday, went down to the House & prorogued it, preparatory to a dissolution in May next, as it had this year reached its last Session by Law.

It is expected that a very general change of Representatives over the Province will take place, a number of the present Members (being illiterate working farmers, tho' sensible men) are not fit persons for public affairs.

Having made all necessary preparations to make a hasty run down to Bermuda & back here, on board the *Forth* frigate, I intended to have sailed today, but our fine weather has failed, and it now blows a gale at S.E. with rain.

Altho' the annual meeting of the Parliament of Nova Scotia has little other business to do than appropriate the disposable revenue towards public works & purposes, the amount of which for some years has been about £40,000, the Session has generally been pro- tracted to six weeks. This has been more talkative than usual, & on the whole the business treated in a less liberal manner, the country members evidently working for popularity, & their known senti- ments on public matters struggling under the apprehension of the approching dissolution.

In proroguing the Assembly I felt it necessary to express myself much dissatisfied with their resolution on the subject of the Militia, some changes on the System of which I had suggested to them. I however concluded by a general approbation of their loyalty & zeal throughout the long course of a 7 years' Parliament, and I believe we have all parted excellent friends.

[*On the 29th of March, 1818, Lord Dalhousie sailed on a short trip to Bermuda with Sir David Milne. He was away about a month and did not resume his Nova Scotian journal until the beginning of May.*]

1ST MAY. On my return a few days ago I found all the mails of Jan. & Feby. & March had arrived in my absence and the homeward bound Packet waiting my dispatches.

By these mails Lord Bathurst writes that it is not his intention to fill up the vacancy in Canada until Sherbrooke shall reach England, that it may be ascertained whether his health may not yet repair so as to enable him to return to that command. At same time he gives me sufficient assurance that I am destined to succeed him. The Duke of York is most kind & most decided in his recommendation of me for the military part of it. I am much pleased with this arrangement as it will enable me to see the parts of this Province which I did not visit last year, & probably leave it for Quebec about August.

I am highly gratified in receiving so promptly Lord Bathurst's dispatch, conveying the Prince Regent's entire approbation of the disposal of the Castine duties, £10,000, in the founding a College, & granting £1000 of it to our young Garrison Library. I am equally so in his decision on my representation of Mr. Crofton Uniacke's claim to a seat in Council, which has been refused to him & to all future Judges of the Admiralty Instance Court.

I shall now prepare for Canada, & if possible lay the foundation stone of the College before I go....

The early ships from England are pouring in now; they bring little news except a report that it is in contemplation to make Halifax a free port. It is an object of the highest importance to this place, & in my opinion the only measure which can reanimate the industry & the spirit of the Merchants, at present failing & dejected.

The American Congress has just now passed an Act to exclude from their Ports all vessels of any Country whose regulations in trade exclude the American flag, this act to take effect after 30th Sept. next. It might be considered as an insult & inclination to quarrel, but it is not so; it is grounded on an assurance expressed by Lord Castlereagh last year in Parliament that no offence would be taken by the British Cabinet at any measure the Americans might think it their interest to adopt, as countervailing to our Navigation Laws or trade regulations.

As we yet live here by the American flour & supplies, we shall be starved next winter unless some remedy to this Act of congress shall be applied, & it has every appearance that some friendly understanding on the subject exists, & that this free port bill is the measure intended. I am however yet uninformed of the views of Government at home upon it.

17TH MAY. It is impossible for me to express the astonishment I am struck with now, by the arrival of the April Packet from England—it brings me a "Private" letter from Lord Bathurst informing me in the coolest manner of the appointment of the Duke of Richmond to the Command over me in Canada.

What can have led to this appointment, not more extraordinary as to the person than the manner in which it has been done, I cannot imagine. I have been deceived to the last minute by Lord Bathurst. I have not a single line upon the subject from the Duke of York's office, nor from any private friend in London, except my own Agent, & he only says that on the morning on which it was gazetted, it was not even suspected in Lord B's office that any other but myself was to have that appointment. That appears to me the most evident expression of a guilty conscience, so to conceal it that no representation could be made on my part before it was actually published.

Indignant & disappointed in the utmost degree in my pursuit as a Military man, I feel that I cannot put up patiently with such scandalous treatment, & nothing is left me but to resign my present command and retire for ever from the Service.

24TH MAY. After much serious & painful reflection on this incomprehensible transaction, I have resolved to bear myself up with as much moderation and firmness as I can.... [*Lord Dalhousie gives the text of a letter he wrote to Bathurst, expressing deep mortification and disappointment, pointing out that he has served his country for 31 years, and had hoped to serve it further with distinction.*] If I could throw up my command here at once without offering violence, a sort of meeting against this appointment, I would do it instantly, & in the strongest manner express & do justice to my wounded honour....

In the astonishment & vexation which this has occasioned, I have been gratified very highly by the expression of the feeling of the Public here towards me. From several of the first members of our Society I have received the most flattering assurances of the attachment & esteem of the people here; to remain amongst them under such feelings must be gratifying to me at present, & attach me to them hereafter, most Sincerely.

1ST JUNE.... I spent two days this last week at Mount Uniacke with the old Gentleman, the Attorney General, a most pleasant, well informed and sensible man. He lives a great deal at this seat of his own making, he is a zealous settler & spends a great deal of money on this place, which is pretty but thought to be sadly unprofitable to his family.

This year I have no complaints of scarcity or want in any part of the Province, the poor have abundance even for sowing & planting &

IV

the fine season it is hoped will ensure them a good harvest.

5TH JUNE.... Yesterday the line turned out to fire in honour of the King's Birthday—it was a very hot day, Therm. 85 in the shade; an unlucky accident happened to the Admiral, riding out one of my horses & cantering out to the field of exercise. Sir David lost his stirrup & with it his seat; he fell off, with great violence, & received two cuts in the head, but providentially it proves but trifling. Today he is quite well.

6TH JUNE. For some time past we have been talking about an attempt to revive a very pleasant and sociable Club that had existed these last 20 years, & met under the patronage of Sir John Wentworth (the old Governor of this Province) at the Rockingham tavern, 6 miles from this on the Windsor road – and today we accomplished it. About 30 of us, Civil & Military, dined there, & spent a very pleasant day, reviving the old & adding some new regulations.

13TH JUNE. The weather this month has been unusually hot and dry, the beauties of the woods opening & growing daily more rich. The improvements on the common south of the Citadel going on with great spirit.

In returning from the Rockingham Club last Saturday a serious accident happened to two of the oldest & best members—Mr. Hill & Morris. Their horse ran off with the carriage & turning into Dutch town of Halifax overturned & threw them with great violence to some distance. Mr. Hill is much cut, but Morris is very severely cut, & not yet out of danger – several ribs broke, with alarming bruises....

25TH JUNE. The fine season being now set in, my public despatches closed for some weeks, I am now preparing to set out on a long ride into the distant parts of the Province I did not reach last year – particularly Cumberland. As Lady D. had very much admired the Mahone Bay when we visited Lunenburg, she wished to go there during my absence, & Miss Cochrane having agreed to accompany her, Sir John Louis offered them the *Forth,* and accordingly we embarked last night. We did not get under weigh untill 10 this morning – then it was a very light air, which drawing ahead with fog, we returned when near Mauger's Beach, dropped anchor, & landed again.

29TH JUNE. We had not been long on shore on 25th when we had a violent thunder storm which brought the wind round to N. in the evening. We went on board, & at day break, 26th, sailed. Off the Light House about 10 it fell calm, & continued so till about 2 when a fresh breeze from S. W. carried us up to our anchorage in Prince's harbour (or more properly Mush a Mush, by the Indian name) an hour before sunset. After breakfast next morning, 27th, we landed the ladies at a neat Country Inn, kept by Zwicker, a German original settler. We spent the day with them, & seeing everything most comfortable we returned on board late at night, leaving the party in charge of Mr. Temple. The admiral with his usual kindness, has sent down to remain with them a small Yacht with a midshipman & 20 men; they have also a rowing boat with which they may go to all parts of that beautiful bay. Next morning, 28th, we weighed anchor, and reached Halifax by 2 o'clock – a delightful day & very quick passage.

The weather has now continued so long dry that Prayers were yesterday offered in all churches for rain, and today I see an awful smoke covering many miles into the interior on the Dartmouth side.

30TH JUNE. I went out today to visit the new settlements of the Blacks at Preston, & was glad to find that the fires raging these two days had not done any material damage. Still, Mr. Fairbanks on Lake Porter, Morris & Fergusson had suffered.

1ST JULY. While in my room this forenoon reading, I observed about 2 o'clock, all at once a very extraordinary darkness – a deep yellow tinge obscured the sun; it appeared to be a tremendous column of smoke driven by a strong gale of wind at N.E. I went immediately to the Citadel Hill where a number of the inhabitants had already assembled – they judged it to be a fire in or very near the other new settlement of the Blacks at Hammonds Plains, but I also see several other fires at different points about 14 miles from this to the North and round to East – spreading rapidly by the force of the wind, and shewing indisputably what I had heard but did not believe, that in these cases the progress of the flames went raging directly to windward more rapidly than it gained down the windd. It is now one of the most awful sights I ever saw – the burnt leaves & the flakes of fire are carried before the gale & have reached even this, and the burning smell & heat of the atmosphere are strong in the rooms of this house.

2ND JULY. Still the fires are more and more alarming. I had today entreaties from the Proprietors of Birch Cove and Rockingham, that I would sent out troops to assist, as the fires were coming down and already within two miles of these places; but that could not be agreed to.

The *Wye* is just arrived from a Cruize in the Bay of Fundy; Capt. Harper tells me that the whole coast is obscured in smoke, & that he saw very extensive fires between Shelburne and Liverpool. Tomorrow, I leave this on my ride thro' the district of Cornwallis & Cumberland. Sir David Milne, Capt. Hay & Schomberg Kerr go with me.

4TH JULY. We stopped yesterday at Mount Uniacke; later in the evening the Old Gentleman positively foreboded rain today from the continued calling of the Loon, a large & beautiful bird that frequents the interior lakes & waters of the Province. Its call is a long & very melancholy but musical sound. By the starlight, and in the solitary stillness of the woods at midnight, this note on a large lake was very pleasing. The night was very fine & we walked about till late enjoying the peculiar call of several of these Loons, but we have had no rain today.

We breakfasted at Spence's, & reached this (Graham's in Horton) early. I see the repairs & improvements on the public roads going on very actively. The road thro' these Horton mountains is really grand & beautiful....

5TH JULY. This being Sunday, we stopt & went to the English church. It is only just built; the congregation is small. Mr. Norris from Cornwallis performed service. After Church, we rode over the hill to the southward, skirted up the valley of the Gaspereaux to the right, thro' some very fine woods on a large tract of land belonging to the family of Alderman Harty in London, which he inherited from the late Lord Rodney's family. This tract is laying waste & shall be inquired into.

We then passed into a settlement begun 20 years ago, called New Canaan – fine land, the farmers & proprietors chiefly immigrants from England are apparently doing well– more rich and comfortable than the rest of the Country. The large fields, extensive crops &

gardens about their houses shew them strangers in this country, & more industrious than others of their class.

This part of the Province was generally settled by Loyalists at the Peace of 1783 from New England, & consequently the Anabaptists & Methodist sects prevail, I am told in the proportion of 9 in 10. The Established Church of England is scarcely entitled to a name here.

The character which the people of this part have generally obtained is by no means favorable—living poorly & chiefly upon rum or worse ardent spirit; they are idle, insolent and quarrelsome. All in debt. They have no faith in one another. They are strongly tinctured with Yankee manners, ideas & principles – canting & preaching constantly, they have no thought of Religion or morality.

The state of agriculture here is wretched. They depend entirely on large crops of hay cut upon the marsh & dyke lands; on potatoes, and cyder made without any knowledge of the art, from heavy crops of apple trees, of every variety sweet & sour. Every one, however, tho' ever so poor, has his horse & gig, or "shay"; at the Church service of the Established Church and that of the Anabaptists we counted 70 of these buggies hung up to the rails or trees near.

7TH JULY. Yesterday we went into Cornwallis township & break-fasted with Mr. Prescott. We then rode to the top of the hills stretching from Blomidon to Annapolis. On that high point, from whence we looked down on Spencer Island in the narrows leading from the Bay of Fundy into that on Minas, the land is strong clay, the wood not large. Between the Horton side of the river & these hills there is a tract of flat land perhaps 8 miles broad, into which the Canard & Habitant rivers formerly flowed, but the French settlers exceedingly industrious carried at successive periods dykes across, which backing off the rising tides gained very extensive meadows of rich marsh. These works are still carrying on, but very slowly, and very insufficiently when compared with the old dykes of the Acadian French. These meadows give the proprietors large stock of hay for winter, & feed very considerable numbers of cattle for the Halifax market, but this easy way of obtaining a living encourages that want of industry that keeps down this district in poverty. In capability this township is considered the first in the Province for the improved system of Agriculture—and I do think it is.

Cornwallis was formed into a township and granted to 150 original settlers, calculated to have 650 acres each lot; 1200 acres have already been lotted to each, & yet there remains very large tracts of wilderness not distributed.

This mode of settling the country has proved to be a most mischievous system, for I have found in Lunenburg, in Truro, Horton and Cornwallis, that nearly a half of the surface of these townships are either in dispute, or not yet granted from the quarrels of the trustees....

At Mr. Prescott's, who is a very superior man indeed in manners, conversation & style of living to all others here, we met a large party at dinner.... I was much tempted but had not time to visit an old Yorkshireman near Mr. Prescott's—his name Jackson—one of the first settlers in Cornwallis & best or rather most industrious farmer in it. He is quite a character, goes by the name of the Honest Man, much past 80 years of age—he has given up his land & property to his son, with whom he & his old wife live quite content & he says independent, as they give him five pounds a year pocket money. We were obliged to return early to Graham's in Horton, having agreed to dine with Col. Crane....

9TH JULY. We left Horton yesterday about 2 P.M. in a very good sloop packet carrying one or two gigs & 8 horses, expecting to have landed here at Parrsboro in 3 hours; but the wind failed us when in mid-passage—a very rapid current got hold of us, Sir David having insisted on taking the helm & obstinately refusing to steer as the Master advised, we drifted to leeward of our Port quite unmanageable—near Sunset a thick fog in the narrows behind Cape Blomidon in a few minutes enveloped us. We lost sight of land on either side, & drifting at the rate of six knots with the current, the Admiral, the Master & Col. Crane all became exceedingly alarmed that we might strike on a bad shoal or reef called the Black rock. Sir David desired the Master to take the helm, he refused to do so, making Sir David responsible for the Vessel and property on board. At that moment while warmly disputing, Hay called out, "Land, Sir D., close to us; I see the trees over our heads." He was then forward in the bow. The helm was put down. The lead told 2 1/2 fathm. Sir D. called to let go the anchor. The master said, "No, we must not do that," in great confusion. A little shipwreck appeared our inevitable fate; however, we droppd into deeper water, & hearing the waves breaking on a shingle beach, the master did let go the anchor. Our alarms soon changed into great good humour, & being safe we were content to wait daylight & make what bid we could continue. We now heard the watch dogs barking on shore close to us, & now & then saw a light, but the Master could not exactly make out our situation. At day dawn today we found we had passed the Black rock & rounded into an eddy in a small bay of deep water to the beach. It broke a most delightful morning and we got up all well to breakfast with Mr. Ratchford at Partridge Island. In all this adventure no one of us dared to say the Admiral was wrong, for his nautical skill was acknowledged, until Mrs. Ratchford, a very mild quiet Quaker looking person, said most innocently, "that she could not but wonder what was the matter, for sure the Packet had not been so well managed as usual." Old Crane then took courage, and blamed Sir D. for all the mishap. Still Sir D. maintained his theory right, & all the arguments imaginable could not gain one jot on him. We have had a great deal of fun & laughing.

10TH JULY. Yesterday we walked all about the little settlement of Parrsbro' which has every appearance of being cut off from the common society of the country. It is however a very clean nice place, extremely retired & consequently under the rule & control of Mr. Ratchford who is everything – keeping a shop for every sort of supply, the whole population is individually indebted to him; selling his goods at enormous profit he makes money of those that pay their accounts, and of those that do not he takes mortgages on their lands, takes that in payment. Such is the practice in every part of this country, & individuals thus are acquiring large landed estates of which they make no use. In this part of the Province many curious specimens of mineralogy are found – iron, lead & copper in large pieces—we picked up some like Amethysts, & curious pebbles.

This morning we started early & reached this (Mr. White's at Amherst) 34 miles, by 2 o'clock. We breakfasted at Mr. Jesse Lewis', a Magistrate. In my life I never met with so perfect a picture of primitive contentment, happiness and worth. Old Caleb Lewis has given up his house, farm & property to his eldest son, Jesse, to manage for him & his old wife. His history is a singular one, tho' I believe many similar (indeed I have already met with several) are

86

found in this Province. About the year 1780 he possessed a small farm near New York, from which he was obliged to fly or serve as a soldier with the Rebels. His family, a wife & two children, took refuge in the City of New York; he himself came to Halifax without friend or relations. For some months he wandered thro' the country and crossed to Parrsbro', where at that time no soul had yet ventured to settle. Lewis & another man with him sat down where he is now about 10 miles inland from Parrsbro'. They found some Indians near them who were very kind to them & supported them by fishing & shooting the first winter. The next summer he returned to Halifax & obtained from Governor Parr a grant of 1000 acres – carried back with him some hatchets & hoes & set himself down to clear a farm. He could gain no information of his wife & children till about 5 years after when she found him out & joined him in the woods. He says that from that day to this he has been perfectly happy. He has now a very comfortable house, about 200 acres of cleared land around it, now managed by his eldest son, also married & has a large family. He has settled 5 other sons and 3 daughters married within 10 miles of him, and now he says he counts 300 relations by blood or marriage within his walk in a forest in which he sat down a single wanderer near 40 years ago. He is a remarkably little man, quick & intelligent – white hair, thin face & person, rosy red cheek, clean dressed in cloth suit entirely made in his family, having clipt the sheep himself, spun, wove & made by his wife. We got an excellent breakfast of tea & coffee, but the sugar was the maple & has an aromatic taste, the bread very good, the produce of the farm – with variety of sweetmeats & common fruit preserves made by themselves. Old Caleb said a long Grace in a manner quite Patriarchal. It is remarkable that his first companion still lives next door to him and also doing prosperously. I did not see him & don't know the number of his family.

There exists at present what may be called the original settlers of Nova Scotia, for tho' the French did settle Annapolis, Horton, Truro and Fort Cumberland (Beau Sejour) & tho' in 1749 Halifax was begun as the seat of Government, yet the great influx of Loyalists in the American Rebellion first led to the real settlement of the forest lands, & this Caleb Lewis & many others still alive in various parts I do consider as having fair claim to be set down as the first who planted the prosperity of Nova Scotia.

The road from Parrsbro' to Amherst is very good, in many parts beautiful—the soil light red turnip loam—at every step we met rivers & trouting rivulets.

As we approached this, the day extremely sultry, the sky o'ercast & gathered a very wild appearance, & about 4 o'clock one of the most awful Thunder storms I ever saw set in with violent gusts of wind, vivid flashes of lightning & instant crash. One particularly loud seemed to burst close around us, Sir David & I standing in the outer porch of Mr. White's door—another followed almost instant & in our view darting like a spiral rod of fire struck a pine tree on the side of the road & shivered it to pieces about 200 yards from where we stood. After that the storm passed away from this to the south East, but still continues about 7 o'clock.

12TH JULY. Yesterday morning we went to see the extraordinary effects of the storm at Amherst. The tree I have mentioned was tore up by the roots, no other touched near it. But in a field about 300 yards behind Mr. White's a most awful scene remained. Under a grove of spruce, fir, perhaps 20 trees, some sheep had taken shelter & with them a cow & a pig. The electric fluid had struck in the midst of the trees, apparently conducted down two of them, & then diverging in every direction had killed on the spot every one of the animals—32 sheep, 1 cow, 1 pig, which last appeared as if running away about 20 yards off; all the others seemed crushed down as if by a weight; their legs failing under them they had settled on the belly on the ground. Two lambs only were tumbled over. On the cow there was no visible hurt, but on all of the sheep there was a line singed as if by a hot iron from *the hind leg into the head*. The proprietor had them all opened & skinned. He found no bone broke, nor any apparent harm to the flesh—however, he buried all the carcases.

After breakfast we rode to the Bay Verte, and returned to Fort Cumberland to sleep at the inn kept by Mr. Weatherhead, who is also sheriff of the county, which is however in New Brunswick. A very wretched inn it is. I got excellent quarters at a Mr. Napp's....

Today we looked at the Fort in ruins, & rode here to Phillymore's on the river Philip about 18 miles from the fort. The road excellent & the woods magnificent all the way.

13TH JULY. Sir David & I taking a late evening walk last night observed a miserable small hut scarcely 10 feet square in which a man & his wife were living close by the road, & with a pool of stagnant water all round them; our attention was caught by the myriads of mosquitoes that attacked us in passing it, & we stopt to ask the unfortunate pair how they could exist in that situation. They allowed that they lived in torment from these insects & nothing could destroy them but smoke of green wood – with which at that moment they were filling the house by closing the door & chimney. In that manner they continued to obtain a little rest at night. The man was a shoemaker, had arrived about a year ago from Scotland, an emigrant, & hitherto had supported himself by his trade, but was anxious to obtain some land to settle upon. His wife was a young active woman of this country & assured me she could chop wood and use the hatchet as well as any man. They were very poor, had no money to pay the fees of office to get land, & the hut was a ruin which they had been permitted to occupy. On further conversation I found that he had served 7 years in the Galloway Militia this last war, had an excellent character on his discharge, & the same from all his neighbours since he had been there. I gave him an order for 200 acres without paying fee. He was quite happy. His name is David Milroy....

17TH JULY. Last night we reached Halifax, the admiral to our great astonishment coming in quite fresh after 47 miles.

We left Phillymore's early on 14th, breakfasted at Sutherland & got on to Flamingo about 32 miles – the road nearly like that from Amherst, green turf with very noble woods all the way along – hilly till within 4 miles of Flamingo in Londonderry it is flat & dry gravel, capital road. In passing one of the bridges next day to Truro we observed what is called the *Boar* – a most violent rush of the tide from the Bason of Minas into all the creeks or rivulets emptying into it. This Boar rushed up with a great noise at 6 or 7 miles an hour, stemming the current of the stream meeting it. The effect of this at the entrance of Shubenacadie river where large vessels anchor to take in Gypsum, is so violent as to upset any vessel that drops anchor in the stream, & there are many instances of this known. The tide on this side of the Province rises 80 feet while in the St. Lawrence at Bay Verte it rises only 8 or 9 feet.

From Truro on 15th we got on to Gibbons', a very poor house, but very obliging people. We got very wet today, the only time in our whole journey. In the Evening Sir David and I, walking out, heard close to us the bird called "Whip-poor-Will." Its call is as plain as I can pronounce these words, slow & distinct, but it was then too dark to see them. Sir David insists that it is not a bird but frogs, & that is a very common opinion, but I am quite persuaded that it is a bird, not only because I thought I saw them flitting about like the night hawk, but also because their call was aloft among bushes, & not upon the ground.

I have frequently heard these birds spoken of but never before met with them myself.

Yesterday breakfasted at Keys, & got home to dinner. We are all delighted with our excursion – the weather has been very hot – we have not met with the smallest accident and the country in every part most beautiful....

I find here the *Grasshopper* Brig of War, Capt. Forbes, come to join the squadron in place of one ordered home, and the Packet from England just coming in.

22ND JULY. I yesterday closed dispatches & the Packet which had been detained & waiting my return this last week, sailed homeward bound.

Capt. Forbes being ordered with the mail to Bermuda has offered to carry me round into Mahone Bay where I had left Lady D. I have sent my horses round there by land, via Hammonds Plains & Chester, and only now wait a wind.

25TH JULY. Day before yesterday we left Halifax.... Today Forbes & I rode by Lunenburg, & returned thro' the Northwest range, a new road well made & settled.

26TH JULY. Sunday. A very fine breeze at N. this morning tempted us to sail in the yacht to see Chester, but we had not gone 3 miles when a violent squall overtook us; our helmsman not minding what he was about, it caught the mainsail, the boom gave and with the violence of the check snapped in two, jamming itself on deck within a foot or two [of] where Lady D, Miss Cochrane and I were sitting. Fortunately nobody was hurt, but it is yet utterly incomprehensible how we should have all escaped such a tremendous crash. We instantly rounded up head to wind and dropped anchor. Forbes, who had put us on board & taken leave on his farther voyage to

Bermuda, was just getting under way in the *Grasshopper* when he observed our accident; he instantly in the kindest manner hastened to us with his surgeon; & all the carpenters of his ship. He was astonished to find we had no occasion for the former, and the latter soon cleared away the wreck. We returned to Zwicker's all well, & Forbes remains with us to repair our damages.

I yesterday rode to the falls of Le Have River nearly 20 miles from this, a very good road to Cook's. People are doing well in this new settlement. The river is navigable, & a very considerable quantity of timber shipped from it every year. All hands are now busy making hay, but I find rum prevails here as in most parts of the province. Cook came in at 2 o'clock quite drunk. He has a fine family & a large tract of land. We got an excellent lunch, & leaving fed our horses & returned home to dinner....

1ST AUGUST. Two days ago I rode to Mr. Crandle's at Chester & yesterday having got two country ponies, we rode into the Sherbrooke settlement. Lt. Ross of the Nova Scotia Fencibles, of which the men settled here are the remains, came to meet us; on being disbanded two years ago they were offered land & rations; about 100 families accepted & came into this wilderness. Mr. Ross, an Irishman, resolved on sharing their hardships & has done a great deal in the way of example & by encouragement, but from want of system on the part of Government when first placing them here, they have had to contend with most appalling difficulties.

The road to Ross's hut is scarcely passable for horses, about 12 miles – to Lance's 3 miles, very good, but we then struck into the woods & what with rocks & bogs & rotten trees I never could have hoped to accomplish the end without broken legs or arms. However, we did reach Rosebank, as he calls his place, in about 4 1/2 hours. He had prepared a very good dinner for us, & invited his neighbour Mr. Wells, an officer of the Navy whose distressed circumstances have led him to fix there as a schoolmaster for the sake of getting land & rations.

Mrs. Wells, a remarkably pretty woman, very cheerful manners & very ladylike – she is a niece of Mr. Prescott's of Cornwallis. I expressed my surprize that she could have dared the hardships of such a situation, but she said that necessity had driven them, and she was quite happy in seeing their hardships disappear very rapidly.

In another year she hoped to have forgot it all, but as yet they were frightful to look back upon. She had been obliged to go out there in May, the snow then so deep that she got into a wretched log house prepared for them by the window, & during the first month kept themselves warm by the thickness of the smoke in the hut. Now she has her little garden, her poultry yard, a piano forte & two sweet little children, she says, that occupy her whole time from morning till night.

Mrs. Ross is also lively & pleasant, but more able & longer used to the hardships of the world. Her family is large & the eldest girl able to help a little. She also appears quite happy & contented. Several of the settlers who have turned to their work industriously have cleared large pieces 10 to 15 acres, & will do well, but two thirds of the number will leave the settlement as soon as the Rations cease.

From what I have seen I think I can powerfully assist them by making a new settlement about halfway between Lance's & Rosebank. 25 men of the 60th now discharged & a Mr. Kien, the Quartermaster of the Regt., have agreed to settle there, and I shall as soon as I return to Halifax send down a detachment of the Regiment to make a road accessible to them. I call this new settlement "Kiensland," which pleases the Germans & they promise great things in very short time. The land is light, easy to work & the wood very fine indeed.

Having reached Crandles' again by 8 o'clock Couper and I mounted our own horses & got to Zwicker's about 11 last night, very tired.

3RD AUGUST. Yesterday the *Forth* was seen standing into the Bay thro' the islands in grand style, with studding sails & every other sail set, but we were still more astonished to see another frigate soon after follow up & anchor near her. Sr John Louis brought with him the Commissioner Wodehouse, with Col. & Mrs. Beresford, and we found that the *Wye* had brought General Smyth to pay me a visit on business. He landed last night for a couple of hours but returned on board. Today it has poured rain incessantly & we have not seen him yet. As we are not in any hurry to leave this, the Beresfords have made this little trip to pass a few days here & see the country.

5TH AUGUST. Again safe in Halifax, but the ladies & the whole party of Mahone Bay are lamenting to have left so delightful a spot. They have been poorly accommodated as to lodging, but the Zwickers have been most obliging & kind, anxious in the extreme to do anything in their power to serve them. The scenery is beautiful, but better described in the sketches I have had taken by Woolford than it can be by words.

They have all enjoyed perfect health; the quietness of the retirement, uninterrupted by visitors or neighbours, has permitted them the appropriation of their whole time; they have disposed of it from the first day to the last with clockwork regularity, and I really do not know which of them all has been most happy in their particular pursuit or play; whether it be Lady D. and Miss Cochrane in their reading & studies in Chemistry & Mineralogy, Mr. Temple in his own private studies & walks, Henry Dundas in his command of yacht & boat, Ramsay in fishing tommy cod, or Jim in his play with two little girls of his own age whom he calls his Squaws, & who have built for him a wigwam in which he fancies himself an Indian Chief, & commands in [as] Master. All of them have been very happy & all seem equally to regret their return here.

We soon heard that General Smyth's visit was not altogether intended for me; indeed he had no business for me; his attention to the ladies confirmed some tittle tattle reports that had been current in this town & to which his visit certainly gives probability, altho' I cannot think Miss C. will approve them.

I started the party at dawn of day; by 5 o'clock we were on board, but did not get up anchor till 8. It has been a delightful day. With a wind quite fair, a sea quite smooth, we made a surprising run here by 3 o'clock....

18TH AUGUST. The Packet brings no news. Elections in England are going on as here also, bearing equal importance tho' on a scale widely different. The good old Queen is failing very fast and her death must now be looked for by every Packet.

23RD AUGUST. We have again had a great deal of thunder & Lightning. A large ship from New Brunswick came in yesterday under jury masts, having lost her Bowsprit, Foremast by the board, and main top mast struck by lightning. The master says that he was standing aft near the helm when a very vivid flash & instant explosion took place, but he was not shook by it, nor was he aware of any mischief done untill he saw the Bowsprit & Masts overboard. Nobody was hurt.

The *Grasshopper* returned some days ago but did not bring up Sir James Cockburn as I had hoped I had persuaded him to come & spend a couple [of] months with us during the hottest period of the year at Bermuda.

The Admiral having offered us another cruize in *Leander,* we propose sailing tomorrow to visit Louisbourg and the Bras d'or in Cape Breton, the Canso Gut, Prince Edward's Island, and land as last year at Pictou, where our carriage will go to meet us....

26TH AUGUST. Day before yeserday we left Halifax and have only now reached Country Harbour about 2 o'clock. Calm fine weather all yesterday. We tried to catch some Cod, but with little success from the shoals of dogfish that seized the bait as fast as thrown overboard. It is a long ugly fish full of oil, and unfit to eat, so voracious as to prevent the cod fishing. Dewar of *Leander,* & young Vogrier, took one of them & passed a piece of wood two feet long thro' its gills, & then threw it overboard. We saw it floating & struggling more than two hours after. The fishermen do this constantly in the idea that it drives off the shoal of that troublesome fish.

27TH AUGUST. We all started this morning on a fishing & shooting excursion to the fresh water stream at top of this harbour; the law for the protection of game which existed last year being now nearly expired, we were anxious to shoot some partridges.

Everyone filled his basket with very fine trout & Sir John & Hay also got some brace of partridges. We dined in Picnic, a very large party, and in the Evening I walked part of the way home to shoot but got nothing. The birds are found by mere accident basking or running on the road, and there you shoot them on the ground or mark them into a tree where it is very difficult to see them again. I made two attempts to follow them but got into such a scramble thro' very large trees tumbled in a mass over one another, lengthwise & crosswise, some rotten, some burnt, some matted together with weeds & undergrowth to a depth from 10 to 20 feet, that I had great difficulty to extricate myself with torn cloaths, scratched face & blackened all over with burnt sticks.

94

Our Picnic was exceedingly pleasant, and as we recollected the day to be the Anniversary of Algiers, we did honour to the Admiral, & those who had shared in that memorable day.

29TH AUGUST.... We intended to have sailed for Louisburg but the wind still hangs to the Eastward. We went with Sir David round into a small bay called Isaac's Harbour, or Hinchinbrooke by Des Barres – at top found a very small rivulet tumbling over some romantic rocks. Caught a few trout.

Others went out shooting. Wellard, a Midshipman of the *Forth*, has been most successful. Wandering alone he put up a covey of partridge which all went to tree. He saw one of them & fired; down came a brace. The others, alarmed, crouched on the branches until he shot 14 of them. This is the real picture of Partridge shooting; the stupidity of the bird is very extraordinary, & still more is the tameness of it. When caught alive, a day or two make it as tame as a dove.

30TH AUGUST. Sunday. Got under way at daybreak but on reaching the open sea found the wind still at S.E. We bore up & dropt anchor under shelter of a large island, but at noon a heavy sea came tumbling in; we returned to our snug anchorage above the Cochran head. Mr. Temple performed divine service to the ship's company.

1ST SEPTEMBER. Yesterday it blew a heavy gale & thick weather. We stood fast, & this morning weighed at day dawn with strong breeze at N.W. When clear of the harbour we found it blew hard & very cold. We run 12 knots an hour—anchored just as it grew dark in Gabarous Bay, having gone our 90 miles in 9 hours.

2ND SEPTEMBER. After breakfast beat up into Louisbourg; the *Forth* led us in. We immediately went on shore & took our guns. A miserable & deserted village. We found great quantities of Plover, snipe & curlew, of which we killed great numbers, & having walked round the ruined ramparts returned on board.

3RD SEPTEMBER. At 6 this morning I again went on shore with the Admiral, Couper & others, to trace the old works & operations of the siege, & having in our hands a very detailed account of it in a book published by Jeffery, called "State of Canada & North American Provinces," with maps, we plainly saw the remains of the smallest batteries & lines both of approach & Defence. Wolfe was here the active & operative officer, most enterprising indeed he appears throughout the whole siege, & shewed himself highly qualified for the subsequent great command against Quebec.

The ramparts & stairs are now laid smooth in grass, & the town quite overgrown is cut in hay annually by two people who have settled themselves there. I went to call upon an old man still hale & healthy at 86. He was in Wolfe's Regiment, the Louisburg Grenade, & present both at this siege & at Quebec. He was reduced with his Regiment and has lived here ever since. His old woman also still alive but quite blind, sits by the fire grumbling & scolding. We could not find any means to put her in good humour. This old Veteran has no pension nor support of any kind, and is now literally starving – to the disgrace of the British Govt. who at present prohibits most severely the giving support or a ration to such objects as this. I have seen several men in the Province in similar distressed circumstances who had also served with Wolfe, & are now living to starve.

I have had several views taken of this by Woolford; it is a small but very safe harbour, the land around it very good, and I certainly think that Government ought to re-establish a town here, as a much more easy communication with Halifax to obtain supplies which might find way into the interior & to Sydney, without the dangers of rounding the headlands East of this....

7TH SEPTEMBER. We left Louisbourg yesterday with a fine wind at N. at 10 o'clock divine Service by Mr. Temple, ship's company attending.

Sir David intended to have gone into St. Peter's Bay to see the Bras d'Or, but none of the Pilots would venture to carry the large ship into it, & we therefore stood on round the Green Island, passed Arichat on Isle Madame, a nice clean tho' scattered village, and near 10 P.M. under a most beautiful moonlight dropt anchor at Eddy Point in the entrance of the Canso Gut.

This morning I was anxious to visit the Light House now erecting on Cape Canso. We sailed after breakfast in the *Chebucto,* but the wind drew to the South, & the access to it being rocky & narrow we returned on board *Leander,* which had in the meantime shifted her berth a little way further into Inhabitant's harbour. This was a great disappointment, as Sir David had expressed an opinion that this light was badly placed. I was very desirous to examine it with him. He thinks it ought to have stood on Green Island. The objection to that is simply that this is a Provincial Light house & we in Nova Scotia could not have demanded dues if it had been placed on Green Island which belongs to the Government of Cape Breton.

10TH SEPTEMBER. Day before yesterday the wind tempted Sir David to make trial of the Lennox passage up to St. Peter's Bay. At 8 we got into the *Jane* tender with our shooting things, & some provisions in case of need. We expected shoal water & some difficulty in finding the channel, but Des Barres' charts are in this particular neighbourhood wonderfully correct & carefully laid down; we wound our way thro' all the turns without touching and dropt anchor at 12 o'Clock at Mr. Kavanagh's in St. Peter's, about 20 miles, passing a continual variety of beautiful scene. The Isle Madame is chiefly inhabited by French, the remains of the Acadians. They are all fishermen, but to judge by the appearance of their houses & the number of schooners building at their doors, they are a very industrious well doing people. A boat full of women passed us, crossing to the opposite shore, we thought going to haymaking. They were rowing and singing very gaily, dressed altogether in the old French taste with coloured handkerchiefs tied in turbans very becomingly round the head. The men being all absent on the fisheries, the women do all the harvest & home work at this season.

Mr. Kavanagh received us with great civility & invited us to remain at his house....

The back of the Lake is thinly scattered with new settlers, to whom Kavanagh is a common father & protector. He keeps a general store of every supply but retails out to these people at very moderate & fair gain. He is paid in return with anything they chuse to bring him, as fish, timber, cattle, & poultry of which he makes a trade to Halifax. They all speak of him in the most affectionate manner. He has also a number of Indians about him, working a little but chiefly living on his bounty.

On one of the islands the Indians have built themselves a Chapel, and the Catholic Priest comes there to perform services, & to which numbers of the settlers go, being chiefly Irish & West Highlands from Scotland.

Having stood up to the point where the Bras d'Or expands into a Sea, the boundaries of which are just seen on the horizon, we bore up & returned home to Kavanagh's to dinner.

By this Bras d'Or the communication to Sydney & thro' this whole interior of Cape Breton is easy & convenient; roads thro' the country, were it settled, would be almost unnecessary, but it is not only not settled, no pains are taking to advance it. The British government is either utterly ignorant of the state of this part of the British dominions, or it is not in its present policy to encourage improvements in it. But it really excites a feeling of disgust to think of & observe the total neglect & apathy of the Colonial department under Lord Bathurst towards all these Provinces.

In that interior of Cape Breton, the land is excellent soil, the timber very fine & abundant, the fishermen all around its coasts are considered the best on these seas. The quantity of fish in the Bras d'Or is quite a natural curiosity, & even in depth of winter are taken in cart loads; by simply opening the ice they rush in shoals at the aperture & greedily take any bait. That source of nourishment is sufficient of itself to encourage the settlement of the country. Coal is found in all parts of it. Notwithstanding these advantages, Cape Breton has no Government; it had been promised a Legislative Assembly, as Prince Edward's Island & New Brunswick, but the promise never has been fulfilled, and on that account the Governor can raise no tax, impose no duty, has no authority whatever by which to promote the interests of the people he is placed over.

We this morning left Mr. Kavanagh's most hospitable house, & equally fortunate in our passage down we got on board *Leander* about 2 P.M., weighed anchor immediately, & now about dusk have crept up slowly into Ship Harbour in the Canso Gut, where we anchor again.

11TH SEPTEMBER. A raw nasty day with heavy squalls from North. Unable to beat up against wind and a very rapid current, which by the bye always goes here with the wind, we stand fast in safe anchorage.

I again recur to Mr. Kavanagh, try to recollect something more of the information I picked up from him. He tells me that General Ainslie's administration of the Government is very popular & only hampered by difficulties not in his power to remove.

Cape Breton never has had a House of Assembly; the Council has not the power to raise taxes or levy duties. The Merchants at Sydney did submit to certain duties for 18 years, but the Chief Justice Dodds now there, lately gave an opinion in court on a trial where two Merchants had refused to pay these duties, "that they could not legally be obliged to it, because no Power but an House of Assembly could impose tax, or levy duty." Under this judgement the Government of Cape Breton has now no revenue whatever.

Lands are held by Lease or Licence of the Crown, paying Quit rent, but it has not yet been called for. Ainslie has lately granted lands in nonconformity to the Royal Instructions under which I act in Nova Scotia, a copy of which I sent him lately, paying fees similar. He has also levied a duty at the Plaster Cove near this harbour of one shilling pr ton sold. The Americans carry it away at 6 shillings per ton.

Altho' Government may not find fault with the system of Grant instead of occupation, I very much fear he may involve himself in difficulties by the authorising of Fees, and shilling duty, as both of these partly go to his own pocket. Mischievous people may take hold of it, and altho' my friend Ainslie is a good, honest & clever fellow, he is in needy circumstances & wildly speculative. The character of such a man is generally most roughly handled by the public, & least able to stand the vindictive, illnatured attack.

The Indians in Cape Breton sometimes gather to the number of 300 at their Chapel to meet the Priest. They do not stop however—a few wigwams only, with a very little cultivation near them, are scattered about, & give the only hope I have yet seen of inducing this extraordinary race of human beings to fix themselves in a civilised state.

Kavanagh told me that Des Barres had the assistance of several Naval & Scientific officers in making the surveys of these coasts. Admiral Knight, then a Midshipman, was one of them, that he had often seen him at St. Peter's & Arichat in his father's lifetime. Knight was then a very active & very clever young man. The surveys were taken between 1766 and 1776.

16TH SEPTEMBER. It came on to blow a gale on the night of the 11th-12th and lasted untill yesterday when the winds & current changed, but so light that about noon we were again obliged to

99

anchor under Cape Porcupine. We all went ashore to walk, fish or shoot, till about 3 o'clock a breeze sprung up and a gun from the flagship with Blue Peter at the fore hurried all hands on board. We cleared the Gut before sunset and now are standing up into Pictou Harbour.

17TH SEPTEMBER. We landed yesterday and have been most comfortably accommodated by Mr. Mortimer. Today we had intended going up to the Coal Mines but it has poured rain incessantly.

We were very glad to get on shore again, for tho' we have spent a very pleasant month with Sir David, we have had generally very blowing uncomfortable weather, having a fire in the Cabin almost every day.

23RD SEPTEMBER. We reached home last night. On the 18th Lady D. and Mrs. Lawson went with us to the coal mines which I have already mentioned last year. Next day, Saturday, we left Mr. M., Hay & I on horseback, Lady D., Mr. Temple, Ramsay in her open carriage with 4 horses, driven postillion. It rained heavy the whole day & made our journey to Truro, 40 miles, a severe one. Sunday we stopped, went to church with Mrs. Archibald, & had a wretched sermon from a dissenting Scotch minister. I don't think I ever met with so respectable a congregation so very poorly appointed. Tho' Mr. Archibald was only recovering from a servere illness, he insisted on our dining with them, & most kind they were. She is a very handsome woman, & he at the top of the Bar, one of the most rising men in Nova Scotia.

Day before yesterday we slept at Key's Inn, 30 miles—a delightful day. The Partridges were so numerous by the side of the road, and so stupid that I killed them without getting out of the carriage. Generally however we did stop to let Ramsay shoot. He had a short little rifle that did not carry shot well, but still he killed 2 brace. I shot 5 hare & tired of it. I might have killed 20 without stepping out of the carriage.

Yesterday cold & rain, not a bird was seen from Key's to Halifax, 32 miles. We got home without any accident whatever and my horses in excellent condition.

27TH SEPTEMBER. I have been these last few days busily occupied in bringing up arrears accumulated in my absence. Nothing material however has happened, and I shall again start tomorrow morning to visit the Musquodoboit settlements as far as the roads will permit us.

3RD OCTOBER. We left this in 28th early, the Commissioner Wodehouse, Capt. Forbes of *Grasshopper*, Dr. Robb and Hay with me. We took our guns & fishing tackle, slept at Keys, breakfasted on 29th at Andrews' on Gay's river. This is a beautiful spot. Forbes & I walked down the river about 2 miles where it joined the Shubenacadie; on our return Robb had to his own surprise filled two baskets of very fine trout. We here left the Truro road & struck into the right. At 10 miles nearly dark we reached Johnstone Colbeck's, a very bad road—saw a few birds.

On the next morning I rode with Forbes & Hay about 6 miles forward to Mr. Cload's farm, road still worse than before. Killed 7 brace without quitting the road, returned to dinner at Colbeck's. Robb & the Commissioner had had capital sport fishing. Till today I never had been persuaded that the Bear is yet common in this Province. However a lad with us shewed me distinctly the foot-marks of one & a very large one along the road; a boy with Robb in a direction quite away from us shewed very recent tracks of one, & Colbeck assuring me that he loses many lambs by them, even when perhaps near the farm houses, I am now satisfied on the point....

A deputation from the upper settlement came down to ask me to visit it & Souiac, but my time did not permit. I shall return there with great pleasure. I was astonished in this excursion to see one of the finest settlements in the Province—a very fine valley nearly a mile broad, large hanging woods of hard timber mixed with pine & spruce, and a fine river winding down in the middle. It is well cleared in some places & well worth the trouble. The people are very poor but indusrious & comfortable; they have little dealing with Halifax, and those in town know scarcely that such a place as Musquodoboit exists.... We returned this forenoon, and the Admiral is now standing in with the *Forth* from his cruize of six weeks.

24TH OCTOBER.... Walking out this evening I have been comparing in my fancy the fineness of this summer day with the climate of home at this time. The air here is like our common summer, but the beautiful & varied tints of the woods at the same time tell that autumn will soon pass into the snow white & dreary dress of an

American winter. This evening the ground is covered with a brushwood mixed of Kalmia, Rhodora and another shrub, bright red, which Lady D. tells me is called "Candleberry Myrtle" – in contrast to this red are the higher woods, Beech, Birch, Poplar & Maple, all shades of delicate red & Yellow leaves, dropping as by every puff of wind. Add to these the Pine, spruce & fir of lively green in great quantity, and the harbour, smooth & warm blue, with several vessels & many boats out. Altogether it is a summer evening of England, with all the varied painting of Autumn & coming Winter—a picture as rich as it is possible to fancy.

26TH OCTOBER.... Some alterations necessary at Government House preparatory for winter have obliged me to bring Lady D. & the boys to Rockingham Inn for a week....

3RD NOVEMBER. In my walk today, Judge Stewart with me, we met Howe our Postmaster—a very sensible, well-informed & shrewd old man. He is just returned from a tour by Quebec, Montreal, New York & Boston. His conversation was so interesting that I cannot help sitting down immediately to take a Memorandum of it.

He says the Americans are making silent but rapid advances into Canada. Whole streets are building at Montreal, brick houses exactly similar to the style of New York, and building by American Merchants settling at Montreal in business.

500 Vessels have loaded this summer at Quebec with timber & lumber, the whole almost sent down in rafts navigated by Americans.

He considers the St. Lawrence at this moment as freely occupied & used by the American trade as is the Mississippi.

On the line of frontier at Plattsburg, the Americans are building a very strong work & have already got up a prodigious octagon tower of solid masonry seemingly adapted for a double or triple range of guns. Further at Albany or Greenbush they have a very fine barracks for 10,000 men. This I have heard from many others.

The tide of immigration which we are told is flowing to Upper Canada, & which the Govt. at home is helping forward at great expense, flows full to the States. The steamboats at Quebec to Montreal are generally loaded with Irish families—all, as Howe was told, going to Upper Canada, but at Plattsburg he saw the steam boat there filled with them as at Quebec – and he is satisfied that these & the far greater proportion of Artificers that come out with the sanction of Government to Canada do not stop a month before they proceed to the States.

In the Plattsburg steam boat, he says, he could not help wondering with himself what object could possibly have induced Sir Geo. Prevost to direct his war to that point – a wild forest, where scarcely yet two settlements are seen at the time. (Sir Geo. acted by orders from home.)

In that boat, he entered into conversation with a tall odd looking man, a Scotchman by his language – not more strange and eccentric in appearance than in his ideas & the view he took of all subjects in conversation, a man such as answers fully to Shakespeare's description, "fit for any treason, strategem or plot." This man he found to be Mr. Gourlay, the noted disturber of Upper Canada at present.

Howe seems much annoyed at the report in Quebec that Bouchette is now persuading the Duke of Richmond to undertake the opening of the road from Quebec to Fredericton, a most unwise & dangerous measure. The road ought to be carried from Cumberland in this Province right thro' the woods by Miramichie, touching the St. Lawrence at Bic.

Govt. ought to open these forests & plant there the immigrants. Having no temptation & great difficulty to proceed to America, they would stay, & from Miramichie, a very fine river, they would load thousands of our own vessels with our own timber.

In Lower Canada, tho' thinly settled, no land is to be had. It all belongs to the Church or to Seigneurs, & not liable to Escheat to the Crown.

8TH NOVEMBER. The weather is still remarkably mild & pleasant. Lady D. in a thin summer dress walked with me this Evening till half past 5 o'clock, when darkness drove us home.

30TH NOVEMBER. At last the Packet of October from England has reached this [place] – a long passage of 40 days, the last 15 very boisterous off the coast, altho' on shore our weather has been very fine. It brings no news of any importance, but that the excellent old Queen was yet alive, suffering torture by spasms from water in the chest. The allied Sovereigns had met at Aix la Chapelle & ordered forthwith the Armies from France. Sir Geo. Murray writes me that the British will be in England by the end of November – and very extensive reductions immediately follow.

All the trading ships from England, which usually bring the Autumn (or called here, the Fall) goods, are yet a-missing – they have generally arrived in October.

1ST DECEMBER. Yesterday I dined with the North British Society, on St. Andrew's Day, Judge Halliburton in Chair – not a very numerous meeting, about 90, but a very pleasant one. I took an opportunity to suggest the forming an Agricultural Society to be resident at Halifax, and I think it will be taken up in some shape or other soon. Some person signing himself Agricola has been writing in the Paper, Acadian Recorder, these last 4 months, Essays on the improvement of the Agriculture of the Province. He has stirred up the Country to the most extraordinary pitch, & certainly writes in very superior style. Nobody yet knows who he is.

2ND DECEMBER. Today snow has at last fallen. *Bellette* has sailed for Bermuda. Captain Pichell is an impudent and insufferable puppy, now called in London a Dandy, or an Exquisite. Lieut. Cheape, the grandson of my old and excellent friend Mr. Guthrie of Craigie, is in this Brig, a very nice young man indeed.

3RD DECEMBER. More snow, now laying deep and likely to last.

15TH DECEMBER. Arrived two days ago the long looked for ship *Castlereagh,* from London, after a passage of 77 days, the last 5 weeks within 300 miles of this harbour, blowing constantly hard, & so dead off the coast that she could not gain a mile upon it.

She brings the public supply for the winter, or the Fall goods – is worth £100,000 to this little town. She brings also our great supply of Books for our Garrison Library, and now completes that work to my utmost wishes. It is comfortably fitted in the center of all our Barracks, a quiet detached building – now an excellent selection of general reading to the amount of £1500, and has a fund in hand for purchase of more books of £600, with an annual subscription of £150 besides the ordinary admission of New Members that come to the garrison every year. The general incidental expenses will not exceed £50 a year.

Letters remarkably well written under the signature of Agricola have for some months past attracted the public attention. Agricultural Societies are strongly recommended by him, and are now forming in every corner of the Province. Being myself convinced that such Societies are alone wanting to give life & vigour to farming here, I have repeatedly expressed myself in public, and in private to this Agricola by post letters, that the object he pointed at was in my opinion of paramount importance, and that I should be happy to join hands with him in giving all the help in my power to his exertions. On St. Andrew's day, I took an opportunity at a public dinner of Scotsmen, to give Agricola as a toast, and to ask why we in Halifax were slower than other parts of the Country? I stated that I knew the great advantages that Scotland had derived from her Agricultural Societies, and therefore felt desirous to throw out the suggestion to them. It has been taken up quite warmly. A public meeting took place today. A provincial Agricultural Society has been formed, and a subscription to the amount of £600 immediately entered into. The meeting was most numerous & respectable; nothing was opposed, and the Proceedings appear to have given the utmost Satisfaction.

Snow is still laying deep. Therm. at 8 this morning stood at 4 degrees above zero. In order to have a correct state of the Therm. this winter, I have placed my horizontal one, which marks the extreme of heat & cold in the 24 hours, at the Garrison Library, and the Sub-librarian is directed to mark it at 3 periods of the day, noting also the state of the wind & weather. Skaiting, Sleighing & walking are in perfection in this steady cold weather.

27TH DECEMBER.... I had occasion lately to send the Government armed Brig to New York to obtain specie or Bills by the Commissary General for the public service. Lt. Stewart, who commands her, is an intelligent smart officer & has had frequent opportunities of being there. He tells me that it was with difficulty the Consul has procured specie. Very large sums are now sent by the Americans to China, having neither produce nor manufactures to offer in trade, money & that in Spanish dollars is the only exchange the Chinese will accept of them. Large sums have also been sent from New York to establish the Bank at Montreal in Canada, and a motion in Congress to restrain the export of Specie had all tended to raise the money market.

Stewart also informs me that the Batteries and defences of New York, tho' formidable, are extremely ill constructed & in bad state. Last summer when President Monroe visited there, a frigate was ordered to fire a broadside at the Battery on Gouverneur's Island to prove the works.

The Congress is composed of violent & needy members of the community. No man who is prosperous in trade or in farming will sacrifice his time to it, and therefore it is only such as consider the daily pay of 5 dollars (30 shillings) that will canvass the honour of a Seat. A few however must be excepted who aim at public station & diplomatic employ.

Of New York, DeWitt Clinton is Governor – a man of very superior station in Society – in appearance & manners prepossessing & Gentlemanlike, in talents able, in acquirements at the head of their literary Societies, which are highly respectable. He has long aimed at the President's Chair, but in politics he is a Federal, a steady Washingtonian, & now the Democrats are all powerful.

As he cannot be President, he is obliged to be content as Governor of New York.

Tomkins was last year Govr. but was content to yield to Clinton & accept the chair of Vice President under Monroe. The Vice President is ex Officio, Chairman of the Senate, but so contemptible is that station – it has no weight of interest in Government, not even a seat in the Cabinet – Tomkins is a poor miserable creature commonly called the "Ploughboy" for what reason Stewart could not learn.

1ST JANUARY 1819. The New Year opened with one of the brightest and most delightful winter days it is possible to imagine.

We held a Levee at Government House, which was but thinly attended, and some of the company dressed in their most common attire; some in boots, some great coats, and a Clergyman I saw in his full canonicals over a dress of coarse brown cloth, as if just come in from the plough or hatchet. Altogether a very motley group. Were it not likely to create a discussion, I would abolish altogether these Levees, but established by custom in the Colonies, it might be unwise to touch them. The people here know my dislike to them, and on that have presumed to neglect the ceremony of dress; this is not right, and as they must go on, I shall take steps to restore the old formality in all its state.

10TH JANUARY. Yesterday arrived the *Grasshopper* from Bermudas, 10 days, bringing the November mail from England. Nothing material in the newspapers. The old Queen still alive on the 13th, dragging on a suffering illness from which she cannot recover. Captain Forbes says the severity of the cold off this coast was beyond anything he could have imagined. 20 of his men have been frostbit. One man will lose both his hands. It was certainly very unlucky his making the coast & anchoring off York Redoubt during the night of the most intense cold we have had this winter. Thermometer at 6 degrees below zero....

As usual on this day the Standard was hoisted at daylight in honour of the Queen's Birthday, but at 9 o'clock New York papers, and the Sun of London of 17th November, were put into my hands. They contained Lord Sidmouth's official letter to the Lord Mayor, announcing the Death of Her Majesty.

The rejoicings of the Day were changed into instant mourning; at 12 I ordered the Standard and the Flags at all posts to be lowered to half mast, by signal Gun from the Citadel; the order for the usual salutes from the batteries & shipping were countermanded and the Ball this Evening at Government House stopt by cards.

As I have been daily looking for accounts of this Event, it is no surprize, but has created very sensible regret. It is not a little singular that our salutes and rejoicings on this day last year were also stopt by the fatal intelligence of the death of the Princess Charlotte, and our Standards then spoke our grief as now at half mast high. The venerable age of the good old Queen leads to feel this as an Event in the natural course of things. Our grief cannot be expected to equal that in last year under circumstances the most afflicting & unexpected, but still the mourning here will be general & deep.

19TH JANUARY. Late this evening the town was in great joy on the arrival of the ship *Castlereagh* from London 77 days passage – serious apprehension has been entertained for her safety. She has goods on board valued at £100,000 for this town....

24TH JANUARY.... The church of St. Paul's was hung today in deep mourning, the appearance as formerly most impressive and solemn. Dr. Inglis delivered a very eloquent funeral sermon on the virtuous & revered character of Her late Most Excellent Majesty, a sermon that pleased me exceedingly as one becoming a dignified clergyman of the church....

28TH JANUARY. This forenoon arrived the *Cyrene* from the Bermudas with the December mails, 5 days. She came in before a violent gale of wind from S.W. with heavy rain....

29TH JANUARY. The details of the death & funeral of the Queen are very interesting at this distance from home. The good old Queen will be long & sincerely lamented, rather perhaps I should say deserves to be. There is something in the whole slow catastrophe of her illness & death that is highly pleasing & comfortable; so much in unison with the mild, inoffensive and domestic course of her life; and so kind, grateful & affectionate the attentions of her children of 50 and 60 years of age, that to die in that way seems truly a picture of an aged Parent in earthly bliss.

5TH FEBRUARY.... Sleighing on the Dartmouth Lakes in great fashion. Lady D. has been up near to Fletcher's Bridge....

11TH FEBRUARY.... Opened the General Assembly in the new Province Hall. It is remarkable that every Member was in his place. Mr. Robie was unanimously chosen Speaker, 39 Members being present including him.

14TH FEBRUARY.... Yesterday the Council and Assembly brought up their respective addresses in answer to the Speech. The latter peculiarly well written by Cogswell, both of them remarkably Loyal, & expressing themselves disposed to meet my wishes.

21ST FEBRUARY. Sunday.... It is a singular thing that this new House of Assembly has met so nearly equal in new Members & others of the old House, that setting the Speaker aside, there are 18 of each; and on the first question they divided equal numbers & required the Speaker's casting vote.

24TH FEBRUARY. The *Forth* sailed for Bermuda. The sleighing on Dartmouth Lakes still in fashion.

2ND MARCH. A delightful summer day. I walked by the sea shore round Point Pleasant. Wet and disagreeable underfoot, but the sun so warm that I sat down on the rocks nearly an hour, enjoying the heat of the day, and the fresh smell of the seaweed on the beach.

3RD MARCH. Another winter. A fresh storm of snow & heavy gale at N.E.

16TH MARCH. Wind S. with rain. The streets in a shocking state, knee deep in snow & water. The *Speedy,* Packet from New York homewards arrived; Capt. Osborne states that the January Packet from England had not arrived 6 days ago – *Chebucto* there still waiting for it....

24TH MARCH. *Forth* returned from Bermuda, just in time to anchor before a heavy gale at S.E. with snow. No Packet from England had arrived 8 days ago. I have therefore desired *Chebucto* to be recalled from New York.

Forth had stormy weather going down, & equally bad coming back, carried away her foreyard both times. Reports nothing new at Bermudas, except that the small trade in Schooners from America was rapidly increasing; 140 sail of them there at a time. This trade does no good to the island, as the Americans have sent there their own Merchants to settle & do their business. I don't understand how this is permitted, as it appears an injury to the resident British Merchants. It is only said that the Bermudians are so inactive & dispirited, & such general want of capital among them, that they cannot carry on the trade....

8TH APRIL. Our Packets of January & February have at last arrived –the former yesterday, the latter day before–and today *Forth* has left us, to the sincere regret of all who have met with the utmost kindness & attention from Sir John Louis & his officers. He goes first to receive Mr. Bagot & family at Washington, & proceeds then to England....

14TH APRIL. Delightful settled Summer now. The writer in the public newspaper under the name of "Agricola" who has excited so much notice & curiosity of the public addressed a private letter to me this morning, offering to declare himself & assume his duties as Secretary of our Society if I approved of it, at the same time stating reasons that led him to tremble at the step.

I had no hesitation in advising him to show himself, convinced that he would be well received by the Public, & that his fears were groundless. He is a Mr. John Young, a small merchant here, & the same person that has long been supposed the author. He is a Scotchman from Falkirk, educated for the Church, a good classical scholar, & fond of study, so much as perhaps to have injured his pursuit in trade.....

24TH APRIL. I prorogued the Assembly today after a very long Session in which very little business has been done. Much party spirit on a claim by dissenters & Methodist clergy to obtain the same privilege of marriage license as is granted to the Established Church. Much difference of opinion; a difficulty in obtaining an Increase to the Revenue, everyone opposing or resisting the proposals as they touched his own personal interest. I was compelled to censure lightly their voting an increase of pay to themselves at a time when they debated the inadequacy of the Revenue to meet the wants of the State. We parted however very good friends, many of the opulent and independent members & all the Council publicly approving the reprimand.

29TH APRIL. This last week, constant easterly winds, cold & raw, but these are bringing in the early spring ships from England in remarkably quick passages. One in 14 days from Portsmouth, one from London in 22 days, and several from Aberdeen, particularly *Louisa,* Capt. Oswald, in 24 days.

12TH MAY. Nothing has occurred this month. Cold N.E. winds, with fine weather generally. I have begun my works on the North Parade, & my College, in town. For the latter I have £5000 pounds in hand to build with. I have besides the interest of £7,000 in the funds, and a promise of at least £500 a year from the Assembly to provide Salary for Professors, quite sufficient to make a beginning of this Institution.

20TH MAY. I have … today received letters from Mr. G. Ainslie informing that he has received official, tho' private, notice of the intention of Ministers to reannex Cape Breton to Nova Scotia. I have no intimation of this. Yesterday the Regt. of West India Rangers arrived here, on their way to be disbanded in New Brunswick. I detain them to clear their mens' accompts, & make all arrangements which otherwise might cause a great deal of correspondence from General Smyth, an officer who is careless in his duty & takes no responsibility on himself in his command in New Brunswick.

The York Rangers also from the West Indies, and to be disbanded in this Province. I don't well know what to think of this measure, or how to avert the consequence of turning loose at once a Regiment composed of convicts from the hulks, deserters, & robbers who have forfeited their lives to the laws of England. They have their option of settling inland, or receiving £10 per man to dispose of themselves as they please. The thought of disbanding 800 such fellows with

£8000 in hand is alarming to a very peaceable community.

25TH MAY. The *Swiftsure* Packet for England is now sailing. By her I sent report to Earl Bathurst of the Proceedings of this last Session. I have transmitted an address from the Assembly on the extending the Priviledge of Marriage license to be issued to all sects in the Province, a Protest against that measure by several Members of Council, a Statement in behalf of the Established Church Clergy by Dr. Inglis in the absence of the Lord Bishop, and my own opinion upon it in a letter, sealed, to Lord B. I do not agree in the extending of it, nor do I agree with Dr. Inglis in his exclusive claim to it, thinking the Ministers & Clergy of the Established Kirk of Scotland justly entitled to it with that of England, but as the Kirk has it not in Scotland I am decidedly inclined to restrict the use of it, rather than extend the privilege. I have proposed that the Bishop should sign them instead of the Governor, that a heavy fee should be put on them in order to place it beyond the reach of common persons, that names of the parties be inserted before it is presented for signature, and that these fees be appropriated to the revenue of the Bishop, which is at present very inadequate to his rank & station. The object I aim at, is to oblige all parties to be called in Church. And now there is no part of the Province in which that may not be done easily.

I have also transmitted an Address from the Assembly on the late Convention, to be presented to the Prince Regent; this treaty with America has laid open the fisheries to them, & admits them to come freely into all our harbours to wood & water when they please—it is to license to them a free smuggling trade into the Province which nothing can effectively check. The supply of fish caught by our own poor people in the distant harbours will be bought up for bad flour, bad rum, or the refuse of the bad American markets. It will of course reduce our own export of fish, while it makes our population friendly with Yankees, & when the day of war shall come, the loyalty of the Province will be doubtful at the best.

This address is accompanied by a Report by a Joint Committee of the two Houses, embracing the general interests of British America; very ably drawn up & expressed in very strong language. If it does not, nothing will open the eyes of our present Government to the falling state of these colonies....

6TH JUNE. I promised last year when in Musquodoboit to return &

visit the upper settlement there and that of Souiac. I left Halifax this morning & sleep at Key's. I bring with me Mr. Wm. Lawson, Hay & Schomberg Kerr. The road is already in good order. Sad havoc appears to have been done last year by the fires for many miles between Fletcher's Bridge and Key's.

7TH JUNE. This morning started at 5 o'clock & breakfasted at Colbeck's at 10. Captain Taylor of the Militia Company came there to offer excuses for not turning out his company, not knowing of my company. He gives a very good account of it. I have promised to send him 50 stand of arms wanting to complete them.

One of the veterans of Wolfe's army came to me there also to ask an allowance of Rations. His name is Allamand—aged 85, his wife 81—and in great poverty. Served in the Artillery. Is a Swiss, a nice laughing old man, quite delighted to find I had authority to give him a supply of rations during his life. He walked yesterday 15 miles to meet me & goes home again tomorrow.

We came on to Geddes' to dine & sleep. The river under his house is deep, warm & still. We fished a couple of hours and loaded ourselves with fine trout but were terribly stung by flies & mosquitoes. This man Geddes has a fine farm but, a rum drinker, he is going to ruin, and all to be sold.

8TH JUNE. We rode this morning early to visit the furthest settlement in Musquodoboit—a little old man of the name of Deans, had been a gardener in his early days. He is very happy in a nice farm where he raises hops in great perfection & proves that they might be cultivated to any extent in Nova Scotia. He has trained up his hawthorn hedges round his garden to a capital fence of 12 feet high, but to his sad mortification the mice have got at the root this year & during the winter, under the snow laying deep, had gnawed the bark entirely round a foot up, so that just now the hedge appears quite dead. His situation is springy bad soil, a white sandy clay, but very fine woods all about him.

He complains of a grant adjoining him of 500 acres to a Mrs. McCallum, housekeeper of Sir Geo. Prevost. Nothing has ever been done on it. He is very anxious to have 100 acres of it, & shall have it if I can do it.

We returned to breakfast with our guide, Mr. Henry, an old land surveyor, who is a rogue by all accounts but civil & intelligent. He conducted us over the hill Northwards into Souiac. Several farmers met us, particularly two Fultons & a Mr. Tupper, a sensible pleasant man. On the hill passed a farm of Stewart's who has 8 sons settled or just about to do it, all around him. Stopt half an hour at Fulton's to feed our horses. Saw the Presbyterian clergyman, Graham, a very sensible man, 30 years preaching here.

8TH JUNE. Crossed the river again in Middle Souiac as it is called, & found the road very good all the way to Gibbon's on the main Truro road, about 18 miles from Fulton's. This middle settlement is very thinly inhabited after crossing the bridges, except by one family of the name of Fisher – the old man is alive, & happy with nine sons married and settled on farms of their own within his sight. The settlement is called from Fisherton – is flat & open, soil light & gravelly but capable of cultivation, & of good pasture. The chief objection of settlers to this point is the want of firewood near at hand. Souiac is I think a beautiful valley & equal in all respects to any part of the Province I have seen.

9TH JUNE. From Gibbon's returned today to Halifax to dinner & found the homeward bound Packet arrived from New York. Also received intelligence of the *Asia* transport with troops and stores having drifted in thick weather on Sable Island. Dr. Almon's family being in this Vessel he is gone down to their assistance.

14TH JUNE. With the view of placing Jim out of mischief while we made a rapid visit to Canada, I got a promise from Rev. Mr. Milner, Principal of the Academy at Windsor, that he would take him on board with his schoolboys, and keep him occupied. I am just about to start this morning with him, to dine at Mount Uniacke & proceed tomorrow.

15TH JUNE. I took the opportunity yesterday to ride into the Beaverbank settlement parallel with the line of road at Sackville Church, and myself enquire into a dispute & petition by Messrs. Hartshorne and Boggs about some land there. The access to it is yet bad, but the soil is excellent. It is a line of road leading centrical between the great Windsor road & the Shubenacadie Lake, into the township of Douglas, & will very soon open into a valuable extent of Country, but as the Surveyor General is either ignorant of it, or more probably unwilling to inform the King's Government of these tracts as their disposal, it is only by accident I pick up my information. I am sensible that my duty calls upon me to report this state of things, but yet to ruin this old man Morris & his family is what I cannot do. The present state of the Surveyor General's office calls loudly for a partial reform.

Put Jim today with Mr. Milner, & dined with the Chief Justice.

16TH JUNE. Lady D. and I paid a visit to Mr. & Mrs. Milner, and spent the forenoon in the College Library which is in sad confusion. About 5 o'clock Schomberg Kerr and Hay arrived with the mail bag that reached Halifax at 10 o'clock this morning in the Packet of May —very agreeable surprize.

17TH JUNE. Breakfasted at Mount Uniacke & reached Halifax early. The Packet brings me the unexpected event of the death of my excellent friend the Duke of Buccleugh at Lisbon on 20th April. I had a letter from him by this mail dated 9th April, in which he says nothing of his health, & I had concluded he was mending. It appears he had been greatly better, but not so in reality. He had taken his usual walk & lay down on the couch oppressed with the heat of the day. In that sleep he died without moving his posture, without the appearance of the smallest struggle.

Lord Melville having desired I would suggest to him a respectable person here to be appointed to the Office of Marshal of the Admiralty Court, I have recommended Agricola for it.

21ST JUNE. Monday. Arrived the *Tamer* frigate, Capt. Gordon, from Newfoundland for stores. Mentions a curious story of the catching there a squaw of the red Indian tribe, which is yet quite savage in the interior parts of that Island. Her husband was shot at the time she was taken. She was now treated with every possible kindness; some persons speaking the Indian language had been able to make her understand them, & it was hoped that a renewed attempt to pacify & soften the hatred of these savages to the English might prove successful at last.

No appearance of the Admiral from Bermuda yet. I imagine he has altered his plans of coming up early in the season, and as I have no time to spare in my short leave to visit Niagara, I shall start tomorrow, if weather permits.

22ND JUNE. A delightful day & fine winds. Embarked from the Lumber yard on board *Mersey*. Capt. Collier had weighed early &

hove to near the red Buoy below George's Island, and by 11 o'clock made sail.

I take *Chebucto* with me, and tho' our party is large we are most comfortably accommodated. In *Mersey* I have Lady D., Ramsay & Mr. Temple, & Major Couper. In *Chebucto* are Hay, Schomberg Kerr, Torriano of the Artillery, a young Aubrey Beauclerc, an Ensign of the 62nd, a distant relation of the Duke of Richmond to whom he was desirous of paying a visit. This evening our fine breeze has brought us very smoothly, but now almost calm....

24TH JUNE. Collier hove to last night at 11 off Arichat, & made sail at day dawn with very light airs Easterly. The wind freshened as we opened the warm channel about 8 A.M. Off Ship Harbour by 10. The woods all on fire, much mischief appears already done there, but a strong breeze now carried us 10 knots an hour, all studding sails set. At 12 clear of this beautiful passage we stood up for the East point of Prince Edward's Island – a steady pleasant breeze, and *Chebucto* close with us. Hay, Torriano & Beauclerc came on board to pay us a visit, but would not stay dinner.

Ranging up along Cape Breton shore to Cape Hood, it appears hilly, an unpenetrated hardwood forest. Near the Gut are several good settlements & farms, but North of that, very few scattered huts. No boating or business of any kind appears astir. On the larboard side, the land of Prince Edward's Island is barely seen from our deck, low & flat. Some heavy columns of smoke rising inshore.

25TH JUNE. At noon today we are close in with the shore of Gaspe, almost under the island rock of Bonaventure, perpendicular all around & top covered in woods.... The thick fog with rain & an Easterly wind setting us on while no one could make out where we were. It cleared however a little & shewed this remarkable headland, & it appears that some strong indraught into this bay had sucked us very wide out of our course. This was clearly the case when we saw *Chebucto* six miles further down & appearing all bewildered as we were.

During the night the breeze had freshened much; we passed the Magdalen Islands, the property of Sir Isaac Coffin, about 12. These are inhabited by a few families of fishermen, some French induced away from the Miquelon islands, & some Americans – this a mad speculation of Sir Isaac's, & a very imprudent Grant by Government, for if the fishery were free to settlers it is a most eligible situation. Many years ago Sir Isaac leased them to a company in Halifax at £500 a year. They soon found it did not pay them. Lawyers made out flaws in the terms, they went to law in the courts of Nova Scotia, & there the dispute will remain forever, & the Magdalens a poor & starving, tho' valuable little commonwealth. Hauled up at noon & stood off the headland for the West Point of Anticosti. Fog & mist with head sea made us very uncomfortable.

26TH JUNE. Last night towards evening the drizzling rain cleared away, but the wind drew round to North & blew directly down between Gaspe & Anticosti so that we stood across doing very little. Day dawned clear & the wind shifted to S.W. By 8 A.M. we rounded Cape Rosier, a bold & beautiful headland of perpendicular sandy coloured rock; on its face large patches of green bush or wood. Inland appears a thick forest of hard wood. Along the beach on a low flat are three miserable houses with a little cultivation around them. In the channel we see seven Vessels, a number of whales, a white porpoise tumbling & spouting....

27TH JUNE. Sunday. About 9 P.M. last night a heavy squall carried away our jib boom. Took in sail & close reefed topsail, but the weather cleared again & wind set steady at west. Day dawned fine with fresh wind at W. and has continued so all day, extremely cold. We see patches of snow laying on the black mountains in Gaspe, and at same time at 12 [noon] the land on the North shore. At first we supposed this to be the point of Anticosti but observations taken, find it to be Labrador, and at 2 P.M. distinctly see the seven islands.

28TH JUNE. When close in with the Labrador coast last night about 9 P.M. a canoe with 3 men came off to us; they were Indians, nearly the same as the Micmacs of Nova Scotia – high cheek bones, lanky black hair and yellow complexion, short men, mild manner & countenance, & well dressed in blue short doublet, red cloth leggins & English hat. Spoke no English. One of them came on deck & brought up a wild goose & a fine trout, for which we offered money but he did not like it. We gave him some biscuit & a bottle of rum, which last to all appearance was well known & a favourite with them. He held it out to show to his companions in the boat, & they bellowed hoarsely, ah! This man had a pen well cut in the band of his hat & stained with ink. We took it out & made signs to him to write with it, which he did immediately. The character was altogether of the pothook kind, but straightly written & distinct. Bouchette says that this part of the coast is let by Government in lease to the North West Company, which employs an Agent to collect the furs & Peltry from these Indians, in exchange paying them with cloaths, rum & etc. The appearance of the coast is rocky & barren in the extreme, with nothing green within our sight....

29TH JUNE.... At 8 P.M. we thought ourselves up to the "Pointe aux Peres" & hove to for a Pilot. We fired guns for half an hour & sent *Chebucto* close in. At last one came off to us. We found we were 10 leagues lower down. At noon we are over on the North shore opposite Bic, creeping up with light wind. The river here is 25 miles broad. The weather hazy, we see both sides, neither of them fine or interesting. Bic appears a low woody island locked in with the shore on our larboard quarter.

30TH JUNE. At 6 this morning I went on deck, a very fine morning, the breeze fair & fresh, passing Hare Island and the Brandy pots very fast. During the night, the current was so strong off the light house on this Green island, that we hung upon it, making no way at all, and had almost found it necessary to drop an anchor. The scene today is magnificent – the land on both sides rough & rugged looks rising into what may be called Mountains; on the lower & nearer, masses of granite sticking up thro' a tattered cloathing of stunted firwoods.

At 9 A.M. abreast of Kamouraska, a long scattered village of small whitewashed houses, neat & clean enough in appearance, but no large barns, nor any outhouses to bespeak a farm or comfortable establishment. The Pilot, an Englishman, tells us that a Catholic Church or Chapel is placed at every three leagues from this to Quebec, very well attended. At the Pointe aux Pères where he lives, there is a settlement of Protestants, but they cannot get a Church or Clergyman. They would do anything to obtain it, & being what he calls uppermost – i.e., the strongest part of the community there, he thinks it very hard that no care is taken of them by Government.

Coming up to near the Isle aux Coudres, the river again expands, & no scattered island to break the space, the view around is less interesting. On the north shore, the scattered hamlets are high on the mountain, white & clean, but all around is a rocky surface with little or no soil upon it.

117

At 8 P.M. the breeze had freshened so as to carry away one of our lower studding sails; the scene was altogether beautifully grand. The current of the river strong against us was running full 8 knots, & made a considerable head sea; the wind very fresh right astern, with every stitch of canvass set upon the ship, studding sails on both sides, lower, top mast, & top gallant, the little *Mersey* delighted Collier in ploughing at the rate of 10 knots way past the land. The Isle d'Orleans is now on our starboard hand close on board; it appears all cultivated in stripes scarcely 100 yards broad; one of grass & another of grain to each little farmer, so that it is studded with houses & covered with fences of woodspars.

On the other hand the shore of the mainland is heavily & beautifully wooded upon the steep & craggy bank; a continued village, or more resembling a straggling & ill pitched camp; the houses small, sharp & white look like the round tents of the troops. In these I can imagine ease and plenty, without comfort or affluence.

As we approach Quebec, our progress becomes more & more beautiful as the scene & river closes into narrower bounds, & the vessels pressing up under a crowd of sail seem straining every nerve to reach their anchorage before night falls.

1ST JULY. The variety of incident towards the close of evening last night, & the constant change of scene, kept us running about so from side to side of the ship with our glasses in hand that it was impossible to fix our notice on any one point.

This morning I particularly recollect the signal post & telegraph on the Isle d'Orleans, about 8 miles down the river. It stands high over a fine woody bank, & so streaming with flags & pendants of all colours that the country might have imagined an Enemy's fleet or some other strange event creating a general alarm & call to arms. Opposite was a beautiful & romantic fall of water with a mill at the foot; I could not learn what it was, & soon after the steeples of Quebec were seen on our left over the low stretching point of Levis— and nearby at the same instant a shout from the starboard side called us to see the magnificent fall of Montmorency, like an immense white sheet over the precipice, & in the distance perhaps 8 miles. These steeples covered with tin look like massive silver; grand & singularly striking at first sight even tho' the sun did not shine, but on the contrary the weather was gloomy and boisterous. By 9 P.M.

we had rounded Point Levis, & with the Montmorency falls astern of us, dropt anchor close up to the Lower town. *Chebucto* & several other vessels did the same in half an hour after.

Colonel John Wardlaw, Commander 76th Regt., and Colonel Frobisher the Duke's Provincial A.D.C., came off to us immediately with the passage steamboat to carry us & baggage all on shore, but we declined untill morning. Unfortunately it has been very wet with violent squalls of wind, thunder & rain; however we came on shore at 9 A.M. to breakfast. The Duke of Richmond had by letters which I got at Halifax requested me to take possession of the Castle St. Louis, but I was unwilling to do so in his absence, & sent Couper on shore last night to take rooms for me at the Hotel. He found these so full of low rum drinking emigrants, & common country travellers, that it was impossible we could be comfortable, & thought it prudent to accept of quarters at the Castle. Lord Frederick Lennox had breakfast ready for us.

About 12 today it cleared, & as the military heads in garrison had called upon me, we walked up to the Citadel & roundabout the fortifications of it. The whole is in utter ruin, & the slight repairs doing are so trifling as to be necessarily annual.

We after that rode out to the plains of Abraham once so famous, now a race course, & so closely subdivided & fenced that it is difficult to trace the ground where the armies fought. Continued our ride to Sillery; this is a flat copse wood of spruce & small oak mixed with scrubby cedar, maple & birch, but the weather lowering we returned hastily to dinner....

3RD JULY. Yesterday being very fine & Col. Frobisher having arranged matters for us, we set out under the [guidance] of Mr. Caldwell to see the fall of Chaudiere. We went up the river in the barge of *Mersey* about 6 miles & landed in a cover nearly opposite to Sillery, & a mile above the entrance to the Chaudiere river. Here Mr. Calwell had provided carriages for us, in which we could not proceed much more than a mile, but they enabled us to cross a brook in flood. We were then obliged to walk full 2 1/2 miles; the heat was oppressive, & Lady D. suffered most severely, but at last we reached the fall at the top and behind it rather. There it was tame & nothing, but we crept forward over shelving rocks & ridges until we got to a point projecting into the full front view. Here indeed it was tremendously grand. A very considerable river (Swollen with late rains to a size it has been seldom or ever known) came tumbling over a perpendicular precipice with bold broken rocks & points that threw the falling torrent into various channels & changed the shape & appearance of the stream constantly & incessantly. We sat down to rest ourselves & to enjoy at leisure this awful & yet delightful scene. It is impossible to describe it otherwise than by pencil, and I am glad I have brought my draftsman Woolford with me. He shall be kept hard at work during my rambles in Canada, so that hereafter I may refer to his sketches for the beauties of the Country. This immense body of foam falling in crash in the deep below threw up spray in vapour & like clouds passing upwards over the woods all around; of course the more dense below, & there it was every now & then enlivened by a resplendent sunshine which caused a perfect rainbow. The colours exhibited were most beautifully bright. In a moment again the sun overcast, & thus at intervals we were astonished & relieved from admiration alternately, as if it had been some piece of mechanism contrived to amuse the company. But when we contemplated all this magnificence as reality and the work of an Almighty Ruler of Nature, it drew from all of us the feeling & acknowledgement, how little & how utterly insignificant are all the works of man compared to this! After sitting there an hour and scrambling all around we returned with Mr. Caldwell to his country house near his extensive saw mills on the river Echemin. It is a sweet little place, tho' quite a batchelor's box; laid out with some taste, it has a beautiful view of Cape Diamond & the shipping on the right hand; on the left a stretch of the river & the Cap Rouge equally fine. We dined with him, but Lady D. was too much overcome. Everything in excellent London style. In the evening his carriage took us to the Point Levis from whence we crossed & reached the castle quite delighted with our day's work. On my return here I shall not fail to pay another visit to the Chaudiere.

Today I walked with Colonel Wilson thro' the ordnance department & along the lower works. Nothing interesting. I then rode to the fall of Montmorency, which tho' very grand does not compare at all with Chaudiere, & ought to be first visited. The road to it is deep in mud. My horse stuck in it so fast that in trotting along sharp, he came down on his head like a shot, and threw me 10 yards from him. When I got up, not in the least hurt, I saw his head had been literally over the ears deep in it; our difficulty was how to clean ourselves to return into Quebec, but we soon dried in the sun & got brushed.

This evening we embark in the steam boat *Malsham* for Montreal.

4TH JULY. We left the wharf at ¹/2 past 8 & moved very slowly & cautiously thro' the shipping. No sooner were we clear of our difficulties, & fairly away, than Mr. Temple called several of us to look at a meteor, or Comet, with a streaming & very perceptible tail, nearly about N.W., when we were 5 miles above Quebec. It was evident to everybody, but did not attract us long, as it soon sunk, & we were glad to get into our berths.

At 8 A.M. we were opposite the seigneurie of Grondines – a very fine fresh morning. The appearance of the river & bank nearly the same as at Quebec, only more flat; it is still rich & peaceable. Our quarters are excellent, being specially prepared in this Vessel for the Governor General. We have separate Cabins below, & a round house on deck entirely to ourselves. This is somewhat enviable as we are nothing better than common strangers, but all the passengers are exceedingly civil & evidently desirous to be attentive & communicative to us as travellers. The assembly of passengers is something extraordinary, & very entertaining. A large proportion of them are emigrants just arrived from England, Scotland & Ireland. They are wretched to look at, but yet are singing & laughing as if quite at home and not thinking where Providence may bring them to a stop. They don't seem to care about it. There are officers going to their Regiments, merchants of Montreal, Kingston, York & all the intermediate ground, with numbers of Rum casks, Sugar Hogsheads, packages of British merchandise, bars of iron, & everything saleable that it is possible to name, laying loose upon decks, out of our way.

With all this confusion there was the greatest order & regularity; no noise, no quarrelling, no complaining of any kind. There was a long breakfast table in the public room below, & we had ours above most clean & comfortable. The wind is now at noon fresh & right ahead, still we go about six knots good. Some of us are writing, some reading, some playing backgammon, & some walking the poop. We [neither] hear nor feel the beating of the machinery in the least degree, & as we progress, the banks of the river becoming more flat & less interesting, our party seems to take it as a day of rest.

At 4 P.M. we dropt anchor at the little town of Trois Rivieres, & landed passengers & merchandise. The banks of St. Lawrence are now low & flat; woods fringing in masses to the edge of water frequently bear a resemblance to the scenery of the Thames near Richmond on a very large scale.

5TH JULY. We again anchored during the night for half an hour at Sorel, also called William Henry on the Richelieu river, landed some passengers, took in others & got a supply of firewood for the furnaces.

We proceeded with the wind still ahead at the rate of 6 knots. Nothing either fine or remarkable, the river perhaps a mile broad occasionally expanding & closing. About 1 P.M. some part of the wheel machinery gave way & obliged us to drop our anchor. I was surprised to find that in such a vessel there were no means of repairing such accident, but were obliged to go on shore to a blacksmith.

We were then 8 leagues from Montreal. Hay, Kerr, Torriano & Beauclerc started immediately in a 'Marche donc' or calèche of the Country, & were asured that they should reach the hotel in 4 hours, if they paid the ferry at the town. That agreed, they set off at a great rate. I took a walk on shore with Mr. Temple for a couple of hours to look at the farming, which is wretched — and we looked also into their houses, which seemed clean & comfortable, the women sitting in half dozens inside with all the doors & windows open, generally knitting or sewing. They are poorly dressed & very ugly.

Having got our damages patched up we started again about 4 P.M.

6TH JULY. We did not arrive at Montreal till near 11 o'clock last night, & then with some difficulty. As the sun set the scene was pretty. The river's breadth was broken by several flat islands covered with wood, the solitary sugar loaf hill of Beloeil, or Chambly in the distance on our left, & the Montreal, or Mountain just rising ahead at 10 miles from the town. The rapid stream passing Montreal was too strong to steer, without the assistance of a tow rope which was sent on shore, & the Proprietor Mr. Molson was prepared with men & horses to give us a pull. Our passage has been tedious by the head wind, and the accident, but it has been very comfortable; the only annoyance we experienced was from the sparks flying from the furnace cylinders when the fires were stirred.

These in daylight were not perceptible, altho' they burnt holes in the Ladies' gowns when they touched, but at night these were illuminated & flew in such Quantities as to resemble the comet's tail, which we still see in the N.W. & rising at the same time about 8 o'clock.

After breakfast I walked out to the parade of the 37th Regiment, Lt. Col. Buren. The parade is a handsome public walk immediately behind the New Court House & Jail—both of them fine buildings, ornamental & creditable to the city. In front of them is a column in honour of Lord Nelson bearing a statue of him on top, but it is very poor altogether—ill proportionate & unpleasing.

While on parade, a Mr. David Ross came up to us & introduced himself as quite intimately acquainted, but none of us could recollect him at first. However it was soon found that he had been down in Halifax last summer, and I had paid him some little attention for which he now expressed himself very grateful. He very civilly walked us all about town. At 2 P.M. he provided carriages & drove Lady D. and myself round the Mountain, nothing more than a woody hill. The view from it is exceedingly rich & pleasing. On the one side the city stretches along the bank of St. Lawrence & is mixed in the buildings with lofty spiral poplars that have very good effect. Off the town lays an extension island finely wooded. This the Duke of Richmond has ordered to be purchased for Government to be made an Ordnance depot, secure in war against any momentary attack of the Yankees. On the opposite shore are many villages with their shining silver spires. In the distance are the sugar loaf hills of Chambly, backed still farther off by a lofty range of mountains in Vermont state, carrying the eye along St. Lawrence from Montreal. The villages on the south bank are Longueuil, La Prairie & Caughna-waga, a dirty hole of civilised Indians too filthy & too debauched to be visited. On this side again I see Lachine, in a very rich landscape of wood & water.

Continuing the drive round the hill by the house of Chief Justice Monk, a solitary man, & a Colonel Ogilvie, a man highly spoken of— the view on the country below, on Isle Jesus, the Ottawa river &

the Deux Montagnes, is a gloomy exent of forest with here & there a peep of water to relieve the eye, but it is also rich & pleasing. The day has been very sultry, but favoured our excursion. Mr. Ross, Capt. Hill of the Staff Corps, Lord Wm. Lennox & several other people dined with me. Our hotel is altogether magnificent, a splendid house furnished from London, & the Proprietor, Mr. Molson, quite a character. Hearing that he was a curiosity I sent for him today to thank him for his attentions last night. He came to me in a light bed gown as is worn in the East or West Indies, told me his whole history & all his speculations & intentions with prodigious volubility of tongue, & at once breaking off in his harangue, he bolted away laughing in a most eccentric manner. He is quite mad in my opinion, but his madness fortunately runs towards public improvements. He is very rich & very liberal, sole proprietor of several steam boats, of an extensive Brewery of Beer & Porter, of large works in the blacksmith trade – a variety of others, & this Hotel, which he has let for £800 a year, but touches nothing, & saying that he broke away from me.

In walking thro' the town with Mr. Ross, we visited the English Church, a handsome building under repair at present. The Catholic Cathedral also a fine building, but not taken care of as is usual with their Priests. The new bank & several houses lately built shew an improving taste, & a general prosperity in Montreal far superior to anything I have seen in America.

7TH JULY. Anxious to overtake the Duke of Richmond at Kingston, & as he had ordered arrangements for us in almost every choice we could make as to mode of travel, we left Montreal early this morning, taking the shore road to Lachine, 12 miles thro' a flat district of rich black loam, quite garden ground. It seems wretchedly cultivated, but improving in their system. I saw some good crops of wheat, potatoes well drilled & cleaned with the plough, a good deal of fallow preparing for wheat in September, & the old Yankee worm fence replacing by others in straight lines. Some of these are close boarded, others open, others rough upright spokes in length, as hurdle fences 8 or 10 feet long by 6 feet high. These are suspended between strong posts with wooden bolts or pins. This last I think a capital fence, cheap, strong, durable & easily moved.

On this road the convents & religious Catholic establishments in

Montreal have extensive & very valuable landed property.

Having breakfasted at Lachine went on to Ste. Anne 18 miles, where a passage boat carried us across the ferry above the Isle Perrot to Vaudreuil, & there getting into the "Marche donc," a calèche with one horse, carrying two people & the driver before us, we drove like fury 15 miles to the Coteau du Lac, a small fort & depot for the protection & convenience of military transport. Our road from Vaudreuil again touched the back of St. Lawrence at the rapids called the Cèdres. There it is truly a grand rapid river, but at the Coteau du Lac it is still infinitely more grand & beautiful. Here the river tumultuous & broken is divided by several islands richly wooded into the very stream. At Sunset I made Woolford try to sketch it, but I much fear he is not equal to it....

8TH JULY. Got up at day dawn, & after an early breakfast went on in our calèches to Macdonnell's point 3 miles, where two large Batteaux with awnings had been ordered for us to proceed to Cornwall 49 miles, & here we arrived at 9 o'clock just dark. The greater part of the day's work was crossing the Lake St. Francis, broad, flat & uninteresting, but the novelty of the Canadian boat song which our fellows kept up merrily for hours together killed the time very pleasantly. They have volumes of songs in variety & as many tunes. They are difficult to understand, being the old gascon, or patois French, & the burden of the song generally Love....

About 4 P.M. we put on shore to get the men something to eat & give them an hour's rest. Enquiring at the house near us, I spoke to the man, Somers, in French as we had done all along at other places we stopt at. But he shook his head & told me we had now passed the Canadian line & should find none but Scotch or English inhabitants as we got on. Very few of the Canadians speak any English, yet they are quite friendly & sociable, and always occupied passing up and down. This is remarkable for they are clever & smart people, but they are averse to our language, and the attraction is on our side, picking up enough of their language to communicate with them.

They brought us up here singing & seemingly fresh to the last after a long pull of 49 miles the whole way against the stream & without any wind to help them. Our quarters at old Cheslieu are clean & comfortable.

9TH JULY. We started this morning in waggons, some on springs, some without. At 6 miles stopt at the rapid of the Long Sault. The river there is certainly very fine, on a scale much larger than at the Coteau du Lac, tumbling in broken waves, & yet boats & rafts go down without any difficulty or danger. On the opposite side, I observed with my spy glass, several men on a stage spearing at fish, chiefly Sturgeon & black bass, the first very bad, the last excellent eating.

Under the bank where we stood is a road or towing path to assist the boats poling upwards. A little way down is a building or Mill on piles in the river, which appears to be in ruins, but adds to the picturesque scenery. A sketch of this will have the disadvantage of a view down stream, but it closes below so richly & so grandly as the river bends suddenly in an elbow to the left, & is lost to the eye altogether.

At this spot the road passes thro' a very fine wood of oak & other large timber, but yet I don't see any trees to compare with oak in England.

Breakfasted at 13 miles at the house of Mr. Baker, a small Inn very neatly kept. Saw the process of making Potash which appears so simple, & the produce of the ashes so valuable, that I am astonished it is not a more general practice.

At 26 miles I got fresh horses to my carriage; the others could not & were obliged to go on 23 miles more to Fort Wellington.

The road is generally good, tho' there were bad places, a bad bridge now & then. The settlement is generally composed of Dutch people, Loyalists from New York, particular in their manners, but industrious, their houses excellent & many of them building new ones of stone with all the appearance of Gentlemen's houses. Farming is slovenly & bad but the crops good, and the system of fallowing before wheat commonly practiced. The soil is black & very good indeed. On enquiry I was told that in that neighbourhood 100 acres, a great proportion cleared, with a house & barn on them, could not be purchased much under 4000 dollars, £1000.

Several half pay officers have settled themselves on lots purchased there, & having obtained grants of land in the rear, have made their first residence on the road as the inhabited world, untill roads are obtained to the back lands.

Fort Wellington is a wretched work, falling to pieces fast &

already incapable of defence; the village of Prescott is growing & a very nice place; an excellent Inn kept by one Wilson, an American. Opposite is Ogdensburg, a very pretty village. A Mr. Parish & Judge Ford have each excellent houses, at least they appear such from this side. A passage boat goes every hour or two, the communication constant, but indeed in Prescott there are more Americans than British, & they avow that were war to break out they would retire to the other side again.

Wilson has laid out considerable capital in building the Inn. Another Yankee of the name of Ellis has set up a Mail Coach or stage with 4 horses which runs the whole way from Montreal here with the greatest regularity.

10TH JULY. After dinner last night went on board the steamboat *Charlotte,* and left Prescott at 3 o'clock this morning. At 6 stopt at the little village of Brockville to take up passengers. At 9 breakfasted on deck. The scenery now was most beautiful. We had just entered what is very properly called the Mille Isles (1000 Islands). The current of the river is scarcely perceptible, & the expanse so varied & so contracted by woody islands that the scene changes every 5 minutes. At many places a stone may be thrown on shore on both sides. The rocks bold tho' not high, the water very deep to the side of the rock. This threading thro' the labyrinth it may be called was most beautiful.

At 4 P.M. stopt at Gananoque, a small village, to take wood & passengers.

We had before taken wood on an island which I shall remember from Ramsay falling overboard from a plank laid to the shore. He escaped with a good ducking overhead and a fright.

At Gananoque an old Gentleman introduced himself, seemingly a sensible, well bred & intelligent man, a refugee Loyalist from New York in 1783. Expressed his recollection of many & a great regard for some of them who went at same time to settle in Nova Scotia. Change led him to Upper Canada. He cut the first tree at Gananoque. And tho' he has often lamented his separation from friends, relations & all the world almost besides, yet times have strangely altered now, the wilderness is full of people; he is wealthy, tho' not rich, occupied sufficiently to be busy, comfortable and content. He cannot yet believe, he cannot reconcile to his ideas the separation of the colonies from England; it appears to him as a dream of an impossibility. He is quite sure that Washington always desired to reunite them, but that arch democrat & atheist Jefferson by his unnatural partiality to France always thwarted the design. He fancies that he sees yet in the conduct of the British Govt. to the United States, in Peace or in War, a feeling that the Colonies are still the children of the Mother Country. He has 5 sisters married & have grown up families in the States; to all of them he is affectionately attached, but has not seen one of them since 1783. "That is wrong," he said, "very wrong. I know it is, but yet I cannot bring myself to go there, and I read & dwell upon the history & discussions in Parliament from 1765 to the present day with a mixture of sincere sorrow and astonishment at the Events." The bell rang to call us on board, & very much pleased with Mr. Stone's manner & sentiments I have put down the conversation in his own words as nearly as I recollect them.

11TH JULY. Reached Kingston last night at 9 o'clock, so stewed and heated as to feel myself really ill.

Found the Duke of Richmond here who had ordered me to be received by a salute & guard of honour—begging His Grace's pardon, honours never paid to a junior officer by the superior immediately in command.

Col. McGregor, 70th, came to me on board & entreated me to join the Duke dining at the Mess of the Regt. Col. Grant, commanding, soon followed to do the same, but I was not equal to it.

This morning called on him at 8 o'clock & was most kindly received. At 9 went with him on board the steamboat *Frontenac,* Capt. Mackenzie; our large party joining his, fully as large, filled this immense vessel. The Duke has with him his two daughters, Lady Mary and Louisa, Major Bowles, Secretary, Col. Cockburn, D.A.G., Col. MacLeod, A.D.C., and Sir Chas. Saxton from Dublin on a visit.

I have with me Lady D., Ramsay & Mr. Temple, Capt. Collier of *Mersey,* Major Couper, Hay, Schomberg Kerr, Torriano, Beauclerc, and Woolford to sketch for me.

The wind blows very fresh & dead against us this forenoon, while hanging along the shore of the bay of Quinte, called the garden of Canada.

12TH JULY. At 9 this morning we had made 90 miles and were off the pointe Presqu'ile, just half way, the wind fresh & obstinate; we don't seem to go more than 3 knots an hour.

I felt very unwell today, my head having swelled & broke out all over as if I had been actually melted two days ago. The Duke & some of them amused themselves by shooting ball at a bottle from a German rifle of his own, and he broke the bottle at second shot. I had at different times a good deal of conversation with the Duke on the state of the Canadas. He laments the present state of representation in their Lower House, and is taking quiet means to improve the body in next general Election. His plans seem well taken & the line, if pursued firmly, is such as will assert a proper weight & authority in the Government.

I find Sherbrooke's administration was weak & palliative, keeping friends on all sides – he had no resolution to enforce, & was too irritable & violent to consult or manage measures, altho' he saw & allowed the necessity of them.

If the Duke is really doing all he says, & is determined to follow up the measures he has planned, I have no doubt he will improve the system in this country & lay a foundation of much better Government than it has yet enjoyed.

One of the greatest objections I hear stated against Sherbrooke's administration, was a marked and distinguished attention he paid to the Catholic Bishop & Clergy. The Duke, I am told, shews him no more than common respect & civility, very seldom invites him to the Castle & thus gives him neither cause to boast, nor ground to complain of neglect. It seems, I think, as if popularity had been the sole object of pursuit by all the Governors in Canada, & to it there were only two paths – the French or the English – Catholic or Protestant – & each succeeding Chief followed in regular opposition to the steps of his Predecessors. There is no steadiness nor prudence in the general course of Government, since the time of Sir Guy Carleton (Lord Dorchester), and the mischief was by frequent changes of Governors.

Sir Robert Milnes was only Lt. Governor in 1799, was mild & gentlemanlike, ruled by Dr. Mountain, the English Bishop of Quebec, who avows open hatred to the Catholic Bishop.

Sir Jas. Craig, Governor General 1807, dragooned the country & was feared by all parties.

Sir Geo. Prevost, Governor General 1811, smooth & flattering;

in manner like a Frenchman, conciliated the Catholics & was at open war with all the English.

Sir Gordon Drummond, Lt. General on the staff administered in 1815, quarrelled violently & suddenly with the House of Assembly, & dissolved it in the manner in which Sir Jas. Craig formerly did it.

Sir John Sherbrooke, Govr. General 1816, cross & ill tempered, staved off difficulties & assumed no decided character of Government during his short administration.

The Duke of Richmond arrived in July 1818, & took up the reins which had fallen from Sherbrooke's hands; the distribution & control of the Civil List & Revenue were the objects of dispute in last winter's session; the Lower House grasped at these & had thought themselves sure of them, by their partial advantages obtained over Sherbrooke. The Legislative Council strenuously opposed the ambitious views of the Lower House, and after a long & angry session, the Duke prorogued the Assembly with sharp, but dignified censure of the Commons, & there the question stands.

In conversation today with the Duke on this subject, he told me he had advised the King's Government to resume immediately the control, by recalling the offer made some years ago, to grant the whole Revenue to be appropriated by the Provincial Legislature, on condition of paying the Civil List from it. If that offer is withdrawn, the question will be at rest, and the *faux pas* yet remedied; but if not, the King's Govt. must bow to the Commons in the Parliament in Canada, who will have assumed the power to grant only what they please for the public service of the State.

Sir Chas. Saxton appears a pleasant, well informed man, a perfect courtier from Dublin, & up to all the stories & jokes of the Duke's time there as Lord Lieutenant.

Col. Cockburn a pompous, bullying sort of fellow, not liked by any of the party. Col. Macleod & Major Bowles gentlemanlike young men. Capt. Montrésor, R.N., is also with him—a soft useless person, I think.

The Duke himself is much broken, looks old & beat down, very thinking & low, untill spoken to; then his manner is exceedingly gracious, kind & lively; a rough but agreeable countenance. I took an opportunity this morning to present him Hay, Torriano & Mr. Temple, and we were all quite captivated by the ease & manly manner he assumed at the instant.

13TH JULY. We reached York during the night; when I got up at 7 o'clock I found the Duke & all his party gone on shore. We also landed to breakfast with Sir Peregrine Maitland at the fort. Walked about afterwards, & thro' the town. At 11 again sailed for Fort George, or Newark, at the mouth of the Niagara river. The Duke starts in a few days inland to Lake Huron, & returns by Detroit & Niagara. They talk boldly of long walks & hot marches thro' bushes & mosquitoes; that I should be very shy to volunteer. How Sir Chas. Saxton will make it out I don't know. The Duke is fond of hard exercise & in the habit of taking it, but he is older than I am by 7 years, & may feel it beyond his time. Colonel Cockburn is a very powerful man, & looks as if he could kill them all.

Sir P. Maitland is tall, thin & silent; very well bred & gentlemanlike, but evidently not a favorite with the Duke who, they say, has never pardoned him for carrying off his daughter Lady Sarah. His conduct in this Province has been firm & decided in putting down a mad Democrat from the Spa field meetings in London – Gourlay – & has gained the confidence of the country.

Lady Sarah Maitland is a thin & delicate little person, with a most sweet & engaging cast of coutenance, not in the least like either of her two sisters here. As Sir P. is a gloomy Methodist in religious points, people were much astonished at the elopement, & the Duke's manly honesty feels yet as if it had happened but lately. He appears very fond of Lady Mary & Sarah, but minds Lady Charlotte very little.

At York, there is only yet the beginning of a town; the harbour is bad, & the neighbourhood so flat & extended that it offers no means of defence. The opposite of the bay called Gibraltar, as a joke I suppose, is so low as to be flooded in bad weather, but if not so bad as that is quite open beach around a wooden Light House. Sir Peregrine seems decided that another situation must be chosen for the capital of the Province, tho' at present it is not sufficiently advanced in population to require a choice to be made. He talks of the Lake Simcoe as the best situation. The country is fine, the retired distance will afford means of defence. A church was built last year, mechanics are gathering & shops forming in town, but as yet all supplies come from Kingston by the steam boat.

14TH JULY. Last night we anchored at Fort George about 9 P.M. & were most kindly received by my old friend Col. Johnston & the

68th Regiment. He insisted on carrying us to occupy his quarters. I have known him since he joined 68th an Ensign in 1791. He commanded the Regiment in my division in Lord Wellington's Army & was wounded in almost every action. His claims of old acquaintance & the kindness of his offer were not to be resisted.

We had a long but pleasant passage over – the common run is about 5 hours.

This morning we left Johnstone after breakfast, in American waggons carrying 4 each. Colonel Hawkins of 68th rode as our guide; the river close on our left is broad & deep, but looks less so, as the banks are high. In Queenstown, the sudden rise of the heights narrows the river at once, & it seems to issue from a trough or gorge of precipitous rocks. We walked up the heights to take time leisurely to look about us; from the top the river moves slow, dead & tame to the Lake. At the mouth stands on the one side the American Fort Niagara, bold & bullying; clean whitewashed, & displaying the "Star-spangled banner" as large as the British standard. On the other side, a small English jack not bigger than a pocket handkerchief, worn & blown to rags, shews an earth fort crumbled down on all sides, utterly defenceless, filled with & surrounded by log huts, in appearance to a military man altogether mean & beggerly – & so the Americans seem to think of us, by their very superior display, & by their constant insolence in all intercourse with them.

Queenstown village stands at foot of the hill, & in the centre of the village the road turns off at right angle. There is the spot where General Brock fell by a ball from a rifleman on top of the heights; the affectionate regret with which he is universally spoken of in this country best expresses the loss sustained in his fall. Tecumseh, the Indian chief, who also fell soon after bravely fighting when General Proctor fled near Detroit, marked very pointedly in their short sentences the character of Brock, compared with Proctor. "Come, say our Great Father, Come with me, seek the foe. Go, says young father, go seek him." An Indian needs kindness & encouragement to go to battle. Brock had by his personal conduct gained their unbounded admiration. Proctor drove them to despair. Tecumseh, refusing to retreat with him, stood until cut to pieces by the Americans advancing.

Immediately opposite to Queenston on the American side is

Lewiston, a scattered village, in no way remarkable.

From the top & on the brink of the precipice we looked down on the river imbedded below in rocks, & yet so deep as to flow heavily along in unbroken surface. Towards the Lake the country is quite flat & woody; these heights extend to the left & to the right, a marked boundary of nature. It is supposed, & it appears to me quite evident, that the Lake in former days covered this flat & that the great fall of Niagara was at this point. Some convulsion had opened a deeper passage into the St. Lawrence, & by so much toward the level of the lake; while the romantic scenery of the "Mille Isles" gives probability to that idea, it is not difficult to imagine that such a vast body of water may have worn its way backwards in the soft & loose composition of the rocks that enclose it now. The scene at this point is however extremely beautiful, & we got into our carriages more in impatience to reach our grand object than satisfied with the picture there.

The whirlpool next arrested us, about 3 miles on. Well worth seeing as very beautiful and romantic scenery; I think however that I have seen in England & Scotland, on a smaller scale certainly, but in proportion, scenes equally lofty, precipitous & woody, equally romantic tho' perhaps not so gigantic. Some of us went down to the bottom, partly by a ladder suspended on a tree, & partly scrambling on hands & knees; below we lost all its beauties, but our party sitting on the crag over us, seemed small as points & lost in mid air; it was bad to get down, but the getting up again made me nearly repent such schoolboy scrambles. The heat of the day and that fag led us to stop under some cherry trees on the high road, loaded with ripe fruit, which we sat under in the carriage to eat of untill cooled.

From this to the falls 5 miles of good road passing the battle ground of Lundy's Lane, where General Vincent was beat, but Sir Gordon Drummond coming up in the evening renewed the fight till midnight, when his perseverance obtained a decided Victory; but that is a subject with which I won't meddle at present. We arrived here at Forsyth's tavern about 3 o'clock, & proceeded immediately to the Falls, where we remained till late; here I shall stop untill having seen all I may take time to think of it, & collect it to refresh my memory hereafter.

17TH JULY. On board the *Frontenac* steam boat our passage from

York to Kingston, sailing very smooth & pleasantly, I now return to take up my story where I left it off on arriving at Forsyth's on the 14th. All of us on the "tiptoe of expectation" set off directly to the falls, but strange to say we could not hear a whisper, or see a particle of spray over the woods to lead us to them. We got a boy as guide. We walked along the worm fence of a hayfield, at bottom of which we turned into a small descending glen, which in a very few minutes led us straight in front of the American part of the falls. At first sight of this white cascade, I felt an instantaneous disappointment, & the whole party seemed struck in the same manner, for not a word was said, & scarcely any noise of the fall yet heard; we then walked on thro' a paling gate about a hundred yards to the brink of the river; there the falls are seen in their whole extent, & then indeed I felt astonished, & so were all, quite lost in amazement at this most magnificent display of nature. The feeling on the first moment is indescribable. Every part of the whole is so far beyond what I had attempted to fancy it, the mind sunk into immediate acknowledgment that it was indeed far beyond the power of human comprehension. Lady D. was so nervous she could not speak, & the first disappointment perhaps added to the wonder & delight of the next step; here however we were again joined by Col. Hawkins, Capt. Vavazour of the Engineers & several officers who had followed us for the purpose of conducting us, & explaining the different points. Capt. Vavazour was particularly intelligent & entertaining.

I suppose the whole of it a picture which we stood admiring. On the left is the American fall, a sheet of white foam falling over a wall quite perpendicular, pure as driven snow & equally spread all across. At bottom it is rocky, & there a body of spray rises about halfway up, rounding in unequal volumes like smoke, & like a running stream of water incessantly changing its shapes. The next compartment is the bold precipitous front of the Goat Island. It is a mixture of masses of projecting rocks, deep soil in places, & streaks of green & flowering brushwood. On top a thick wood of large sized trees of great variety. The remainder of the picture, perhaps equal to a half of it, is the Horseshoe fall, so called from forming a sort of half circle, but this is not perceptible so much when standing as we did in front of it.

Over this rolls the far greater part of the river, and it comes tumbling down at a great distance, broken & raging like a sea dashed among the rocks by a gale of wind. This horseshoe may be again subdivided into three parts; the two outer, particularly that on the extreme right, tumble over in masses of foam, and shaped like pillars from top to bottom, visible even thro' the volumes of smoke rising & curling half way up or more. The centre part has a most beautiful & rich transparent green colour, from being less broken by projecting points of rock, yet it is also touched with streaks of foam, pure & white. Here we remained some time, each of us pointing to the beauties that struck him in the fantastic & ever varying appearances of the water as it fell pondrous & heavy to the eye. A passing cloud, or a Sunbeam bursting out, changed the scene like magic; and every now & then a most magnificent rainbow forming a complete circle in the depths below of the highest colours seemed as if intended to exhibit nature in all her most beautiful dresses. Our senses were fixed in wonder & astonishment and admiration.

After some time we moved perhaps 50 yards nearer to the fall, & again forward to the Table rock 50 yards more; at this last point it is certainly seen in its greatest grandeur. While the eye was delighted with the beauties, the ear was deafened by the tremendous noise. With difficulty we heard one another speak, and at last sat down to contemplate the stupendous cataract before us & below us.

The fall on the American side is so much smaller and so regular [on] the top line that it gives the idea of a cascade built by art, altogether so inferior to the other that I felt a desire to set it aside as scarcely worthy of the Grand picture. The bold front of the Goat Island, covered at top in wood & patched with brush & flowers, is a beautiful contrast to the broken & tumultous tides rushing from the distance to tumble over the precipice into the depth below.

The hour of dinner, tho' ordered late, had arrived, but with difficulty I could get the party away, each turning & lingering at every step to take another look at the wonderful work.

Next morning (15th) it was agreed that Lady D. could not attempt the scramble below the crags, & we therefore started at 6 A.M. to go under & behind the fall. Torriano, Hay, Schomberg Kerr, Mr. Temple, Ramsay & myself turned out at the hour named. [At a convenient spot] we stript to our shirt & pantaloons, with cap, handkerchief or night cap on our heads; we went along the path singly perhaps half a mile before the fall of the spray affected us, but all the way water trickling from the rocks, & little falls of it, soon drenched us. As we neared, the rain fell more & more heavy, & the noise grew more & more awful. When just under the arch of the Table rock, looking up I saw the sheet of water falling not upon me, but wide of me to the left. We certainly & literally were behind it & under a canopy of rock. The walking became very bad, on loose stones & fragments too small to rest firmly upon, & so slippery as to make me hold on constantly by the shelving slope above me, on which the water now run down like a rivulet; from that point we crept on perhaps 30 yards; the column of water, falling into a depth apparently bottomless, threw up outwards the volumes of vapour rolling & rounding like clouds on a distant horizon; inwards it had scooped out a cavern & created a strong wind like the blowing of a pair of bellows in Vulcan's Workshop. Every puff dashed the water in buckets in my face with such violence that tho' crawling on hands & knees a foot or two at a time, I gained ground with difficulty. When sitting on the shelving rock I could neither open my eyes nor hold my face to it.

Mr. Temple & I, tho' resolved to go as far as possible, were compelled to stop. The rest of us, 10 or 12 yards behind, had already given it up; at that time, speaking to Mr. Temple, it was scarcely possible to make him hear my words, tho' bawling at his ear. After a little while we retired out of this tremendous conflict of the elements, to where we could draw breath freely, & hear ourselves speak. We did get behind the falling sheet & looked from behind or thro' the white curtain without being crushed by it, but it is not literally true that the traveller may go into the arched cavern & stand secure under the cataract.

I know of nothing to which I can compare the noise of the storm raging below the fall; it was truly awful. Ramsay, when close under it, killed some small brown adders of harmless sort; farther in, small eels about a foot long were laying in shoals on the shelving rocks, and every step we made put in motion the whole surface of them rushing into deeper water.

In viewing the falls from below, the scene is neither so beautifully pleasing nor so grandly astonishing as above, particularly when on the Table rock.

After breakfast some of us drove, others walked to Chippewa, &

visited "the burning spring," as it is called. It is a strong mineral well into which a tree hollowed like a water pipe is planted upright & built in; into that again, a gun barrel is fixed with a mouth piece into which 3 dutch smoking pipes are inserted. From these a gas issues of strong sulphuric smell. It readily catches fire & gives a very clear flame, a gas light. We blew them out & lighted again, frequently by a bit of paper, & they burnt strong while we remained, nearly half an hour. The apparatus has been fitted by some kind person to gain a trifle from travellers for the poor people who are the proprietors; they did not understand & could therefore give us no information upon the qualities of the spring of water, of its depth or contents. They would not drink it as medicinal.

Returning from this about 3 o'clock, Lady D. & our party (except Couper & Torriano who had gone over in the morning) set out in the intention of crossing over to the American side, but while we waited the return of the ferry boat, a small cockboat rowed by a lazy fellow, a thunderstorm with heavy rain came on & forced us to return home, & it continued too late for us to attempt it in the Evening. I believe we have lost nothing. The view of the American bridge above the fall is pretty from where we stood. Woodford has taken a collection of sketches & those small pieces of the whole are very good.

Yesterday morning (16th) Lady D. with some of the party again went down to the falls for a short time, to take a last farewell, and at 7 A.M. we got into our carriages to breakfast with Johnstone, 68th. Hay, Kerr, Beauclerc & Torriano remained to pursue their tour thro' the States, by Buffalo & Albany to New York & Halifax, Torriano alone proceeding to England. With him we parted with great regret; he is a very fine gentlemanlike young man. His father, a captain in 30th Foot in 1790, was an old friend of mine in that day.

Forsyth's tavern & accommodation at Niagara were very good indeed, and the man himself, tho' a Yankee & reputed to be uncivil, was quite the reverse to us, obliging & attentive in every way.

The land is poor gravel & sand in that neighbourhood, yet the woods grow well. Pine, Oak, Butternut & other varieties of the Walnut & Chestnut, all loaded with fruit, as also Cherries & Peaches at every step, the former generally the bitter kind, the latter, I should say, fit only for feeding pigs. The people are unhappy & discontented with the British Government, partly that they are generally Yankees settled on our side, & partly that this frontier is so weak, so ill guarded, & constantly so much exposed to the depredations of the Enemy in war. No one has any security in his property, nor any encouragement to permanent industry. I must confess their complaints are but too just.

After breakfast I rode with Capt. Vavazour to the Mississauga fort on the point opposite the American fort Niagara – the former a miserable starwork in decay. Our fort George at the landing place is still worse, that of the Enemy in tolerable good order – yet a thing that any 20 gun ship ought to lay in rubbish in a forenoon. Capt. V. at first is a very entertaining pleasant man, but we found him soon to be a Bombastic & discontented soldier, constantly speaking without any regard to truth.

At 11 o'clock sailed & reached York by 5. I had just time to walk up to Sir Peregrine Maitland's quarters & thank the Duke for all his kindness and attentions; at 7 we sailed again with a fair wind.

On our first arrival at Niagara we were surprised that we saw no clouds of vapour rising over the woods, nor heard any noise of the Falls. While there, we both saw the one & heard the other roaring at times. It depends entirely on the state of the atmosphere & the course of the wind. During the thunder storm the vapour towered to prodigious height in dense column; while on our passage to York, we distinctly saw it in a cloud, at least 40 miles distant at the time. Our grand object has thus been accomplished to our utmost satisfaction, not only without difficulty, but with the utmost ease & comfort, not yet a month from Halifax.

This steam boat is the same we came up in – is an immense Vessel, as long I believe as a 74 gunship & cleanly & comfortable in the extreme.

18TH JULY. We had an excellent run all yesterday, and anchored late last night. Several Members of the House of Assembly came down with us; among them the Speaker, Mr. Maclean, a mild placid looking man, a lawyer in Kingston, a Member for that place. I walked with him a good deal & found him a sensible intelligent man.

Col. McGregor of 70th was on board of us early, insisting upon our occupying quarters at the Government House which he now was in, and his offer was so urgent & kind that Lady D. and I did accept;

the rest of the party went to the Inn, which tho' large & commodious is abominably filthy & ill kept. After breakfast went to Church, heard Divine Service most poorly performed by Mr. Stuart, a young man educated at King's College, Windsor, in Nova Scotia. Dined today at the Mess of 70th, where several Ladies were invited to meet Lady D. Among them was Mrs. Scott, wife of the Paymaster of the Regiment. I mention this because he is the brother of Walter Scott the Poet, and to this person & his wife, public report at present generally gives the credit of being the anonymous writers of those numerous & entertaining novels which have lately appeared under the names of Waverley, Guy Mannering, Tales of my Landlord, etc., etc.

Mrs. Scott is a lively pleasant woman, but has no appearance of the abilities for such works; he [Mr. Scott] has an uncommon slow, precise mode of speaking & turn of language, with a most joyous laugh in telling a story, which rather inclines me to think him capable of some rude work which his brother or others may have improved & polished. But no officer of the Regt. could tell me that he is ever much occupied in writing. No industry of that kind has ever been observed; on the contrary, he is thought an idle man, eccentric, and was at one period disposed to very hard living.

19TH JULY. In our passage down I had a good deal of conversation with the Speaker on the general state of Upper Canada at present. Sir Peregrine Maitland is exceedingly popular from his quiet gentle-manlike manners, & the firm unassuming tone of his Government. The burst of democratic principles under Mr. Gourlay last year was checked very easily, & that person, who is still in jail at Niagara for a libel on the Government, is considered little better than a madman, a great deal more pitied than considered.

The Session of the Legislature has just now broke up, & all seem highly pleased in the measures that have been adopted. The interior parts of the Upper Province are settling very fast, particularly upon the Ottawa river, & the description of people, generally half pay officers & pension soldiers, will form in a few years a very valuable militia force for its protection. In this view the House has turned its attention particularly to opening roads into it, and an Act has just passed laying a tax on property, a mere trifle, but absentees are made liable for their lands as well as those that are in the country. Rich &

poor both pay, either in money or labour in their respective townships. The objects are roads, churches, jails & Court houses, making it a local tax for their own immediate good, & not going at all into the Treasury. It is so low as one penny in the pound sterling of valued property. Taking an acre of land at an average rate of four shillings, thus a poor man possessed of 100 acres is supposed worth 400 shillings or £20, & his tax is 20/-. But there are absentees who are proprietors of 10, 20 or even 50,000 acres, and at present doing nothing & paying nothing....

Extensive tracts such as these last are purchases made long ago from the Indians, sanctioned by Government & confirmed to the Proprietors.

When the assessment remains unpaid 3 years, it increases 1/4; 5 years 1/2; & in 8 years it doubles. But the Speaker confesses that there is no clause yet to authorise the sale of the lands to pay the debt. At the expiry of the Law, limited to 8 years, he has no doubt that it will be obtained hereafter.

The Speaker tells me that Sir John Johnstone is not considered a very great landed proprietor. The immense tracts which his father, Sir Wm. Johnstone, acquired from the Indians were on the Mohawk river & in the Gennesee country south of Lake Ontario. But he has kept the large island which forms Kingston harbour & contains 16,000 acres. This island is the subject of the story of the dream, so characteristic of the cunning & shrewd sense of the Indians. One of the Sachems had a great desire to have a gold laced coat or uniform of Sir Wm. about 1757, & came to tell him that he had dreamed how Sir Wm. had made him a present of it. Sir Wm. gave it him in great ceremony, but some days afterwards sent for the tribe & gravely told the Sachem that he too had dreamt that his good children had given him that Long Island. The Sachem soon saw his meaning, ceded the island in form, but said that Sir Wm. dreamt too hard for a fine coat. It is a very fine estate, but not a tree yet cut upon it.

Large tracts are also reserved for the Crown & for public purposes, such as for a College, Church & school endowments in the military settlements, and these are now letting on leases, where roads make them accessible, at 7 dollars for 100 acres for the first 7 years, 14 D. 2nd 7 years, 21 D. 3rd 7 years; & then the lease is at an end. No attempt at settlement was made in this Province until 1783, & now

140

a farmer arriving who takes a farm with a proportion of it cleared and is commonly industrious, is supposed will be able to purchase it in 3 years.

The Crown places no fund in the power of the Governor to pay even the common business of the Government; Sir Peregrine told me he was paying the Surveyors of the Lands laying out by giving them a proportion or lot which they are authorised to sell, and lands are now daily purchased at auction in York & Kingston at 2, 3 or 4 dollars an acre, uncleared.

After breakfast today we visited the Dockyard and Fort Henry. There are 2 three-deckers on the stocks which can be got ready in 4 months. Several frigates & smaller craft are laying in ordinary, some of them rotting, some rotten. I am told that in Sackett's harbour the Yankees have let all go to ruin & decay, the land defences even are crumbling down. The opinion seems decided that had the war lasted six months longer, Sackett's harbour & the fleet would have been utterly destroyed.

Fort Henry is a hill rising immediately over the Dockyard & commanding all around. It appears to me too distant to protect the town of Kingston. I was surprised to hear that in 1813 not a tree was cut in the Dockyard or on this hill; it was thick forest to the water edge. Now it is a star fort of very respectable strength, and makes Kingston a most important post. Considerable repairs are going on, & capital Bomb proof Barracks building for a Regiment. Capt. Paine of the Engineers superintends. He is a fine young man.

20TH JULY. Col. McGregor procured us horses today, & I rode with him in a circle of 3 miles round Kingston, going out by the inlet called Cataraqui & the shore road on the Lake; it is pretty enough. The ground is rocky, but it is all limestone, a thin covering of soil, in some rich, in many places so thin that it produces almost nothing. The more distant lands are extremely rich black loam. Kingston is abundantly supplied from the country with everything, but an Enemy may cut off these easily, & the town could not get even enough of milk for breakfast, so entirely dependent just now.

I walked early to see a collection of Indian dresses & curiosities which Capt. De la Haye, 70th, has made during his stay at Drummond's Island near Michilimakinac. They are well worth seeing. He offered me any of them I chose, but [I] declined any. He tells me it is a mere military post – no settlement made. Officers & men employ themselves in gardening & rearing what seeds he can get as vegetables. The island & all around it is a wild & thick forest. The Indians sometimes come to beg gunpowder – very peaceable & honest. Provisions are sent to this post from Detroit....

A number of Indians I see laying about the streets infinitely more wretched than our Nova Scotia Micmacs – all of them in rags, differing from ours chiefly in their painting their cheeks with broad streaks of red paint. All of them brutally drunk even at noonday. One motherly looking squaw, I observed, had lost her nose; on enquiring I was told that her husband had in quarrel with her bit it off. During the whole night they made a hideous howling noise in the streets like so many wild beasts.

21ST JULY. Last night at 10 o'clock we embarked in the steam boat *Charlotte* for Prescott, & took leave of our most kind friends Col. & Mrs. McGregor. Col. Grant & several Officers accompanied us to the wharf. We sailed at 2 A.M. this morning; at Gananoqui at 6, took on board more passengers, among whom was Col. Stone, the sensible old Gentleman I met here on passage upwards, also a staff surgeon, Mr. Bigsby, a very well informed & clever young man. He has been employed some months past in a study of this Upper Province as to its Geology & mineralogy, of which he has some very curious specimens. About 12 we stopt half an hour at Brockville, went on shore & directed our walk to the Court House on a rising ground. It, occupied below by several families of lodgers, had much the appearance of a jail. The courtrooms are above, convenient enough, & fitted to serve as a Church as well as a Court of Law. A Church however is also building hard by. On the door in Court, I observed a long list of names with the lots numbered of each man's property & a column of Remarks. This was giving notice to these names, that having left their abodes when the American Army attacked, & not having joined the Militia, they were declared aliens, their lots were forfeited, & to be sold the week following unless they could account satisfactorily to the Commissioners for their absence. The fact was, they were all Americans & had passed over to the other side as soon as the Enemy had been heard of. This is unhappily the description of a great proportion of the population on the bank of the St. Lawrence from Cornwall to Kingston, but such measures as this will thin them, & the back range on the Ottawa can always protect this front line from any permanent occupation by an Enemy, and in that view I think these new Military settlements deserve the liberal aid & the protection of the Government.

The approach thro' the islands to Brockville is most beautiful, the passage in breadth being frequently little more than the length of our boat, & the perpendicular rock wall topped with heavy timber, brushwood & vines overhanging its face, the water smooth as the surface of a glass. My friend Stone was by no means so talkative or entertaining; he had found out who we were & was shy of us. He promised however to send Lady D. & Mrs. Bigsby some specimens he had picked up among the islands.

We reached Prescott (Fort Wellington) at 3 o'clock, just as a thunder shower came down upon us. Found here Capt. Barry of the Navy, on his way to Kingston as Commissioner of the Dockyard, a very odd & pleasant fellow. We were soon quite intimate, & he amused us with an account of his journey up from Montreal without any servant, because he said he did not like the trouble of taking care of a servant & a Portmanteau too. He gave a ridiculous description of an Irishman & an American in the coach disputing about the late war. Words grew warm, & at last the American said, "Don't you be surprised, Mr. Britisher, if I give you a thump for your observations." "Faith," said Pat, "it would be mighty prudent in you, Mr. Yankee, to think twice about that, for I have felt myself ready for some time past to pay it back with tenfold interest."

Capt. Barry, a thorough Pat himself & a good bruiser, was delighted with the skirmish, & told it admirably, but he put a stop to blows.

As the Evening became fine, we crossed over to the pretty village of Ogdensburg on the American side, but soon found it looked best at a distance. The tavern is good & kept by an Englishman. He was very civil, but could not procure us any carriage to drive a few miles into the country, which is said to be pretty & roads good. Just as we stept into the boat to return, a Mr. Ross came up to me & introduced himself as a Scotchman from Montrose, & well acquainted with my brothers in that County. He says he is related to the family of Ross of Rossie, and an Agent of Mr. Parish, but he smelt so strong of Rum & appeared to have got so much of it, that we soon left him. The

Yankees were laying & lounging like Spaniards in the streets & shade; they stared at us without any offer of civility or incivility.

Lt. Shaw of the artillery, & a Mr. Massani, a half pay officer, accompanied us over. The latter gave me an account of Lord Selkirk's settlement on the Red River; he had been sent there by Sherbrooke with others in a Commission to investigate the late quarrel there. He blames both parties, & attributes the whole to the feeling they have of being out of the reach of Law.

22ND JULY. We now embarked in our batteaux to proceed down the river, all anxiety & desire to reach the rapids of the Long Sault.

We pushed off from Prescott at $^1/_2$ past 4, just as the Sun rose upon the horizon, beaming in all its glorious splendor, a light breeze against us but the stream strong with us. Our rowers worked therefore lazily, but gave us the Canadian boat song willingly & in great variety. They did not however sing near so well as our former crew. We reached Col. Fraser's, 20 miles, by 7 o'clock. He came down in the *Frontenac* with us from York, & had kindly made us promise to breakfast at his house, a neat comfortable cottage immediately on the bank of the St. Lawrence, which has there all the appearance & all the everlasting noise of a rapid running river. A few good trees— Butternut, Locust, Oak, Poplar, all planted by himself, spread prettily in front, affording a delightful shade on a smooth carpet of grass sloping to the water edge. On right & left are small plots of kitchen garden, & behind his house is the great public road, parallel with the river. Nothing tidy or tasteful, but still it has all the appearance of contented comfort.

Col. Fraser is an old half pay Officer of the American War settled here with the men of his Company at the Peace, 1783. Like others he purchased a number of lots of land which his men abandoned. He has by that great landed properties in acres, but no great extent cleared. He lives in the style of an easy farmer.

He has several sons & daughters with families settled around him & doing well. He tells me there is there the finest tract of land he ever saw, a rich black mould, extending back to the Ottawa, and beyond it as far as has yet been explored in that Northerly direction.

We had arrived upon him much before the hour he had calculated upon; there was great bustle in the house & we had to wait a full hour for our breakfast. Mrs. Fraser & two elderly ladies made their appearance; the former, very large, had a most tremendous cough, which apologised for much apparent violence of temper & vulgar manners. One of the others, a remarkably funny & clever old wife, altho' she was called Miss—seemed to be as much pleased with us as we were entertained with her.

We were somewhat annoyed at our delay, but after breakfast bid them good bye. They were extremely kind & the old Colonel much gratified with a long talk over the American war, & particularly the affair of Saratoga. He was there an Ensign in the 21st Regt. of which my uncle Malcolm was Major & wounded. He was quite delighted when I told him the connexion, as he seemed to remember his Major with great affection. He expressed rather a favorable opinion of General Burgoyne as a clever & brave man, but an inexperienced soldier & so flighty and irresolute in plan that the Army never knew what he was flying at. He laid great blame on Sir Wm. Howe, who gave them no assistance or countenance as promised from New York.

At a few miles before we reached Fraser's we passed the rapid called "Le Galop," a rough stream. At Fraser's the "Rapid du Plat" is finer, more broken. At 12 o'clock we reached the Long Sault, described as being 9 miles & dangerous. Running those in 20 minutes, our expectations highly wound up were altogether disappointed. The islands, in masses of heavy woods, contracting the passage, were beautiful, but the stream, tho' more broken than the rapids we had passed, had nothing to alarm or even surprize us, except perhaps the extraordinary boiling of the current, like innumerable cauldrons. We did not go down very fast, and might have gone much faster, had the boatman plied their oars, but they several times set the boat broadside to the stream, as if they wished to make it appear dangerous; by doing this we once shipped a wave that struck the boat, but even that could not give the smallest idea of danger. Great caution & perfect coolness seems necessary in the helmsman who pilots the boat with a strong Indian paddle, shifting from side to side with great dexterity & quickness. It was also necessary to keep clear of the boat following us, as they could neither stop suddenly nor pass us in the rapids with precision, and it was a most curious & interesting part of the scene to observe the violent rapidity with which the following boat gained upon us when we laid ours broadside to the stream; & how she tossed & tumbled in the swelling & poppling sea. The grand stretch of this Long Sault which we saw on our road going from Cornwall to Prescott lay on the other side of the woody island. It is more rapid & dangerous & passed only in time of war when it is more safe from the American row boats which haunt the creeks & inlets about these wild islands.

We left the Long Sault with one universal confession of being disappointed in our ideas of it, and soon after entered into the Lake St. Francis. There the river expands very wide, & becomes dead smooth. Having passed Cornwall a couple of miles we went on shore to dine on a green bank near a poor looking farm house. We had cold meat, bread & wine with us, & got excellent milk & butter.

In the Evening the wind freshened upon us, & having rather trifled away our time, we had now every prospect of being benighted. The boatmen however cheered themselves & us with songs, & at 10 o'clock quite dark we reached the Pointe au Bodet, a resting place on the line drawn between Upper & Lower Canada.

23RD JULY. As we approached last night, we were amused with the appearance of numbers of lights flitting about here & every where on the Lake, sometimes extinguished in an instant, at others blazing out like prodigious flambeaux. It was the Indians & inhabitants at their usual occupation of fishing, spearing into a flat fish by torch light in the bows of the canoe. It was a fine Evening & the darkness of it rather shewed that scene to advantage. About midnight they all retired as if by general agreement, & in a few minutes not a light was to be seen.

On first arrival the comforts of the night were futtering. The house at Pointe au Bodet is very poor, the usual stop of the batteaux going upstream, & which are generally filled with hundreds of wretched Irish Emigrants. The Landlady, a sort of Virago calculated to keep the Peace in the house by her own authority & strength, was not over civil. She had some time ago peremptorily refused admittance to the Duke of Richmond, who had been obliged, as we were, to stop there. On entering, we found the large room full as possible of common people, the floor covered with women & children laid down to sleep, while others – men were drinking, women talking, children squawking, all formed a most outlandish scene. The Landlady however shewed us into an inner room & soon became very civil

& obliging. Lady D. was very happy to see this, & after some speeches to please the old one, set about getting tea, got down the tea cups from the cupboard & washed them herself; we spread a table & the old Lady brought excellent butter & milk; we had plenty [of] bread with us, & in a few minutes our prospect of hardship changed to a very merry party. Meanwhile the old one opened another room still within us; in it we got a bed made on the floor for Lady D. & her maid. The Gentlemen made the best of it in the other room. Ramsay and I got upon a bed. Collier, Couper & Mr. Temple lay down on the floor in their cloaks; this morning Mr. Temple complained of his bones & we found that having walked about later than we, he had to extinguish the lights, & then wrapping himself up had laid down on a broken brick pavement, the stand of the stove in winter. He roughed it however as well as any of us.

As day dawned we were astart & thanking the old one for her civilities. We parted excellent friends, & reached the Coteau du Lac for breakfast. Here again Mr. Nicoll was prepared for us with every possible attention. We proceeded down the rapids at the "Cèdres" & then the "Cascades," both similar to the Long Sault, but both more rapid & broken & consequently finer than what we had hitherto passed. We reached Lachine about 4 o'clock, & finding Capt. Hill of the Staff Corps waiting us with carriages, we proceeded in them immediately to Montreal, not by the same road we left it but by the inner road which is very good & very prettily wooded. As we entered the town we passed Woolford who had left us at Kingston to proceed down the river slowly by himself for the purpose of taking sketches at his leisure.

24TH JULY. Here we are again at a halting place [Montreal], & I feel it a great relief after 17 days of almost constant travel. It is today oppressively hot, so much so as to prevent us from going out. On my arrival I expected to find the Admiral & Sir Jas. Gordon both here, but the latter is already returned to Halifax, & the former hourly expected. 1819

26TH JULY.... We have engaged our passage in the *Quebec* steamboat. Admiral Griffith arrived late last night & called here today with Sir John Johnson, whom I had a great desire to see. He is a very tall gaunt looking old man, very lively in countenance & speaks rapidly. Very gentlemanlike manners, & with all that a kind of wildness, as if he wished to appear a character tinctured with the habits and the intercourse he has had with the Indian tribes. I am told he never ceases grumbling at imagined ill usage by the British Government, altho' a very different opinion is held here as to that. He appears to have quarrelled with society generally here, being visited by nobody, altho' the Ladies of his family are most pleasing & agreeable. The Admiral has brought up his daughter here lately married to Capt. Johnson, Sir John's son, & is so little disposed to better acquaintance with his new relations, that he returns with us in the *Quebec* tomorrow.

I took a long walk today with Mr. Ross to call upon several of those who civilly visited us on our way up. Their houses are excellent & all fitted from London. I am told their style of living is also more expensive, but they suffer inconvenience from want of servants, & Mr. Ross today described the state very strongly in making an apology for not having asked us to dine in his house; he said "that Mrs. Ross (who is very near her confinement) was unable to attempt the fatigue, as upon any such occasion we must do everything in our own families. The Gentlemen all go to market in the morning & our Ladies are our chief cooks & managers of the feast; they make the broth & the puddings, and you strangers would have no suspicion at dinner that they had been cookmaids all morning." Notwithstanding that trouble, there is an incessant eating during the winter months. At present everybody is in the country that has the means of leaving town.

Among many discussions & opinions on the conduct of the late war in Canada, & the probably result of any future contest, I find here as well as very generally in the Upper Province, that Sir Geo. Prevost is esteemed a weak, undecided & irresolute character, but an able man, amiable in private life & harshly dealt with latterly. Sir Jas. Yeo is abused as ill tempered, incapable from bad health & deficient in that dash or enterprising talent that is essentially necessary in the Commander of the Lake Squadron.

The Canadians are supposed not to like the British, but to detest the Americans, and would defend Lower Canada to the last.

This Evening we attended a concert in the Great Ballroom here. The Music was only a few songs by an American lady, who chiefly recommended herself by a pitiful story of the misfortunes of her husband who had failed as a Merchant, & whose broken fortunes she was attempting to repair by this public exhibition. The Ball room is very handsome indeed & lighted by several of the most magnificent crystal lustres I ever saw, all done by that eccentric & extravagant creature Mr. Molson, the proprietor of the Hotel.

27TH JULY. It rained all morning, but clearing about noon we went to see a collection of Indian curiosities & dresses, very valuable. After that went by appointment to meet Colonel Ogilvie at the Bank where he was going to deposit the extended Survey & plans of the St. Lawrence so far as the Commissioners for fixing the boundary line between the Americans & us have yet completed. It is well worth seeing; upon a scale I think of 4 inches to a mile, beautifully executed, partly by us & partly by American draftsmen. Upon ours the base lines are taken afresh every ten miles, & the triangles of the survey accurately laid down, so that there cannot be any mistake, & if there is one imagined, it can be remeasured any day.

That of the Americans is not so done, but Col. Ogilvie intends to return upon these surveys by the Americans & require them to certify as to what has been done by him. He seems a very capable man of business & a very pleasant man to act with. The Americans are loud in his praise.

This Survey has proceeded as high as the falls of Niagara & the Commissioners are at present in camp on the Grand Island at Chippewa. Ogilvie is absent for a few weeks on private affairs, & now about to return, has deposited as public property in the keeping of the Bank those very valuable Plans. The rough sketches of the summer work are in the winter extended clean & carefully, & then deposited. Col. Ogilvie expects to accomplish as high as Detroit this summer, & the next year conclude his operations at the head of Lake Superior.

28TH JULY. Last night late we embarked in the steam boat to which Mr. Ross & Capt. Hill very kindly accompanied us. We found the Admiral & Capt. Fanshawe already on board, and we sailed at dawn of day. We have unluckily a head wind, but cool & pleasant. Several passengers among the others are Mr. & Mrs. French, the American lady who sung at Montreal; they are very unassuming modest people. He is a Yankee but speaks without the prejudices or vulgarity which generally marks his countrymen....

29TH JULY. We did not reach Quebec in time to land last night, but hove to for some hours & anchored with daylight, after a very pleasant passage of 30 hours. The boat is smaller, but every way more comfortable than the *Malsham*. It is surprising that so many of these boats (8 of them) plying between Quebec & Montreal should all find sufficient employment to pay the heavy expences attending them. It is the case, however, & speaks the immense quantities of manufacure & other import forcing way into the Canadas.

We landed to breakfast at the Chateau, & were received by Lady Charlotte Lennox with her little sister, Col. Ready, the Duke's civil Secretary, & Capt. FitzRoy, A.D.C.

Mr. Temple had hoped to profit of this opportunity in seeing the Lord Bishop of Quebec, to get ordained in the Priesthood; the absence of our own Bishop in Nova Scotia having prevented it from being done there. This morning I wrote a few lines to the Bishop to state the request, & to beg he would appoint a time when I would wait upon him with Mr. Temple. He called upon me soon after, but objected some informality, trifling as Mr. T. thought; His Lordship was however immoveable, & declined in a way evidently to say, Let your own Bishop do the work of his own flock. Dr. Mountain has long been Bishop of Quebec, is here spoken of as a clever man, amiable in his outward manners, but now a lazy Preacher, very haughty & imperious in Society.

30TH JULY.... After calling on the Bishop with Mr. Temple, from a feeling of respectful civility I walked thro' the Artillery Barracks & the Armoury in which about 20,000 stand of Arms are generally kept in good order.

31ST JULY.... We had to ride fast home [from a second visit to the Chaudière Falls] to dine with the Commissary General Wood, a very good fellow indeed to all appearance. Here I met the Chief Justice Sewell, a mild, gentlemanlike, sensible old man; also a Mr. Ryland, Clerk of the Legislative Council or House of Lords; a resident of many years in the Province. He was Secretary I believe to Lord Dorchester, the first Governor General, of whom he speaks in the warmest terms of esteem & affection. Mr. Ryland shewed us in the morning the Hall of Assembly & of the Council – very small, but handsomely fitted up and appropriately.

In this country where toleration in Religion is constitutionally granted, & the best Security for that cordial union in all classes of the people, so essential to the happiness & prosperity of the country, I am shocked to find that the Catholic & Protestant resident Bishops are on terms of personal enmity. Both must be to blame, because there is no disposition on either side to smooth an approach.

The Catholic is said to be a cunning monk, has very extensive influence over the people, & knowing that, his political line is to foster that rooted dislike to mix with the British subjects, or to open any intercourse by marriage or by language that might in time tend to wash away the manners & national distinctions which exist at this day as strongly characteristic as when Wolfe decided that Canada should be English in 1759. Quebec is entirely a French town, & the whole neighbourhood is French as much as if it stood now within 10 leagues of Paris. The streets narrow & filthy, the people noisy & vociferous, with bonnet rouge, long queues & wooden sabots. Nothing scarcely is spoken but French in the market & in shops. Monks & friars at every turn. All gives the idea that we are travelling, & here in France among Frenchmen.

A thousand pities that it had not been ordered at first, that in Law Courts, & in Parliament, the English language alone should be used. It is too late now to be ordered; convenience or some other distant & growing remedy can only do it; such as a preference to those that shall qualify themselves for offices under Government by acquiring a proper knowledge of English, by an English Catholic Priesthood & etc.

1ST AUGUST. Being Sunday, went to Church; service was performed as [in the] Cathedral, & very respectably indeed. The church is handsome but contains few people. The organ fine. The Bishop occupies a stall by himself, & neither reads prayers nor the Communion service, nor preaches. The King presented the Church plate & a Chime of Bells. The Queen built the Church from her private purse. The plate is plain and handsome. The Bells were taken during the American War & have not been replaced; that surprises me, but the more so, as Sherbrooke neglected it & presented a large & fine toned Bell to the Catholic Cathedral, which that Bishop seems to exercise powerfully; it tolls incessantly, & even in time of the Service of all the Protestant Churches. It is close by, & today tolled 5 minutes at 12 o'clock so loud that not a word from the clergyman could be heard while it lasted. It seemed bullying or crowing over her sister Church; I felt it both indecorous & indecent.

The Catholic Bishop has lately been granted a seat in the Legislative Council. He expected as is usual to sit next in seniority to the President, but that was not said in the King's Mandamus, & therefore opposed, but, curious enough, chiefly resisted by the Catholic Members, who would not yield "le pas" to their Chief Priest. He therefore sits at present as Junior.

2ND AUGUST. I walked out to breakfast with Col. Harvey, the Adjt. General at Wolfe's Cove where he has purchased a very nice place & small farm; he calls it Marchmount in compliment to Lord March the Duke's son, a courtier compliment which I exceedingly condemn, as paid at the expence of the honour due from every British soldier to the memory of General Wolfe. & yet Colonel Harvey is a very spirited & very distinguished soldier. His house actually stands upon the battery first taken on the morning of that glorious day. In my idea, the name alone of Wolfe's Cove is the most valuable part of the property. I am however much inclined to think that the old name is so firmly fixed that a modern Governor might as well change the plains of Abraham to any modern title, as that Wolfe's Cove can become a Marchmount.

When here before I went out early one morning before breakfast with Mr. Temple & Ramsay & Hay, having in my hand the plan of the battle on the plains of Abraham. We traced it all thro', & sat on the granite stone on which Wolfe laid down to die. It has been hammered to a smooth surface by the curiosity of strangers & is now almost sunk into the ground. The ground is now laid into enclosures & strongly fenced. A large field for exercise of troops has been retained, & is I believe used more as a race course than any other purpose. Various individuals have acquired property & built villas within pistol shot of the Glacis, to the disgrace & scandal of the Governor whoever he was that permitted, & now finding how improper it is, the Duke of Richmond is purchasing back what he can get at 10 times the value a private man could get it.

As to the battle I can say nothing. It appears to me that Wolfe had great advantages in standing all ready, prepared to receive the attack, & his Army knowing there was no retreat acted on his orders with heart & soul. After a very short fire he rushed on with the

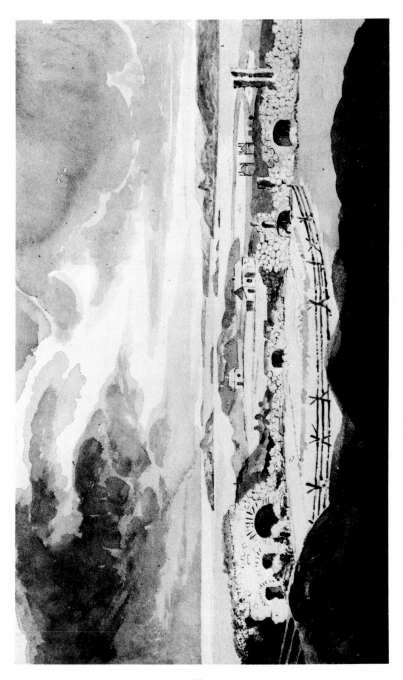

V

bayonet, overthrew Montcalm's army & pushed them headlong down the sloping steep which they had just hurried up and had not been allowed even time to recover their breath. The whole was over in a couple of hours, & the whole sum of misfortunes seems to me to lay in the want of judgment in Montcalm, chusing his post beyond the St. Charles instead of that of the plains of Abraham, having his right on St. Charles, his left on St. Lawrence, a few light troops extended to Montmorency or advanced to the Cap rouge – there he was inaccessible, his retreat into Quebec easy, & the situation of his Enemy helpless in one month more by the certain approach of intense winter.

We pursued our walk down the bank to the St. Lawrence, not so precipitous as at Wolfe's Cove, but so steep as to make us hold on by the bushes in crawling down – skirted along under Cape Diamond by the Lower town, which is abominably filthy & occupied by boat builders. By this road we traced the attack of Montgomery in 1776, who was killed at the barrier, but where that barrier stood is already unknown. "It must have been here or it must have been there," was all the information I have been able to obtain from many I have asked. Still more strange is it today, that no one individual of the staff in this garrison or of the Duke's family staff, had ever walked the path I had done, or enquired about the matter.

Arnold's attack at that same time was on the other side of the town by the river St. Charles, & along the basin where it empties.

Colonel Ready and Harvey are able men, and conduct their departments much to the satisfaction of the country, but there are sad complaints of all others doing business near the Duke.

We had for some days prepared our departure for today, & the wind being fair, we went on board *Mersey* at 1 o'clock; soon after we bid an everlasting farewell to Quebec, where we have been most kindly received, & where every honour would have been paid us had we been disposed to be anything beyond private travellers. So sensible have I been of this, that I yesterday addressed a letter of thanks to the Duke for his great attentions; and informed him of my resolution to tender my resignation of my Government in October, so as to return home early in the Spring. It has been reported that Sir P. Maitland wished to get Nova Scotia, & with the Duke's interest in time in England he has good prospect. I therefore felt it due to His

Grace to make him early acquainted with my intentions. At 2 o'Clock we made sail for Halifax direct.

3RD AUGUST. Last night at 9 o'clock we were obliged to come to at the narrows of the Traverse, tide & wind both against us; weighed again at 2 A.M. but again forced to anchor off Goose Cape at 9 A.M. Several ships from London 50 days passed us going up. Weighed at 3 P.M. & dropt at 10 P.M. off Kamouraska, thus regularly guided by the tides. It is pleasant, being in no hurry.

4TH AUGUST. We weighed at 2 A.M. and dropt again about 10 o'clock off the Brandypots, quite calm. At 4 P.M. weighed with a light breeze but strong current. As we passed the Light House on Green Island, the Pilot asked leave to return, to which Collier readily agreed. He is a drunken useless fellow, as they almost all are here, tho' under regulations of Branch Pilotage. This morning we are gliding down stream at 8 knots an hour, tho' scarcely know we move. The calculations of sailors in this are not very clear to me. We now go 3 knots thro' the water & the rate of current in our favour is 5 knots. Therefore they say we go 8 knots. But it seems to me that if we go at all faster than the current, it can be of no use to us. We have however argued it stoutly & I conclude myself wrong....

6TH AUGUST. Early this morning close in with Cape Gaspe, the craggy face very beautiful. Wind fair but light.

7TH AUGUST.... About noon passed the Dead Man's Island, one of the Magdalens, not more than a mile distant; it does not seem to be inhabited, a barren precipice of white sand or clay with streaks of red. The south head appears to be washed clean by the wind & rain, a dark hard rock with pointed crags, totally inaccessible. The name is truly appropriate & many a shipwreck have no doubt confirmed it a title. Saw several schooners busily at work fishing, sent a boat on board & got some fresh cured cod, but they had had very poor success this season.

8TH AUGUST. Sunday.... This morning off the Seawolf Island on Cape Breton shore; wind has veered round to N.W., quite fair to carry us thro' the Canso passage & to Halifax if it holds. At 11 o'clock divine Service was performed by Mr. Temple on the quarter deck, very neatly closed in with awnings & flags for the purpose....

10TH AUGUST. At 6 A.M. the breeze suddenly sprung up from S.W. after some heavy showers. Got instantly up anchor, & by 8 were off Arichat. Telegraphed the *Bellette,* Capt. Pechell, who soon after tacked & passing within the rocks & Light House of Canso, gained so much upon us, that when we had got round the other ledges, he was full 8 miles ahead of us. About noon it fell calm; Pechell came on board & dined with us. We learned from him that the Admiral had arrived a week ago, the *Active,* Sir Jas. Gordon, with him. That Commissioner Wodehouse had sailed for England with all his family in the *Spartan* & that the Dockyard was nearly shut up. That a most unfortunate duel had taken place in Halifax, in which young Richard Uniacke had killed Mr. Bowie, a very respected merchant. That the Supreme Court sitting at the time had proceeded in a few days to the trial for murder, & had acquitted him. Pechell is cruizing on the coast to watch the Yankee fishermen & smugglers, had not seen any in the harbours East of Halifax. This evening calm; all hands had leave to fish in 25 fathoms. In less than an hour they caught as much cod as was reported to Collier abundantly sufficient for the ship's company....

12TH AUGUST. A fresh breeze at West enabled us to beat up as far as Jeddore Head, but too late this evening to venture into our Port.

13TH AUGUST. Stood off & on during the night. A thick fog this morning and light wind at S.W. Cleared away frequently and as often came on thick again; about 2 o'clock when walking on deck, all impatient & fretting at the provoking disappointment, I accidentally mentioned to Collier that these fogs often hang so low on the horizon, that at the mast head it is all clear while on deck one can't see the ship's head. No sooner said than up he went, with his two Lieuts, Trail & Renou, and they saw clearly without glasses up into Halifax, the Light House about 3 miles distant bearing N.W. & the *Chebucto* at anchor, as we also were, 2 miles S. of us. All overjoyed, he weighed & landed us in the Engineer's Yard at 4 o'clock. The Admiral kindly sent his barge with young Stopford, Lieut. of *Newcastle,* for us, and we were welcomed home by all our friends.

14TH AUGUST. As I had directed the dispatches by the June mail to remain here for us, I found last night heaps of letters. The public ones were of importance from Lord Bathurst: Cape Breton to be again annexed to Nova Scotia. The counties of this Province to be subdivided as I had suggested. The question of marriage licenses but we sat an hour with him. His memory & conversation are both very good, and the anecdotes of Lord Strathmore's family in which he was brought up he told with perfect recollection of the facts.

10TH OCTOBER. Sunday. We came on here yesterday to dinner, 26 miles from Mr. Prescott's; & this morning went with Dr. Inglis to his parish church of Aylesford. A young man, Gilpin, who is missionary here read service & preached, altogether a well appointed & well conducted country service....

11TH OCTOBER. Rode with Dr. Inglis over his estate in this neighbourhood towards the North Mountain & the Bay of Fundy. He has 12 or 15,000 acres laying together near Clermont, not much of it cleared, but he is doing a great deal & will leave it a very fine property. Mr. Buskirk & Agricola rode with us. I was particularly pleased to observe that all his little farmers were delighted to see him. The inference is natural, that he is a good landlord & kind master to them....

14TH OCTOBER. We left Parker's about 6, a foggy drizzling rain, and rode thro' the Dalhousie settlement, entering where the road cuts across that from Liverpool to Nictau. To this cross road it is very good riding & the land at this place light loam, producing large crop of potatoes this first year. Sergt. Harman, the depot issuer, has an excellent lot & several of the settlers of 98th Regt. very good houses. From this to Orde's, an Artilleryman, 12 miles, the road is bad — seven miles of it a swamp, but it appears to me that a dry line might have been found, as I observed the land swelling & sloping on both sides of us. At Orde's we breakfasted; we brought tea, sugar & milk with us & got from him excellent potatoes & partridges.

From Orde's 10 miles to the depot on Sergt. Dargie's lot. These are depots of provisions which are issued by these two sergeants; Major Smith, 62nd, superintends the whole concern and is extremely careful that no man receives who is not industriously employed in clearing his own ground. From Dargie's depot to Annapolis 10 miles very bad road, tho' easy to mend & much public money has been already voted for it.

The soldiers have made more progress than I expected, for a discharged soldier is loose & unruly & unwilling to work. The constant attention of Major Smith has alone effected this, by stopping rations & by that driving from the settlement all the idle build another new one. This Dockyard has been efficient & acknowledged most convenient for 40 years past. It is at present in excellent order & full of stores. It is ordered to be reduced, and that at Bermuda to be the only one on this station. But it is only begun a few years ago, it has no store houses like these here, no wharves of safety, no means to heave down more than a sloop of war, & that is dangerous at present; the anchorage is dangerous, & the access to it is thro' amongst rocks visible under water, a narrow navigation of more than 20 miles; thro' the whole distance the pilot stands on the bowsprit to steer his way by the eye. The same dangers are there when the Vessels have got the repair, & the narrow escapes from striking are the usual subject of conversation of officers arriving here from thence. Little has yet been done at Bermuda but that little has cost half a million. It is impossible to say how much more will be expended but this is confessed that all the millions of England can never make it equal to the Dockyard of this harbour....

Undoubtedly in times of war, the situation is important as a Military post of offence against America, & ought to be well provided for that purpose at the time as a depot of stores & provisions. But to place there a Dockyard & Naval arsenal at an expence of millions, while there is one complete & efficient at Halifax appears to me an Act of Madness.

28TH AUGUST. Sunday.... The exertions in Agriculture stirred up by Agricola are going on with great spirit everywhere. He himself is doing wonders on a small property of 30 acres he has purchased near to the town. I go out to see his progress frequently. It is exceedingly interesting as differing from any attempts to bring in Nature that I ever met with. The surface is covered with large blocks & masses of granite, generally like a scab on the face; below is a deep soil of loam, sand & clay, or of gravel. He has first to prize up with iron crowbars & tumble loose these huge stones. They are then carted & built into dykes of enclosure, sub dividing his farm. The plough, a light iron Scotch plough, with a pair of oxen; sometimes it requires four tears up the sod which never in this world had been ploughed before, two men attending with pick axes to take out any more large stones laying below surface. These again are carted away & the field cross-ploughed is left to the operation of frost & snow. Manure will be prepared during winter & he intends to be ready with the earliest spring to sow out every part of it in crop. He had calculated on a first expence of £25 an acre, but by his own constant attendance, & by piece work on contract, he thinks that including the sowing, his expence will not exceed £10 an acre, and if the season favours in weather, does not doubt that his first crop will pay all his outlay.

5TH SEPTEMBER. Sunday.... This morning Lt. Col. Arnold, Comm. Engineer, sailed in *Chebucto* for the Grand Manan to fix a spot for a Barrack & Battery. Government has at last operated to this on my suggestion that it is a post which must be in war of the utmost importance, as commanding not only the entrance of the Bay of Fundy but all the harbours on the American line near us which swarm with lawless smugglers & Privateers, even in the present days of profound Peace....

9TH SEPTEMBER. Having long proposed to visit the Shubenacadie lakes & the road leading across from Hall's on the Truro road to where it meets that from Halifax to Windsor, near Mount Uniacke, I started last night with the Admiral, Mr. Jeffrey, Collector of the Customs, Hay and Schomberg Kerr.

We slept at Fultz's, & early this morning in a foggy & light rain proceeded to the Fletcher's bridge, where Jeffrey had provided two flat boats for us, sad cobles. The first Lake is small, rocky & unpleasant all around, and in many places very shallow – passed a narrow where the stream is banked in to deepen it for canoes, but still we had to go on shore & walk a mile while the men pushed the boat before them.

Again we embarked & proceeded 6 or 8 miles on the Great Lake, a very fine piece of water; as it blew fresh & had cleared to a fine day, it was rough & agitated like a sea. We landed at Indian Point, a farm of Jeffrey's just begun to be cleared, a beautiful situation, not more than a mile & a half from Truro road, about 23rd or 24th mile stone from Halifax. Here he has 4 Irishmen clearing by contract at £5 an acre, cutting down, burning, log fencing all round, & leaving it ready for potatoes or seed. Having eat our supplies of cold meat, we took two of these stout Irishmen, till now employed in the Newfoundland fisheries. We left the Lake to enter the river which issues about the middle of it, and in a course nearly North, empties into the Minas bason below Truro. A canal has long been talked of by this river & these Lakes, to connect the interior country by water carriage with Halifax at Dartmouth, and it is in the desire of seeing the practicability of such an attempt that I am come up here.

From the place where it issues & becomes a current stream to the bridge near Hall's, it is quite shallow, filling up every year more & more with logs of wood which form sandbanks; in these are beds of strong reeds which we got thro' with difficulty, & could not have got thro' them without the help of these strong Irishmen pushing the boat with the Admiral, Jeffrey & myself in it for 3 full miles. No small labour to them, up to the knee in water. I was greatly surprised, when I offered them a dram of spirits, that they both refused tasting any, but hot as they were dipped their heads to the stream & drank freely, telling us they had kegged themselves for two years, i.e., taken an oath not to taste spirits during that time. They had both nearly killed themselves with Rum while fishermen, & had now quitted it for ever. Fine promises.

We quitted the boat at Hall's bridge, & mounting our horses sent on there, rode to dine & sleep at Key's. I can see nothing very favorable in this line to induce so heavy an expence as a Canal would cost.

10TH SEPTEMBER. We had today intended going on to Gay's river to shoot partridges, & return to dinner, but altered that plan to shoot across the interior road of Douglas township & sleep at Colonel Smith's in Newport; the distance we were informed was 12 miles from Hall's. Accordingly we proceeded at leisure thro' a very nice dry country, a good road till near 3 o'clock, when the Admiral inquired at a farm house at the 9 mile river, how far to Smith's. I was surprised to see him coming after me in prodigious haste, & still more on hearing his intelligence, that we were then 21 miles from Smith's. So seldom is this road travelled, so ignorant everybody proved to be about it. However, we mended our pace, & overtaking our servants & light cart baiting at a blacksmith's named Taggart, we ate some cold meat & reached Smith's just at dark. Hay & Jeffrey had gone on early to prepare for us, & having shot six brace of partridges as they trotted on, we have found excellent quarters & hearty welcome from an honest old farmer settled on that spot with nothing but his hatchet & gun 40 years ago – now a Colonel of Militia, comfortable in his circumstances, and 5 sons settled on lands of their own near him & having all families. He is besides an old man of very entertaining conversation & perfectly contented with the world....

11TH SEPTEMBER. After breakfast, rode 7 miles to Rawdon Church, 7 to Jeffrey's at Lakelands, and 5 to Mount Uniacke, excellent road all the way. The Rawdon township is beautiful, both in farms & woodlands; of the former, many are now laying unoccupied, and selling commonly at the rate of £150 for 250 acres, half of them cleared with a house & barn. The road touches that of Halifax to Windsor at Jeffrey's house, 32 miles.

We have dined here at Mount Uniacke & had already separated except two or three to go to bed, when a loud knocking was heard at the gate. An officer was announced with dispatches from Quebec, and I received the melancholy intelligence of the death of the Duke of Richmond in Upper Canada. This officer, Ens. Ross, 76th, has hastened thro' New Brunswick in 10 days, which is considered quick. Hearing of me on the road he sought me out. The unlooked for event has confounded & stupefied us all.

14TH SEPTEMBER. Day before yesterday I returned early to Halifax and having since then maturely considered the emergency, & the letters I have received requiring my presence at Quebec, I called the Council together this morning. I stated my own ideas, that as the Law provided for the Civil Administration in this case, & as the Military department may be carried on with the same facility [from] my Headquarters at Halifax, & as there were no circumstances of a public nature to call for my presence there untill the pleasure of the King was received, I was inclined to wait orders here. In this the Council fully agreed; & more, that in the Civil part I could not act without special warrant of His Majesty or Prince Regent in his Name, as the Senior Member in Council at Quebec would assert his right to it.

I have this day accordingly intimated my intention to Lord Bathurst, the Duke of York, as also to the Chief Justice Sewell and the Adjt. Genl. at Quebec, and to Major General Sir Peregrine Maitland at York in Upper Canada, directing him to assume the temporary command of the troops & to report to me. I further gave orders today for a General Mourning on the death of the King's Representative, the Governor in Chief of His Majesty's American

Provinces, the Military during one month, the Community generally 14 days.

15TH SEPTEMBER. Closed my dispatches & sent them by Lord
Frederick Lennox, the Duke's son. I was induced to do this on his
own earnest entreaty to be allowed to see his Mother & family in
their deep affliction. The packet will sail at day dawn.

In the official situation in which this Event places me, it is my
desire that nothing should stop or interfere with the usual course of
public business; I make no change whatever in the civil department
and I leave it in the option of Sir P. Maitland to place himself at
Quebec or York as he thinks best for the public service. With regards
to myself, I have not made any request of the command; ready to go
up if ordered, I shall retire from the service if again passed over, and I
shall now wait quietly for the Prince's decision.

19TH SEPTEMBER. Sunday. In reflecting on this most unexpected
Event which now leads to the necessity of my leaving Nova Scotia,
either by moving up to the Chief Command, or by retiring from the
service, I see in it consequences the most serious & important in my
future days. It is not one of these occurrences in life which are all
interesting today & forgot tomorrow. It hangs upon my mind &
pictures to my thoughts all the difficulties of high command, all the
chances of great honour, or still greater misfortunes. New connexions to be formed where I am an utter stranger, & in a country where
violent party feelings have long separated the two distinct classes of
the King's subjects, the English and the French. In this command I
must stand the cast of the die, prospering, do honour to myself, or
failing, I must lose the little share of my Country's praise which I
have already received; let the result be what it may, it is pleasing to
think on the other side that I have hitherto done my duty without
censure in 30 years; new connexions need not dissolve the old, &
particularly as regarding this Province, no change can ever make me
forget the years I have passed in Nova Scotia in health & happiness,
while the country has enjoyed contentment, peace & prosperity to a
very great degree.

21ST SEPTEMBER. I left Halifax yesterday & stopt all night at
Mount Uniacke. This morning after breakfast we came on to attend
the annual meeting of the Governors of the King's College at

Windsor. We met at 12. Very unpleasant business was brought before us, in charges of habitual drunkenness, immorality & profane conversation against the Principal of the Academy, the Rev. Mr. Milner, by his usher, a Mr. Torry; it has occupied us all day, hearing stories of witnesses, servants, blacks & whites of the most infamous description. Dined in the hall and came this evening to sleep at the Chief Justice's.

22ND SEPTEMBER. Walked early into Windsor this morning, inspected the fort & stores, & after breakfast again met at the College. A charge of ignorance & incapacity having also been laid against Mr. Milner, the Governors yesterday referred that point to the President, Vice President, Dr. Inglis & Mr. King, by examining Mr. Milner. On our meeting this morning, Mr. M. presented a written paper, positively refusing to submit to examination, as he considered it an affront, & derogatory to the character of a Clergyman who had kept a school of known repute for many years – refusing to submit particularly to Dr. Porter & Mr. King, as having been decided enemies to him, & the latter a known instigator of the calumnies circulated.

In answer to this paper, the Governors resolved in fully acquitting him of every part of the charges of drunkenness, immorality, &&, but as refusing the examination, they find themselves in the necessity of placing another person in that situation. We then proceeded to the examination of the boys at the Academy school. Mr. M. again refused the wish of the Governors that he should himself examine the boys, & sat quite mute. Dr. Porter & Cochrane were then desired to examine them; they did so, & the boys not accustomed to them, nor they at all informed of the progress of the boys, of course they did not shew to advantage, & no opinion was expressed on this subject by the Governors. It appears to me that Mr. Milner's conduct in general has not been consistent with that which becomes the Headmaster of a school, & if he is competent, he has been certainly neglectful of his boys; I am decidedly of opinion that he is not a proper person to be in that place.

It is impossible to express sufficient disquiet at the villainous conduct of Mr. Torry, in this foul attempt on the character of his superior & a clergyman. It is almost incredible also, but it appears too true, that the Rev. Mr. King, Rector of Windsor, took a strong part in circulating these reports; that the President himself (Dr. Porter) has been very hostile to him by receiving & giving credit to them. The Vice President (Dr. Cochrane) has been his friend generally, gave strong testimony in his favour, having from his arrival a year ago received him kindly into his family and seen him often there. He considers the whole as foul & infamous calumny, void of any truth. Dr. C. however on the other subject, has not been his friend. He advised him to resist the examination required by the Governors, & which alone led to the decision to remove Mr. Milner.

Such is the sad state of the College. The President & Vice President are at variance. They don't speak to each other. What the one does or says is opposed by the other, & there is the cause of Dr. Porter's hostility to Mr. M. I never in my life met so violent a hatred in private circumstances as these two Rev. Gentlemen bear to one another. The Rev. Mr. King is at war with both, & while these three are preaching all around the doctrines of peace & good will, they are striking examples of unchristian conduct to every inhabitant of the country.

23RD SEPTEMBER. This morning early walked with old Jas. Fraser to the Grove, where we spent the summer two years ago. After breakfast rode with the Chief Justice to the Ponhook Lakes about 8 miles from this. A new settlement has just been opened on it by Jas. Hunter, a farmer from Colin McKenzie's estate near Peebles; he is doing very well, the land is light & good. A number of people are going out there this winter.

24TH SEPTEMBER. Returned to Halifax this morning....

27TH SEPTEMBER. A mail from Quebec brings many private letters giving circumstantial details of the death of the Duke of Richmond, particularly one from Judge Pike of Montreal. From such authority little doubt can be entertained that it was Hydrophobia, & yet the invincible impression on my mind is that fatigue & hot sun in the woods caused nervous affections; fever in his constitution & broken frame soon terminated the life....

5TH OCTOBER. I left Halifax this morning to visit the military settlement called Dalhousie near Annapolis, & took with me Col. Darling & Hay. Stop tonight at Spence's tavern near Windsor.

6TH OCTOBER. Breakfast at Knowles in Falmouth; while there we walked into the field with our guns, shot some snipe, a Bittern & a

Curlew. Good sport for an hour. This is a property of Judge Stewart's, capable of great improvement, a large cleared farm on a sloping hill of sandy loam, at present laying wet & covered with rushes. At 2 stopt to feed our horses in Horton, & again we walked out with our guns, but found nothing; at 4 went on to dine at Mr. Prescott's in Cornwallis, one of the hottest days of this summer....

8TH OCTOBER. According to a promise I had made to Agricola, I went this morning to the cattle shew at Horton corner – on my arrival received an address from the agricultural society of this part of the Province.

This shew is the first that has ever been attempted, & was but poorly attended. One half of the neighbourhood never had heard of it, & the other believed it to be nothing more than a drinking frolic, & staid at home. The prizes however were awarded & paid immediately in cash, which will prove an effectual method to bring better attendance next year. After all that has been published & said upon the subject, Agricola finds that the farmers are not yet moved in the business cordially, & he was assured of it by a conversation on the road with a man of the name of Eaton, a substantial proprietor in Cornwallis. This man did not know Agricola personally, & entered very freely into the opinion entertained of him by the farming classes. It is too long to put here, but I got today Agricola's promise that he would at his first leisure day put it in writing for me.

9TH OCTOBER. This morning we visited an old Yorkshireman hard by Mr. Prescott's, by the name of Jackson. Came out to this spot 30 years ago, has cleared a large farm & acquired considerable property. On his lands he has settled several sons & now lives an inmate with the elder one. He is 75 years of age & his wife about the same. I never saw human contentment so strongly exhibited, nor a man whose mind appeared so free from self reproach and so perfectly ready to leave the world. Mr. Norris, the clergyman here, tells me that Jackson had frequently opened his conscience to him in solemn conversation. He is entirely at ease except as to a sum of seven shillings & sixpence, which he wishes he could now repay with 100 fold. 2 / 6 of it he owes to an old woman in Yorkshire for curing a sore on his leg, which he did promise but never paid. The old woman is dead long ago. And 5 / - which he found in a purse & kept for his own use. I should have thought this a simple story of old age, answered to my satisfaction, and with Instructions how to act, if the subject be again agitated on the meeting of the Assembly. The Grand Manan to be occupied as I proposed, & a Plan & Estimate for Barracks & Battery to be sent home.

My private letters bring me the long dreaded intelligence of the death of my excellent friend & neighbour the Chief Baron. A better man or warmer friend never lived. His memory I shall revere, & lament his loss to the latest hour of my time. In my absence the *Spartan* frigate has brought me £150,000 in dollars for the Military Chest, & Tozer in *Cyrene* had gone to Quebec with as much more, also brought by *Spartan,* which after 7 days' stop proceeded to England with Wodehouse & his family.

The New York Packet homeward bound arrived today. Hay came in her, but Schomberg Kerr is left at New York; idle, absent & humming a bit of song, he could not be moved at the active pace of the others. But by Hay's report they have spent their time very pleasantly. They cut their jokes & humbugged the Yankees in the travelling carriages in the most ridiculous manner. Torriano, well set up & having naturally a pompous military air, was easily passed off for a General Officer. Beauclerc, silent & distant, passed for a Judge. Hay's servant, a fat fellow, not dining with them, was said to be a Methodist preacher not very fond of their company, & yet one of the party, but as to Hay & Kerr, a fellow told them he had come more than 100 miles to find them out, & at last he saw that the farther he went, the more he was confounded.

21ST AUGUST. Sunday. A seat in Council having become vacant by the removal of the Commissioner, I have called to it Mr. Hibbert Binney, the Collector of the Provincial Revenue, a very upright clever little man, whose character stands deservedly high in the community....

The lamentation here on the break up of the Dockyard is loud & general; a great number of families long employed in it, & resting their whole hopes of provision for life, are cast adrift at once without any notice or compassion. Many consider the Dockyard as the foundation & support of Halifax & that its loss will be general ruin. That is going too far, but I do think it a very unwise and ill advised measure. It is said to be on the principle of economy, but I cannot see the great prudence of shutting a good & sufficient house in order to fellows & forcing the others, even the best of them, to do more than they were inclined to do. We rode about 27 miles of new road opened within these two years, & I left 12 miles more to the Eastward, leading to Sherbrooke, behind me on turning from the Liverpool road, nearly 40 miles length with more than 400 people on it.

We were unfortunate in weather as it poured rain the whole day; consequently we saw the people and their work to great disadvantage. I am however quite satisfied that very few years will shew it a thriving settlement.

After breakfast this morning I inspected the fort and barracks, & then took a long walk by Easen's House to a spot called Gray's clearing, a new & shorter line which Major Smith is desirous of opening into the settlement, & which seems to be the proper line for the public.

15TH OCTOBER. Early this morning we left Annapolis & rode 30 miles to breakfast at Lennard's, & then 18 more to dine with Dr. Inglis at Clermont.

16TH OCTOBER. Took a long shooting walk with Dr. Inglis, along a large drain he has cut to dry some very valuable flat land, but his drain is nothing – perhaps it may measure 4 feet wide at top, 2 at bottom & 2 deep, yet it is the largest drain in the country, & quite a work of wonder. He will probably enlarge his scale when he sees the effect in a year or two of his operation already. From the lands on the north side we went to his woods on the south side of the public road, & had a delightful walk for two or three miles along the bank of the Annapolis river. A broad, dark & deep stream, choked with rafts of floating timber particularly at the turns, where it is speated up into immense piles, & carried off again in Autumn & spring when the river swells to a prodigious torrent.

The woods on the banks are by far the finest I have seen in the Province, & the only woods I have yet seen that may compare with the fine park trees of England. Mischievous people are cutting & stealing it, but the Dr. is so much pleased today with our praises of it, that he has promised he will henceforth preserve it with care & give it my name as a compliment & remembrance of our walk today. Hay & I shot some partridge, but they are so stupid, & we were so much more delighted with the scenery, that we took no pains to look for them.

18TH OCTOBER. Yesterday being Sunday, we stopt with Dr. Inglis, but it poured rain the whole day, & he released us from attending Church with him. We spent the day in his excellent library of very old & curious books.

On leaving Clermont this morning, we took the line of road under the North Mountain to see the progress of the settlement there. We crept along at a foot pace on very bad & greasy road for 25 miles, all of it rich loam. Now & then a good farm laying fit for plough but wholly neglected. We joined the great line of road again at Horton Corner, and rode on to dine with old Colonel Crane.

19TH OCTOBER. Early this morning I indulged the old Gentleman in riding with him on the Grande Pré (grande prairie), an immense extent of salt marsh land diked from the overflow of the tide. It is portioned off in very small lots of 5 to 25 acres, & the wealth of a proprietor here is estimated by his share of the marsh land. At present it is almost all cut in hay year after year, but by & bye when better farmers, they will get very heavy crops of wheat from it. A strong & rich grassy clay, similar to the carse lands of Strath Earn & the banks of Tay.

After breakfast went on to Knowle's in Falmouth, where we baited our horses & walked up to the Castle Frederic, a beautiful place belonging to old Governor Des Barres. The view from this down to Windsor with the winding turns of the Avon under our eye was rich, but nothing equal to the mountains behind it, covered in massy woods, & these now exhibiting the most beautiful tints of autumn. The fading yellow leaf of the oak & beech, & the deep carmine red of the maple, mixed with the rich deep green of the spruce & silver fir, under a warm & bright beaming sun, forms a picture I think I have seen but in this Province. We wandered about untill late, shooting snipe, & about sunset came on to dine & sleep at Spence's.

20TH OCTOBER. Left early & reached Halifax today by 2 o'clock. We have spent a fortnight most pleasantly, we have seen a great deal of the country I had not had it in my power to see before, and without the smallest accident whatever.

24TH OCTOBER. Sunday. Nothing has occurred for a long time that has caused so much general sorrow as the sudden death lately of Mr. Mortimer at Pictou. As a country Gentleman residing on his property he did much good, not only by his advice but by his example, & the state of improvement in that district strongly shews how important are the effects derived from the influence of such a man in this early period of our prosperity. Mortimer was a sensible man, no great speaker in the House of Assembly, but still he was active & forward in public affairs & his opinion was much listened to & respected. His death is universally lamented. He came out from Inverness when a lad of 16, with a view of getting employment as a Clerk. He was wrecked on Cape George & crawling along shore without a shoe on his feet, he reached Pictou, was taken by the hand in charity by a Mr. Patterson, whose daughter he afterwards married & has left her a widow without any family.

30TH OCTOBER. Day before yesterday I left Halifax to attend the cattle shew at Truro. Couper went with me, & we were joined in party by Judge Halliburton & by Mr. Robie, the Solicitor General. We reached Gibbon's, 47 miles, by 3 P.M., and to pass the time I walked to the farm lately purchased by Mr. Wilson, a farmer from East Lothian. I feel a warm interest in this man's welfare, having known him personally for several years, holding Lord Blantyre's farm at Bolton close by Coalstoun. When I left England he was like all other farmers, embarrassed in his circumstances by the sudden check given to Bank credit on the re-establishment of Peace. Unable to recover from his difficulties, he failed in paying rent to a very considerable amount & lost his farm. He has emigrated & brought his wife & young family, too young to be of any use to him, but he has brought also a little money & has purchased 500 acres for £300. On the farm is a miserable house & a good barn. 200 acres have been formerly cleared, but are grown up in bush again. He will have little difficulty in putting this much into crop, and make it a valuable farm, but tho' he has good hopes himself, his misfortunes have broken him down very severely. Old age seems growing fast upon him, & I fear the hard labour he must himself undergo. If he prospers he will shew an excellent example in practical agriculture & of great service in the present state of the Province.

Yesterday we drove into Truro to breakfast with Mr. Archibald,

VI

the weather most delightful summer day – a great concourse of people and a more numerous exhibition of cattle than I saw at Horton – they were also in better condition. Some excellent pigs imported this season from England. Sheep very wretched. A good Bull of the Ayrshire breed imported some years ago by Sir Alex. Cochrane, but none of the cows good. The general spirit of the people assembled was to me the most pleasing circumstance, & the best assurance that they are anxious to improve.

I had heard that the prize Bull at Horton, only 4 years old, & of the Ayrshire breed, was to be sold to the Butcher. I bought him, & offered him today to Wilson if he could afford to keep him this winter. He accepted him, & I think he is a valuable gift to the neighbourhood. A Mr. George Gracie & Mr. Blackwood, a Scotch dissenting clergyman at Gay's river about 4 miles from Wilson, both very active, industrious & intelligent farmers, also lately from Scotland, promised me to support Wilson if necessary & let me know of any difficulties distressing him.

I received at Mr. Archibald's an address from the Agriculture Society, and immediately left Truro to return to Gibbon's to dinner, as we had agreed with Halliburton & Robie.

This morning started early & breakfasted with the Minister Blackwood at Gay's river. He is a young man of a good family near Kinross, but his father's property having been sold, & having no interest at home, he has adopted his present course; is married & some small children. But Mr. Blackwood very wisely does not depend altogether on the stipend of a dissenting clergyman and is working very busily on a good farm he has purchased. He & his wife are quite satisfied with their situation, & look forward in a few years with perfect confidence to ease & comfort.

31ST OCTOBER. During our excursion we had much laughing at what would be generally thought a very awkward party between Halliburton & Robie, who, Couper tells me, had a violent argument on politicks the Evening before we started; so violent that the party broke up, & everyone supposed that a duel must have been the consequences. Quite otherwise – by 7 o'clock next morning they were on the road before us in the same gig, travelling as cordially as if nothing had happened – and certainly it shewed their good sense, as well as a picture of lawyers' debates. When we came up with them, they both expressed how they had exposed themselves by their violence, & turned all their quarrel into joke. They are pleasant men both, but very different characters indeed.

Halliburton is quick, lively, & good humoured. Early in life was an officer, Capt. of the Light Company in the Fusiliers, but not liking the severity of the Duke of Kent's discipline, & persuaded by his relations who are natives of this Province, or rather came to it from New York in 1783, he quitted the Army and studied for the bar. He pushed on rapidly, & is now on the bench – a Judge, perhaps 45 years of age, highly respected in publick & private life, a loyal subject, & a morally good man – he is peculiarly distinguished by great fluency of conversation, & a loud & vulgar laugh at every word.

Robie is like Halliburton in quickness, & superior in abilities, but in all other respects inferior, a strange mixture, more likely to be mischievous than loyal in times of trouble. Extremely fond of dispute and argument, he is in one company an ultra Royalist, & next day in the opposite extreme, crying down nobility & all distinction in society while he praises to the skies the Institutions of the United States. Rude & violent in company, he is always disagreeable & offensive to some part of it. Speaks of the Church as a "Gospel Shop," and of the good old King as a very "bedlamite." He is on his guard however when I happen to be present, & I hear these traits only in general conversation. I am quite decided in my opinion that he is a man of no fixed principle in any subject; a man who "neither fears God nor honours the King." But with all these faults he is a pleasant man in company....

11TH NOVEMBER. A fire broke out at 2 A.M. this morning in the Naval Hospital, which reduced the whole to ashes in less than three hours. It was caused by an old woman in charge of it. She had gone to bed drunk & was burnt in it. Her bones were found today. It is a public loss of considerable importance, perhaps £25,000, and I fear is only the beginning of the decay of the Dockyard, which being generally all wooden buildings requires the utmost care and attention. The reduction of this Establishment lately exposes it to a thousand risks & accidents.

14TH NOVEMBER. Sunday. I have during my stay in Halifax made it a rule of going one Sabbath in each month to the Scotch Presbyterian Church, which is connected with the Established Kirk of

Scotland. I went there today. Dr. Gray as usual preached. He is much respected by his congregation, which was more numerous some years ago than now. Dissenters & sectarians are pulling the people all ways, but aim chiefly to seduce from the Established Church. Dr. Gray is naturally corpulent & very lazy – gives himself no trouble, pays none of those visits in family devotion to which Scotch people are accustomed, writes & reads his sermons, an unpardonable offence. Of late I think I observe his lazy habit & want of animation in the pulpit growing upon him – a languid & sleepy appearance that forebodes apoplexy. He is a good man, I believe, but would be no loss to the community. We want men active in their calling, whatever that may be. The Kirk has in him a very indolent supporter, and the dissenting preachers are gaining ground fast.

I had lately a conversation with Dr. Inglis on the frequent change of clergymen from their missions or curacies in Nova Scotia. I maintain that it is a source of much mischief; & that unless a Clergyman rests happy & contented among his parishioners, gaining their esteem & affection by long acquaintance & known worth, he does no good at all. A wandering & discontented Clergyman is a character no way respectable. Dr. Inglis is the Bishop's commissary, & as Rector of St. Paul's is the head of our church in the Bishop's absence. He has the regulation & placing of the Missionaries from England. They are constantly changing about, one situation is more profitable, another is more pleasant, in a third the society is more agreeable. These are points in my opinion that ought to give way to the study of being useful. But Dr. Inglis says, it is the only & proper reward of merit, or superior ability, & is the constant practice in England. Very true, & very right in England where a great difference of talent is found. But here there is scarcely a shade of difference – all of them being very inferior indeed, & the new comers worse than the old by a great deal. It is from this cause more than any other, I am persuaded, that the Methodists are spreading so wide & with so much ease. They change about, it is true, by rotation & by the laws of their society, but they do not shew any personal desire to move, any dislike to their employment, & of course do not create that feeling which the others naturally excite.

21ST NOVEMBER. Sunday.... Yesterday the Packet from England was telegraphed, the wind at North. Couper, in impatience to hear if any decision had taken place as to Canada, went down with Capt. Collier in his boat, & brought me my dispatches last night. The Packet did not get up till today.

Lord Bathurst informs me that the Prince had appointed me Governor General in British America.

Altho' I have entertained strong hopes that this would be so, yet former disappointment warned me not to be confident, & I have held my mind prepared to receive a refusal. It has been my resolution to be firm & temperate, so shall I now continue in no degree elated, nor changed in the smallest tittle. I feel very sensibly the manner in which Lord Bathurst has acted towards me. He has not hesitated, even in his great domestic affliction, to recommend me to the Prince. His letter is expressed in terms the most kind & flattering, whether as a public or private dispatch, & if my feelings have been rubbed & ruffled by past events, these may well be forgotten in the "amende honorable" now made.

22ND NOVEMBER. My orders are to proceed forthwith, & a Royal Warrant is sent to authorise me to assume the Civil Government in Canada untill my regular commission shall be forwarded. But should any circumstances prevent my immediate departure, the warrant is also addressed to the senior Officer Commanding the forces there. After most serious consideration, & with the friendly advice of the Chief Justice, I find it impracticable to reach Quebec at this period of the season. The St. Lawrence is closed in ice. New Brunswick is not passable untill February, & the access by New York & Lake Champlain objectionable for many reasons. Here then I must remain at present, & I have therefore sent forward the warrant to Major General Sir Peregrine Maitland now at Quebec. This arranges everything in the most desirable manner both for the comfort of myself & the benefit of the public service, & in this I particularly feel the consideration of Lord Bathurst in providing for the difficulties of the season.

In Canada, nothing particularly requires my presence, as no Instructions have been yet received on the Financial concerns there, the great question which agitates that Province; and if these were received, I think it would be imprudent to discuss them in the House which will die in April next. It has shewn for several years a turbulent temper & cannot be expected to change that tone which it has so long attempted to hold in opposition to His Majesty's Government at home. I shall meet a newly elected Parliament & I hope a better temper.

In Nova Scotia, my presence is particularly necessary in this session of Assembly. Various matters of importance will come under discussion. The question of marriage licence to dissenters & sectarians; the annexation of Cape Breton as in 1763 to this Province, & the subdivision of the Counties of Halifax & Annapolis; and the farther confirmation of the Agricultural Societies are all objects of great interest here. Closing these I deliver over this Province to my successor without any embarrassment, without any existing cause of complaint or difficulty, overflowing with the necessaries of life, & roused to a spirit of Industry that gives the fairest promise of happiness & prosperity in times to come. I leave it with that pleasing satisfaction, in being conscious that I have done my duty fully & faithfully.

In regard to myself, it is a change in my plans & prospects for the future, full of honours, of hopes & of fears. I must no longer look towards retirement at home, I must give myself wholly to Canada. The consequences to my two boys give me the most serious uneasiness. Their education requires, & they must be, sent to England. That thought is sufficient to dampen the joy of having attained a chief command, the object of 30 years in steady pursuit. That command too is one of the highest & most honorable under the Crown. Success in it will carry distinguished honour, but if the reverse, I have a dreadful example before my eyes in the unpitied fate of Sir Geo. Prevost.

Which of the two may be my lot is a question that rests with that Providence which has mercifully guided me thus far in life. My conscience does not reproach me, & I have a veneration for the Character of an upright man that makes my mind easy as to the motives & principles that shall lead me.

My first step in assuming the Government today by being sworn into office in Council was to request Colonel Ready to retain the confidential situation with me which he held under the Duke of Richmond. I shall disturb no man in his office untill I shall see him unfit or unworthy of it, & I will give no promise of appointment to hamper me on my arrival. My own family & my own personal staff alone shall accompany me, & it is my declared maxim, that the good of the service, & the known character of individuals shall alone recommend them to public office.

24TH NOVEMBER. A vessel from England this morning brings the London Gazette of 20th Oct. announcing my appointment, as also that of Sir Jas. Kempt in succession to me here. I rejoice in this, because he is an officer I have long known & esteemed.

1ST DECEMBER. Yesterday being St. Andrew's Day, a Levee & Drawing room were held at the request of the people in town, who wished to congratulate me on my appointment; and very cordially they did so. I received a very flattering address from the Magistrates & respectable inhabitants, as I did also from the Council some days ago. Indeed the general expression of kindness on this Event is not less pleasing nor less honourable in my mind than the appointment itself as Gov. General....

5TH DECEMBER. The *Active,* Sir Jas. Gordon, sailed today for England, carrying home all the half pay officers & their families from the reduced Establishment of the Dockyard.

My business in Scotland has been of late very badly & imprudently conducted. So much has it vexed me that I have sent by this opportunity a Deed to place my Estates in trust till my return home. I have asked Lord Succoth & MacLean to do me this act of friendship. They are mutual friends themselves & for them individually I have always felt a great regard & sincere esteem. John Smith, my agent, is perfectly honourable & honest, I believe, but I cannot depend upon his prudence & judgment. He is young & overwhelmed in business beyond his abilities. He has contracted heavy debts on my acct. since I left home, & my instructions are not attended to when I write. This step I thought necessary, & therefore decided upon it at once.

I have also resolved upon another point of still greater importance — the future disposal of my boys; however painful it will be to send them away from us, their good requires it, & that is conclusive. I have seriously conversed the matter with Mr. Temple. He strongly urges a public school for Ramsay, whose temper is high, & who might be spoilt in the station in which he is placed among aide de camps, & in a manner superior among other boys of his age. He is clever, active, smart & desirous to make himself a scholar fully equal in every thing to his companions. These are valuable qualities which will be encouraged by the emulation of a public school, while his temper & the danger of his station will be checked. I have decided that they shall go to England next October, Ramsay to be an inmate with Dr. Butler at Harrow, & Jim to Dr. Pearson at East Sheen. Mr. Temple is willing to continue on his salary, while pursuing his own studies at Cambridge; he will watch over them & carry them to Scotland in times of Holiday. In all this arrangement I do my duty to them & in a manner that gives all possible comfort to myself, knowing Mr. Temple at their hand within constant enquiry of their health & occupations.

By the *Active* I also send home a letter soliciting from the Prince Regent a Charter of incorporation for the College now creating – a copy of which I have kept as also a plan of the building.

7TH DECEMBER.... I received today three Indians sent by the Abbe Sigogne, Catholic Missionary in the western district near Sissiboo river. They have been lately chosen the chiefs of tribes in that part of the Province & disposed to settle themselves in it.

The abbé requests for one of them, Francis Mune, a letter of confirmation as Chief, & protection from the Governor. I am glad to encourage any of them that shew disposition to settle & plant potatoes, which is the utmost that may be expected from their industry. I gave him a diploma with the immense lump of wax appended to it, but I also gave each of them a present of 2 blankets, a Gun, powder & shot, and a hat with which they were delighted, & taking leave, they very fervently expressed their gratitude in a hope that we should meet again in Heaven. The abbé also made request of a tract of land of considerable extent for the Indians, to induce & enable them to settle. This is a measure I have long thought advisable & I will without delay place tracts in several parts of the Province in proper trust for this purpose....

15TH DECEMBER. The anniversary meeting of our Agricultural Society was held today, & very well attended. The Charter of our Provincial Institution was presented as finally executed. Mr. Young (Agricola) was appointed Secretary & Treasurer, a joint office & entitled to salary. All other offices are considered gratuitous & honorary.

The report states that there are 220 members enrolled at 20/-

annual subscription. £750 were subscribed last year in this town to set it agoing and £1500 granted by the Legislature to make its benefits generally useful. Such has been the spirit of the Country that now instead of one, there are 20 district societies already formed; 18 mills for grinding oatmeal have been created this summer, & now the whole East half of the Province uses oatmeal cake & porridge instead of fine American flour bread, with beef steaks at breakfast, dinner & supper. I shall be astonished indeed if this does not lead to great improvements in a very few years, say 5 at farthest....

25TH DECEMBER.... We have reached the President Monro's Message on meeting Congress on the appointed day (4th December); it is no ways important; setting forth a very lengthy story of their quarrel with Spain about the cession of the Floridas. He says England & France have approved it. I don't believe that, but I rather imagine that neither care about it. Spain is in this, like a man of loose principle who admits his debt, but catches at any loophole to escape payment. America is a rogue who had caught him in the snare, & knowing a scampish claim is eager to press it, & close a nefarious bargain. The president pretends to know nothing of the swarm of pirates at present issuing from Baltimore, under his own nose, armed & manned from the States to plunder anything unarmed – reviving the days of the Buccaneers.

The Quebec mail has at last arrived, three weeks later than usual – the plan of the route has been sent me by a Lt. McLaughlin on the half pay of the 104th, settled with his Regt. near the Great Falls above the Presqu'ile on St. John river, New Brunswick, & exactly halfway between Fredericton & Quebec; this plan marks the stages – the distances where I must take sleighs, snowshoes, or travel on the "taubogan" (dogsled); but such is the state of New Brunswick now, that McLaughlin, who is himself accustomed to the utmost hardship of the woods, & actually capable of attempting any severity to reach his home, has been detained in Fredericton by the impassable state of the river & country. On that I may feel perfectly at ease if any doubt did exist as to the practicability of my reaching Quebec in haste. McLaughlin gives a very flattering account of the land & district where his military settlers have been placed, but complains sadly of the cruelty & ill temper with which Gen. Smyth had treated them from the first, refusing to listen to any statement of wants, to afford them any help or give them any encouragement in their very arduous undertaking. Last winter many of them left the settlement, fearing they should starve. They came back in spring to plant their little stock of potatoes & seed corn. They are rather better prepared for this winter, but are not satisfied as they know that Nova Scotia settlements have been better treated. I have authorised an issue of six months' rations to that settlement, in order to retain them upon it. There are already about 400 people, & that surely is a good foundation on which to commence measure to make a better & more easy communication with the three Provinces....

27TH DECEMBER. Very intense frost today. Yesterday afternoon a ship was reported from the Light House & came up cloathed in ice from stem to stern.... The news of the altered state at home are very pleasing. Parliament had met, & the largest attendance ever known on a first day of meeting. The Regent's speech mild but firm, & calls for constitutional measures to secure the peaceable part of the country, & of the people from outrage & insult. The Address was voted by a great majority in both Houses. Of 531 present in the Commons, the Minister divided 381 to 150, and still stronger in the Lords. The voice of Loyalty was heard in every corner of the country. Addresses to the Throne were pouring in assurances of firm & resolute affection for the King & Constitution, every county in England & Scotland were forming their Volunteer Corps & Yeoman Cavalry, and all fear & alarm had disappeared. How glorious indeed to contemplate at this distance & in this peaceful Province, old England sustaining the violent attempt at her existence, & unhurt by the utmost fury of her foes, sitting calmly down under the safe protection of her Constitutional Laws, & of her Parliament, the Guardian of their power & their healthful vigour....

31ST DECEMBER. A schooner from Boston came in during the night, brings London papers of 2nd Dec. received there by a Liverpool ship in 17 days' passage, the quickest run ever known outwards. Homewards it has been often done in 14 days. At this season we have none of the fun or riot of old fashions at home on this day. The last of the year passes away like any other day, unnoticed, & will be forgot with all the days & all the circumstances that have gone before it.

IST JANUARY 1820. As usual the New Year opens with a most delightful bright winter day, white in snow & hard in frost, excellent walking, altho' but yesterday it was soft & stormy. The Levee has been omitted from some neglect in not giving public notice of it, but I do not regret the omission.

To look back on the events that have occurred in the year now closed affords me much satisfaction; my time has not been spent idly. I have not neglected my public business of Government, and my leisure time has enabled me to visit Canada as high as Niagara. The opportunity then appeared to me the only chance or hope I should ever have to do so. That excursion was attended with everything pleasant & fortunate, & these six weeks have been stamped as an epoch on the mind of every individual of the party. But other events have occurred that leave a very different impression; & more doubtful in prospect than any part of my life yet has been, teach me to look with no small apprehension to the new scenes that open to me.

An awful lesson on the uncertainty of this world has been given in the sudden fall of the Duke of Richmond, & the no less sudden change in which all my fine spun plans & hopes of home have vanished. Home must now be banished from my thoughts, & I step into a new career full of difficulty & trouble. I must assume a station of preeminence that places my every word & act before the uncharitable criticism of the world, and I rest upon no ground of hope, but that of a good conscience and an ever lively trust in an Allwide and All Merciful Guide.

I have been seriously thinking upon these things in order to view the change in all its bearings, & to fit myself to it while I may. In every way I turn it, I see prosperity on one hand & difficulties & dangers on the other, like clouds that darken the sunshine of my hopes. The heaviest of these is the separation from all friends, all concerns and all the happiness of my private life. I may truly say that I have never yet had it in my power to sit down my own master. All this last year I had framed my mind to that close of service; it was fully made up to it, & I felt contentment & happiness in the prospect. All that is gone like a dream, & I am now perhaps farther from it than ever.

I have reached a Chief Command, the object of my 30 years of service. I feel myself now chained to that public service by honour & by duty, while I have health, or while my service is approved by my Country; myself & my private concerns are as nothing in the scale. But I feel myself also willing to the sacrifice necessary, & have a just sense of the important & honourable command conferred upon me. The circumstances of this command are peculiar, & known only to those who have crossed the Atlantic & enabled to judge of it by a personal knowledge of the country.

This new world, when compared with Europe, is in almost every feature, a picture of youth entering on manhood, while the other declines with old age.

Europe, exhausted in strength & failing in vigour. America, British America I mean, is bursting forth with powers of which neither the Government in England or the country here is yet aware. Here are the resources of a great Empire, & we don't yet know how to call them forth; but here they are rapidly expanding, as if in due preparation for a great struggle at no distant day.

The United States & British America are growing up rivals; a hatred rooted in their cradle is growing up with their strength, & will make them for ever irreconcileable Enemies. My station at the head of one of those rival nations, at so critical a time, perhaps at the very moment of explosion, tho' I do not think that moment at hand now, is one of which any man may be proud, but in which also he must contemplate both difficulty & danger. While I look with great pleasure to the honour & the distinction on one side, these reflections darkening the other are the feelings of a mind naturally attached to Home, & to the friends found nowhere but there. If for an hour I give loose to them, sit upon them, & talk them over with myself, I will not give way to them. I'll go to my work with pleasure with an ardent desire of honour, and "I'll do my best in the best way I can," as Archbishop Tillotson expressed himself.

4TH JANUARY. I called today upon the old Lady (Mrs. Swann) whom I visited last year about this time, and with whom I was very much delighted. Without looking back at my papers, I must take a Memo today of her, altho' at risk of again repeating what I thought of her.

She had got notice of our visit, & received us with the greatest politeness – Judge Stewart, Mr. Temple, Couper & myself. We found the Attorney General with her, who I am inclined to suspect had also heard of my going & had thus as if by accident thrown himself in the way.

She is not in the least changed, "in good health & spirits," she says, "thank God, altho' I have outlived all the world of my own times." She told us today, on Judge Stewart asking whether she or Sir John Wentworth were youngest, that she was in her 87th year, and believed Sir John rather younger. Quite right, as he is just at the good old King's age, now 82.

She knows old DesBarres—"Oh, I know that fellow, but am not acquainted with him," — very significantly expressing the opinion which I find generally entertained of him. She thinks her memory as good as ever, & when asked on matters of old date, her answers are instantaneous. She remembers Halifax a green bank nearly covered with wood, & with only half a dozen houses, but she also perfectly recollects seeing from the house she now lives in, the first town of Halifax, on the side where Dartmouth stands, burnt by the Indians —that night they murdered & carried off 28 whites; the rest escaped to this side.

She remembers Governor Cornwallis, & every governor from that day to this; personally acquainted with them all.

She says Mr. Cornwallis was an excellent man, & perhaps the best Govr. that ever was in the Province—a younger brother of the late Marquis. He left all his property to the late Admiral Cornwallis, his 2nd brother.

Horatio Gates was his A.D.C. and she remembers he was the first person married in St. Paul's Church here; "the fellow," she added, "the ungrateful fellow afterwards went over to the American Rebels."

Mr. Bulkeley is recorded as Lt. Govr. at one period, but the Attorney General mentioned that he was Secretary of the Province & Clerk of Council; afterwards Member of Council, & fell into the temporary administration for a few months, on the death of Govr. Parr. "Mr. Bulkeley was a sensible & very good old man."

Such was the tenor of her conversation, lively and entertaining in her manner, but unluckily other visitors calling upon her, it was broke off, & we came away under pressing invitation to visit her again....

11TH JANUARY. Yesterday Lady D. with a party of 13 sleighs again went to the Dartmouth Lakes, driving round by Fletcher's Bridge & Fultz's Inn, a distance of 30 miles. An unlucky accident however happened by which Mrs. Col. Goodriche has had her arm broken by the unsetting of her sleigh.

I am not surprised at this, having dreaded some accident every time they have gone out. It is a feat of hardihood & danger for Ladies, tho' nothing for Gentlemen to perform. I have all along discouraged this romping fashion, & my apprehensions have proved but too well founded....

13TH JANUARY. Passed this morning in the boys' schoolroom. Jim in Phaedrus & Latin Grammar, doing very well. Ramsay, in Virgil & Horace, Xenophon & Homer, French, writing, Geography & Arithmetic is very forward in all, & doing exceedingly well under Mr. Temple.

18TH JANUARY.... Yesterday *Cyréné*, Capt. Tozer, sailed for Bermuda, after many delays & recalls by Admiral Griffith, the most undecided man I ever yet met with. None of the Captains of the Squadron think themselves sure of his orders until they have lost sight of his flag, & the cant phrase is, that the wind is very changeable at the Admiralty House. Tozer has been going every day these 10 days. At last he did sail at daybreak yesterday. At noon the weather began to lower & threaten a southerly gale. At 2 P.M. the admiral sent an order to Citadel Hill Telegraph, to recall *Cyréné*; fortunately the military posts have not the naval signals, otherwise Tozer must have returned from beyond the Light House. Such want of decision in an Admiral is lamentable.

20TH JANUARY. The Nov. mail from England arrived this morning, six days from New York, having passed Bermuda by orders without stopping. As my publick dispatches & most of my private letters have been addressed to Quebec they are gone forward there. I learn however that all are well at home. I am much gratified by an offer to be chosen Govr. of the Bank of Scotland in room of the late Duke of Buccleugh. Sir Wm. Rae, the Lord Advocate, my old & intimate school companion, had proposed it to my agent, Mr. Smith. I have written him immediately a hasty letter to say that I would consider it an honour done me in two points of view—the one, to fill any situation that had been accepted by my valued friend the late Duke of B. – the other, that so strong an expression of the favourable opinion of my Country is to me doubly gratifying in that part of the world in which I should most highly value public esteem.

25TH JANUARY. Day before yesterday, the weather being fine, & the roads in good order for sleighing, I went up to Mount Uniacke to spend a day or two with the Attorney General.

We went up the 27 miles in two hours & half without refreshing, & returned this morning in some minutes less. I detest sleighing as an amusement, cold & uncomfortable, but as travelling it is very easy & expeditious.

I had some time ago requested the Atty. Genl. to look into the Record Books of Council & make an index to the contents; he is doing this with great assiduity & ability.

27TH JANUARY. Old Paul, an Indian, brought me in today the head of a very large Moose. Talking with him about it, he tells me he had followed a pair of them for 8 miles & shot them both....

28TH JANUARY. The *Mersey* arrived this Evening from Bermuda, no mail. Reports that Island free of fever. Sir Wm. Lumley had arrived & assumed the Government in succession to Sir Jas. Cockburn.

30TH JANUARY.... A party of Gentlemen lately explored the woods from Horton Corner, South to Sherbrooke settlement, with the intention to ascertain the distance & nature of the soil. They took an Indian to guide them in the path thro' the forest. They soon saw he was not leading them correctly, but rather trying to mislead & confound them. At last he stopt & said there was no more path & attempted to run away; but they persevered by compass & soon found not only a path, but a sort of bridge over a stream, made after the manner of the Indians. He then told them, that there was there the only hunting ground left them in the Province, & that he did not wish the English should find it, as they soon would go take it like other parts. I did not imagine there was any such feeling as this remaining in the mind of the miserable tribe of Micmacs yet left. They returned by a more direct line, & made it about 16 miles thro' some good land, but also a great deal of swamp, and loose granite rocks. I conceive this to be the general face of the Western half of Nova Scotia....

2ND FEBRUARY.... The *Mersey* has just sailed for Bermuda, all crusted round in ice, & the sails & yards so frozen that her topsails alone are dropped to thaw by exposure to the sun....

8TH FEBRUARY. Visited the grammar school of Revd. Mr. Twining; I have long thought it might be made more useful to the community, by cutting off the infant branch which only learns the earliest lessons of English, & by restricting it more to older scholars, furnishing a supply to the classes of the College now building. Tho' Dr. Inglis & Judge Stewart, two of the Trustees, fully agree with me, & also Mr. Twining, yet various difficulties & trifles are urged by them, & so they say, "It is better to let it alone"—such is the stupid aversion that I find everywhere, even among the most respectable & most sensible men of this Province against any innovation for improvements....

13TH FEBRUARY.... On 10th I opened the Session of General Assembly, & yesterday received very gratifying addresses from both Houses. Little business of any importance being expected, there is but their attendance.

A very indecent mob pushed into the Hall of Council so as to make it almost impossible to obtain a proper passage to the Speaker & Members. When this grand Provincial House was opened last year, I urged strongly with the Chief Justice, as President of Council, that Regulations should be adopted from the outset to exclude the rabble. It was thought unnecessary; however the experience of the noise and tumult has convinced both Houses that it is now necessary. I yet doubt & dread their natural aversion to all innovation may let even this pass.

15TH FEBRUARY. Yesterday the *Carnation,* Capt. Hall, brought the Dec. mail up from Bermuda. Violent debates in Parliament on the state of the country, but happily tending strongly to support Ministers, & expressing the utmost Loyalty of the country to the Constitution....

27TH FEBRUARY. Sunday.... Our Scotch Presbyterian Church has suffered a severe blow this morning in Dr. Gray having been struck with Palsy, & lost the use of speech & of his whole right side. I have long dreaded this misfortune to the public, to himself & his large family.

A Micmac has brought today the annual winter dispatch from Gen. Ainslie at Sydney, Cape Breton. There also the winter has been more fine & mild than ever before known.

29TH FEBRUARY.... Dr. Gray is better & hopes are entertained of his yet recovering....

8TH MARCH. The General Meeting of the Provincial Agricultural Society was held today in the House of Assembly. A great deal of envious & illiberal ill will has been lately shewn by the public towards Agricola. Now that his name is known & that he can be attacked in the newspapers, anonymous writers assail him in ungentlemanlike language, & a strong disposition to annoy him was shewn today in the House, in voting him £250 for his labours as Secretary & Treasurer during this last year, but which after smart debate was granted.

I have found that Dr. Almon & a son of Dr. Cochrane at Windsor, not uninfluenced by the venom of the Rev. Dr. himself, are the chief writers & promoters of all this virulence against Agricola, and I do believe it proceeds entirely from malice, or an envy of the credit which these letters of Agricola have obtained him, & which honours perhaps he does not bear with prudent modesty amongst his class in the community.

While the one is more vain & overbearing than could be liked, Dr. Almon is mean & cunning, & Dr. Cochrane bitter & biting in his language.

Within these few days accounts have reached us by the States, that a Revolution has at last broke out in Spain, & that large bodies of troops are marching at once on Madrid from Cadiz, commanded by officers who have declared moderation to be their guide, but have taken a resolution to re-establish the Cortes. Such has long seemed to be the certain consequence of the cruel and senseless conduct of the King since his restoration from confinement in France. Instead of gratitude to those who supported the Royal Cause & the Cortes, while the Kingdom was occupied by the French, to those who actually restored to him his crown, Ferdinand has shewn nothing but harshness & injustice, allowing the influence of Priests & Ministers whom he has changed every month to send Patriots to prisons, and dungeons, without consideration or mercy.

14TH MARCH.... The Packet from New York homeward is just arrived. I bought today a very fine sow, one of a Cargo of live pigs

184

VII

brought here from Boston; big with young, I could not have her weighed, fearing to hurt her; I have taken her at a guess by her owner, 390 weight of 5 1/2 pence per lb., £9. A very fine animal from the stock of a Mr. Pearson at Bayfield near Boston. My object is to give the young ones away to improve the breed of hogs in this Province.

I have had much plague with the corps of Officers of the 60th; a number of improper persons had got commissions in this Regt. & it is only by degrees that we can get the mischief remedied. An Ensign Hutchinson, lately broke by sentence of Court Martial for striking the Paymaster Jellico without any sort of provocation, was a Porter at the Horseguards.

18TH MARCH. As usual I dined yesterday on St. Patrick's Day with the Irishmen here. Young Richard Uniacke, again in the Chair, did his duty in the same excellent style in which he acquitted himself last year; his toasts, tho' the common set on all public occasions, were eloquently & elegantly expressed, & the Evening passed very pleasantly. I left them about 11 o'clock after much laughing at a speech & blunder of the Attorney General. The old Gent., fond of speaking, but more so now in the midst of his countrymen & his son in the chair—perhaps too having filled his glass more fairly full than he usually does, opened a long thanks on his health having been drank, heaping compliments upon me without any measure or any mercy, his words flowed in full stream, while his fancy wandered. With great animation he burst into a new sentence, "But, Gentlemen of the Jury"—his habits at the Bar, generally addressing a Jury, got possession of his mind in the flight, & without losing the object he forgot to whom he was speaking. The room rung with cheers for some time; at last having pleaded the frailty of an old man's head & the natural habits of an old whip, he brought himself back very neatly to the very sentence he has been expressing.

Still going on at the same rate & with the same flow of words, he had very nearly once or twice again let go the "Gentlemen of the Jury."

Yesterday the joys of the day were nearly broke off by a report from Boston of the death of the good old King, but as it brought also an account almost circumstantial of that of the Duke of Kent, it may be a mistake or false report altogether. Of the former, however, it cannot surprise us. The latter does so exceedingly, & will be cause for deep national concern....

27TH MARCH. The mail brings us today London papers to 29th Jan. containing Gazette notification of the death of the Duke of Kent on 23rd Jan. & assurance, tho' not official, of that of the King on 29th....

28TH MARCH. The Duke of Kent must be lamented not only as a Prince of the Blood whose age & general health gave him the fairest prospects of one day wearing the Imperial Crown of Britain, but also as the Father of the Presumptive Heiress to it, & offering hopes of yet a large family. I think his loss a great national calamity, not inferior to that even of the Princess Charlotte of Wales. His virtues, his talents, his acquirements as a Prince, his services as a soldier & his knowledge of men & of society in all the variety of Rank & subordinate classes in which he has interested himself, fitted him for any station under the crown, & held him forth as eminently qualified to bear the sceptre of his venerable & revered Father.

I have served personally under the Duke of Kent, & in that opportunity of knowing him an intimate acquaintance was founded, which he has always encouraged to a degree farther than I was inclined to go in it. He was extravagant & foolish in squandering money of which he had not the command; he pushed upon society wherever he commanded, a French woman whom he kept, in a manner that was always offensive; altho' he always found some part of the Ladies who acceded to his request to visit Madame St. Laurent; his greatest fault was an overbearing & tyrannical system of military discipline, inconsistent with the nature & the feelings of Englishmen.

This he pushed to a height that was fatal to his own ambition as a soldier, & the source of all his disagreement with his elder brothers the Prince Regent & Duke of York; it was the cause of his removal from the command at Gibraltar & the obstacle to his military employment since 1804. With these foibles & faults, a more plain & easy man in private life, a more honourable, upright & religious man, a more kind, sincere & faithful friend never lived upon earth. His recollection of Officers & men generally at 30 years now gone by always astonished me, and his letters which I receive by every Packet

186

to his old acquaintances in this Province confirm my assertion. To myself for these 20 years past he has been at all times most easy, kind & gracious, & his last letter which I answered on the very day of his death will best record my feelings for him with his manners towards me. The good old King also has sunk to his peaceful rest, venerated & blessed by his People, a name to live in Honour while England's name shall last. His reign has been a period of trouble & ferment in politicks; of mixed disaster & glory more ruinous & more splendid than any other period of our history. We who have witnessed the Events of the last 30 years, while we censure & condemn the disgraceful proceedings of the first 20 years of the reign, may well exult in the glory of the setting sun of George 3rd.

With these mournful changes in our own Royal Family, we have now just received accounts of the Assassination of the Duc de Berri at Paris, one of those Kingly murders which are found so often in the history of that cursed nation. At the moment H.R. Highness came out of the Opera leading his Duchess to her carriage the ruffian seized him with his left arm & plunged a dagger to the hilt in his breast. He lingered it is said quite sensible till next morning.

30TH MARCH. The *Carnation,* Capt. Hall, sailed for Bermuda this morning to return immediately....

Capt. Hall gives us an interesting account of Newfoundland, on which station he has been these two years past. The red Indians there whom we have always understood to be mischievous, savage & watching to attack the white inhabitants, are quite the reverse; he says they are the most miserable creatures imaginable, wild as foxes & timid & cowardly as hares. Very few now remain & the repeated attempts to approach them have failed only from their wary timidity.

Of the country, the East & South coast is all rocky & unfit for cultivation. The inward coast fronting on the Labrador is good land. There the sailors kill vast quantities of wild fowl with sticks. From St. John's, vessels cut thro' the ice at all times of the winter, proceeding to the northward on the fishing of seals, or rather killing of them on the ice, which is done with sticks, approaching them while asleep. They are boiled up to extract the oil from them, & obtained in great quantities.

2ND APRIL. Easter Sunday, cold and raw feel. I received a notice

187

today from the Speaker, that the House of Assembly was ready to be prorogued tomorrow & desired leave to present to me an Address of Farewell, to which I agreed. Accordingly, notwithstanding a fall of snow during the night as deep as January, the House presented their address, very kindly expressed & making offer of a star-sword, value 1000 guineas, as a testimony of their regard. Altogether a very honourable & flattering distinction to me, of which in my answer I assured them I felt highly sensible, declining the offer however untill I had obtained His Majesty's permission to accept of it.

At 2 o'clock I went down & closed the Session, earnestly recommending a continuance of the measures I have begun & intimating my intention to revisit the Province in a few years in the hope of seeing progress made.

I confess I have very serious apprehension of a continuance of the good understanding that has existed in my time between the two Houses, and the Lower House and Governor. The Council & Governor are very cordially together; but the Council and Assembly have had several collisions this session, & the latter is petulant & grasping at more than their privileges; they do not abide by the rules of Parliament, & neglecting these seeming trifling formalities, they throw aside all regularity & order of proceeding. They have taken a fancy to be jealous of any interference or communication with the Governor during their session, & argue measures of Legislation without consulting whether such measures would be approved by the Council or by him in last stage. Incredibly ignorant, & too much self-interested, they have thus wasted a whole session, ending in some blunders of taxation, without giving rise or consideration to any one measure of prospective good to the country. The Council has rejected their Bills almost as fast as sent up. Several debates have been violent, particularly that on giving due encouragement to Agriculture, and the Speaker, Mr. Robie, an ill-tempered crab, deeply tinctured in Yankee principles, broke forth on one occasion into the most outrageous abuse of the Council "as a composition of Placemen & Pensioners, paid enemies of the people." This created a feeling of indignation in Council. I have not heard what took place, but that the Attorney General had urged to make the Speaker explain himself or apologise for these words. Since then, Robie has been so impudent as to say in public, laughing at it, that he supposes of course he will never fill that Chair again, that he does not care about it, as he has had neither honour, profit nor pleasure in it. I have ever entertained a bad opinion of him, & that is now more than confirmed, & I declare him not only an unfit person to be the Speaker, but equally unworthy to be His Majesty's Solicitor General, to which situation he was raised by Sir John Sherbrooke as a "grand coup de politique" to stop the mouth of an opposition member in his administration. Several members of whom I had a favorable opinion have shewn themselves very slippery gentlemen, & I fear will disturb the harmony of the Legislature unless Sir Jas. Kempt begins with a firm hand in the steps which I should have adopted had I remained here. These I shall express on paper before I go, & put into his hands.

7TH APRIL. Yesterday *Cyréné* arrived with the Feb. mails, bringing the official intelligence of the demise of H.M. George 3rd, and the order of Proclamation of George 4th. Having been prepared by the old Journals of Council for the Ceremony on this occasion, & due notice given to the Public, I went down at 10 o'clock to the Council Hall, where the Council being assembled, as also all the Judges, Clergy, Officers of the Army & Navy, many members of the House of Assembly & Gent. of the Bar, I stated to them that I had received dispatches from England which notified to me officially the death of the King, & which I desired might be read.

That done, I desired to proceed according to the enclosed instructions to proclaim His Majesty King George 4th our most gracious Sovereign, with a declaration of our allegiance & Loyal obedience to H.M. Government....

With all present I then went down to the front of the Province Building, where the Proclamation was read to the People, & again most heartily cheered. The Procession then formed with the Herald in an open carriage, and escorted by the military, & stopping successively in the market square, at St. Paul's church, & at the North Barrack parade where the troops in garrison were under arms to receive it. There a Royal salute was fired from six field pieces & the Procession returned to the Province Building. Meantime I had returned into Council & taken all the oaths administered to me by the Chief Justice, & then by the Clerk of Council by my order to the Members present.

At 1 o'clock the standard was lowered to half mast and sixty minute guns were fired, being the exact number of years the King had reigned. The standard was then hoisted up & a Royal Salute fired on the accession of George 4th. It remains hoisted all this day, but on Sunday to be hoisted only half mast & so untill further orders. As soon as the garrison salutes had fired, H.M. ships *Mersey* & *Cyréné* commenced their sixty minute guns, but reserve until tomorrow the further ceremony of salute on the accession.

9TH APRIL. Sunday. The church was hung as formerly in black cloth, and a funeral sermon preached by Dr. Inglis. Rather a weak & poor production than what I could have wished, & did expect from him, upon a subject so full of matter & so capable of exciting the highest colouring of language, without any risk of overstepping the bounds of truth or simple justice. The church was full as it could hold, & the congregation in the deepest mourning. It is a singular circumstance that at this moment the old Sir John Wentworth has sunk under the late intelligence from England. Of the same age as The King, upwards of 16 years Lt. Govr. of this Province, & latterly retired upon a pension of £1400 a year – deeply indebted to & attached to the Duke of Kent by the ties of friendship & gratitude, he felt that part of the melancholy intelligence as if he had lost his own son.

Sir John was a very good little man, & beloved in this community, but in his administration he was weak. He was made the tool & mischievous instrument of several men whose self interest was the sole guide of their advice; by large & improper grants of land he has greatly impeded the improvement of the country, & several of these yet lay altogether untouched in lots of 20,000 acres. They are liable to escheat to the King for non compliance with the conditions of all grants, but delicacy towards the old man has hitherto restrained me from ordering an enquiry into them. But that ought not to be delayed longer now....

12TH APRIL.... Six vessels entered yesterday afternoon from West Indies & States; the latter bring papers with London news of 2nd March. A very strange report of a plot detected to assassinate the whole of H.M. Ministers, when assembled at Lord Harrowby's at a Cabinet dinner. A man named Thistlewood & several Radicals taken in the act of consultation with a number of others in a stable &

hayloft. Thistlewood run a constable thro' the heart, with a sword or dagger; several other people wounded in the fray.

14TH APRIL. In considering more attentively the proceedings of the Session just closed, & hearing in public conversation for some days past a great deal said of the tone & temper of the House of Assembly, I have found that matters have been conducted very differently from what had outwardly appeared to be done. This secrecy is carried on by the House not permitting their daily proceedings to be published or communicated out of their own House; consequently the Govr. is kept in a state of ignorance untill the proceedings of the Session are published some months afterwards. I find now that several matters of public interest which I had recommended have been passed over & rejected in a manner secret & uncandid, exhibiting a sense of guilt while to the public eye they fawned & flattered.

I have therefore at once addressed a letter to the Speaker charging to him & the House with conduct such as I had not expected, retracting my former answer to their address, refusing the Star & Sword offered me, and requiring him to communicate without any delay my letter to each individual Member of the House. A copy of this letter I have kept with their address....

20TH APRIL. Met in Council today & dissolved the Assembly in consequence of the demise of the King. Writs at same time issued for a new Election, returnable on 10th July.

A fellow named Wilkie, of Radical Politicks, has lately made some noise here by a slanderous libel published against the Magistracy, & some associates have been writing threatening letters to the Judges, during this man's trial. I thought them altogether unworthy of notice, but the Judges do not think so, and a sum of £100, a large sum for this community, was ordered in Council by Proclamation to any person who shall lead to the conviction of the offenders....

23RD APRIL. Sunday.... For this week past I have been plagued with an inflammation on my left eye, almost blinding me. It is so unusual for me to ail at all, that I take very ill with the inconvenience, for it is nothing more. The Judges have thought better of the Proclamation & requested it may be withheld for the present. I believe Mrs. Halliburton & Mrs. Stewart had been alarmed by the letters, & their good fool husbands had been obliged to pacify them by the offer of reward.

28TH APRIL. I returned today from a short excursion into the country to try if a change of air or a few days of quiet walking & shooting exercise would remove this cloudy dimness from my eye. Hay & Schomberg Kerr & Dr. Strachan went with me, & took up our quarters at Fultz's. We passed our time very pleasantly & comfortably, but my blindness is the same, very little improved, and as my departure draws near, my arrangements become more pressing, my writing more necessary, & with all that my blindness more annoying.

I could not see to shoot, & was content to wander about with Strachan, a sensible & pleasant man, with the broadest Scotch accent I ever heard out of the country. He has served all his life in the Army, knows a great number of those whom I have also known in the various occurrences of Service, & he has an excellent memory to recall a propos the anecdotes of times gone by. He has an abundant conversation on subjects of Science connected with his medical study, mixing well with a good share of eccentricity in points of common. In short he kept us all alive with Colonel Harris, who came out a visitor to us.

There was little shooting but robins & a few scattered snipe & woodcocks. They found however a curiosity, a woodcock's nest with 4 eggs, & the bird sitting upon it, which removed all doubt. They were laid in an open ill-formed nest on the ground—singularly large, dark & speckled. They do not breed in this latitude. At this season they are seen one day & gone the next. Smaller than our woodcocks in England, & the breast feathers tinged with a reddish colour, I have got one to add to my little collection of stuffed birds which I have been endeavouring to gather for the museum of the College at Edinburgh, in compliance with a request of Principal Baird.

We have been looking very anxiously for the spring ships from England & Scotland; they are now 10 days later than usual, & it is unlucky they should be so this year, as they bring us a large & valuable supply of seed corn & implements for our agricultural societies.

2ND MAY. Yesterday was as usual a delightful May day, bright, warm & gay; all the lower orders turned out at daybreak to gather Mayflowers in the woods.

The examination of the Grammar school under Mr. Twining occupied me the whole forenoon. He has brought it forward very much indeed within these two years, and were it properly supported by the higher people, would soon prove a valuable school, but the indescribable aversion to any innovation, altho' of improvement, in this place opposes all attempts at it. The school is loaded with a number of boys of paupers, learning to read English without paying anything. 5 classes of Latin, 2 of Greek, writing & Mathematics to those who wish it, make a jumble beyond the reach of any one man to conduct with advantage to the boys. There are now 48 Latin scholars, 40 children in English; these last I have strongly urged should be taken away & placed in the national establishment which teaches only English & particularly applicable to the poor classes, but strange to say, after two years' trial, I am not a bit advanced. Dr. Inglis coolly states on the part of the Trustees that there are several objections & that they think the community would not like it. I should be glad to know what is the use of Trustees at all, if it be not to watch over & direct the improvement of the school for the general interest, without consulting the wishes of individuals?

This morning Lady D. gave a breakfast in the woods at Point Pleasant to a large party of children, after having gathered their loads of Mayflowers; they have remained out till Evening & are come home delighted with their sport. Ramsay over head in Love with a Miss Despard, and Jim not less so with his Bessy Boggs.

6TH MAY. Our first spring ship arrived from London, & fortunately is that on which are sent our agricultural seeds. Great fears were entertained that they would be too late for the season, but they are yet in good time.

7TH MAY. Sunday. I laid the foundation stone of Dartmouth Church two years ago, & this morning I went over to hear divine service performed in it, now quite finished. It is a very pretty village, growing fast.

8TH MAY. Today seven vessels from England & Scotland, generally long voyages, 34, 39, 42 days. The *Louise* from Aberdeen brings me a nice assortment of breeding pigs from my brother John. I have given them all to my aid de camp Agricola as his private property to use them as he thinks proper, certain that he will spread them in a way to improvements.

9TH MAY. I am much flattered but more plagued just now with addresses pouring in from distant parts of the Country as farewell compliments. I am pleased with the general feeling of the Province in regard to my administration, but I am disappointed & vexed, that a very few cunning Yankees in the House of Assembly this last session should have outwitted & defeated me in what I think one of the first objects of attention, to maintain a proper spirit & system in the Militia.

11TH MAY.... A copy of Sir Wm. Lumley's speech to the Legislature of Bermuda is sent to me; so violent an abuse of a House of Assembly perhaps never was penned, and must lead to unhappy results in that Government. Altho' the Executive has rights & prerogatives to check any ill advised measures of the Lower House, it has no right to speak unqualified abuse or deal severe censure on their deliberations. I am told he is quite a madman of a piece with some of the Lt. Governors nearer me here.

14TH MAY. Sunday.... In England the Elections are nearly over, with very trifling change of members, altho' there may be considerable change in Politicks in favour of ministers. Riot and outrage are still committing in Glasgow, Paisley and the manufacturing districts, where the lower orders are ill educated & prone to mischief.

My own private affairs are all put to rights by the friendly interference of Lord Succoth & MacLean. My farms are all let & well let to good tenants, tho' the rents are lower. My decided reference to them in November last has done me most essential service, for John Smith still confesses that he would not have let them on such terms, and the consequences must have been not only loss of rent, but an addition of debt of £5000 at least. I feel a load off my mind that made me very uneasy....

18TH MAY. I attended yesterday a dinner given to me by the Members of Council & all the respectable inhabitants of Halifax. Mr. Wallace in the chair, & old Pyke his croupier. About 200 sat down, & all went off very pleasantly. I am a bad hand at a speech, but on this occasion I was obliged to attempt it. My health being drank in very neat expression immediately after the King's, I felt really truly grateful & gathered my nerves as well as I was able....

[Lord Dalhousie then gave the text of his speech.]

I left them at 12 o'clock. The only strange exhibition of the day was His Majesty's Consul from New York, a Mr. Buchanan arrived in the Packet and going home. His health having been drank as the help & friend of distressed emigrants at New York, he made a most extraordinary speech in return. A wild roaring Irishman with a rank brogue, he praised the blessings of the British Constitution, & in the utmost search of abuse execrated the horrors of the democracy of the States. "As for these traitors to their King & Country, these Radicals, he declared to God that if he were their Judge, & to pass sentence upon them, he could think of no punishment so heavy as to send them all to the States, to that land of Liberty as it is called, there to taste the sweets of American liberty & protection."

23RD MAY.... Major Couper is gone home in the Packet sailed this morning. After being 12 years on my staff, it is a trial to part.... Couper ... naturally dislikes now the idea of Regimental duty. I have strongly urged upon him that that is the only road to military success, & tho' not so agreeable as a staff employ, it is much more sure. Still he casts a longing look to my staff, & has earnestly asked to be held in remembrance as military secretary on a vacancy, but he is not fit for such a situation....

Yesterday I laid, not the foundation stone but the corner stone of the College of Halifax. The lower part of the building being intended for shops, the College apartments are on the second range & front upon an upper parade ground or terrace. We made full ceremony of masonic and military honours, and as much insidious & secret influence has been used by Dr. Inglis & the Clergy of the Church of England against this Institution, so much so that the Bishop, now absent, has refused to be a Trustee to it, I thought it but Justice to myself & to this work to address those near me in a few words....

"This College of Halifax is founded for the instruction of youth in the higher classicks, & in all Philosophical studies. It is formed in imitation of the University of Edinburgh. Its doors will be open to all who profess the Christian Religion, to the youth of His Majesty's North American Provinces, to strangers residing here, to

Gentlemen of the Military as well as the learned professions, to all in short who may be disposed to devote a small part of their time to study.

"It does not oppose the College of Windsor, because it is well known that that college does not admit any students unless they subscribe to the tests required by the Established Church of England; & those tests exclude the great proportion of the Youth of this Province, and it is therefore more particularly intended for those who are excluded from Windsor. It is founded upon the Principles of Religious Toleration secured to you by your Laws; and upon that paternal protection which the King of England extends to all his subjects...."

31ST MAY. Most anxiously expecting & looking for Sir Jas. Kempt. This my last day is arrived, & no intelligence of him.

I have written to Lord Bathurst & to Canada that I should wait until the 31st & no longer. I must go, and I regret it exceedingly. I wished much to see my friend, & I had much to say to him on public matters here which I can't well put upon paper; & yet they are things necessary that he should know. All packed & almost all on board *Newcastle*. My horses sailed a week ago in a transport. I dine tomorrow with the Admiral & if possible shall sail next day.

2ND JUNE. In my life I never met with a circumstance so singularly fortunate & so apropos as the arrival of Kempt yesterday. At 12 o'clock a report of a ship to the Eastward was sent me from Citadel Hill, the weather so hazy could not be easily distinguished. At 2 P.M. she was made out to be a frigate, & at 6 P.M. an Aide de C. of Kempt's brought me his dispatches at the Admiral's.

As the day cleared & the ship neared, the anxiety of the town was all astir, & every countenance seemed overjoyed, all running about the streets & enquiring if it was true. I walked out to see the bustle, and could not have believed that the people felt so warmly alive to his arrival before I left them, tho' I knew that many of the leading merchants were desirous that I should have remained here to see him.

Sir James was anxious to land immediately, but as Lt. Governor I could not allow him without the honours usually paid, & these he received on landing this morning at 11 o'clock. At 3 P.M. I have just carried him down to Council where he took the usual Oaths, and I resigned the chair to him, wishing him the same happiness that I have enjoyed there. Sir Jas. is accompanied by a Major Raitt as Military Secretary, Hon. Major Gore and Lord Frederick Lennox as A.D.C.s.

5TH JUNE. These few days have enabled me to turn over all my papers quietly to Sir Jas. and to explain the actual state of the Province to him, so as to lead in the same course & to objects which I have not been able to overtake. I hope most sincerely that he will pursue his plans with patience & perseverance. There is an obstinacy & an aversion to improvement that may be led but will not be driven in this new world; a slowness that is sickening to a man of the other hemisphere, who has seen the rapidity with which art & science is bursting upon the intellects of the nations of Europe, & who feels the desire to open the eyes & the energies of men here as there. But it won't move out of its own pace & will require the patience of more than one man's life to do what seems to me within the accomplishment of a very few years.

Altho' the fog was unusually thick today, & sometimes so that we could not see across the street, I was resolved to embark this forenoon & put an end to all the form & ceremony the townspeople wished to shew me. At 11 I went down with Sir James to the Council Hall where the Council, Magistrates & Officers of the Garrison were assembled to receive us. The Militia flank were on the stairs & the troops lined the street down to the King's wharf. After remaining a quarter of an hour in the Council room, I proceeded to the Barge, attended by a very large assemblage.

I felt too much to dare to take leave of anyone, but simply thanked them for the honour done me.

On the barge giving way, the Militia guns & the Fort on George's Island commenced their salute, & whole shores gave us 3 hearty cheers. In a few minutes we were lost in fog & smoke. Reaching the *Newcastle* it fortunately cleared up & we saw the frigate in bright sunshine, yards manned all in clean white; a very pleasing & unexpected sight. Stepping on board we were again saluted.

No chance of sailing. I came on shore again in coloured cloaths, & feeling as a stranger relieved from all care or business.

197

6TH JUNE. A thick fog still holds, & weather variable. The wind is at North & fair for us, but I have resisted the Admiral's urgent desire & troublesome fidgeting to get us away, and stay to dine with Col. & Mrs. Harris, who regret as much as anybody does.

7TH JUNE. At 10 o'clock the *Newcastle* got under weigh & hove to for us below George's Island. The barge took us from the Engineer's or Lumber Yard, & we left the good people of Halifax, perhaps for ever.

I go now to higher honour & more extended command. I assume more important station in the eye of the world & undertake duties of greater consequence and of wider influence than I have yet been placed in. These ought to bring me to a most serious consideration of the change & make me think how dangerous it is for any man to give way to ambition & grasp at honour, from whence want of ability or want of acquirement & study may compel him to retire in mortification & disappointment; where a little too much rashness or a little too much caution may equally pronounce him unfit to stand, or where either the nature of the people on this side the Atlantic, or the unsatisfied or perhaps unreasonable expectations of those at home, may make his situation irksome & his life unhappy.

I have thought of this change in all these shapes, & in many others of more private nature which are not less important in my view of happiness in life. I do sincerely regret to leave the peaceful command in Nova Scotia, but I feel also that this is not an option for me to chuse in. As a soldier I can't shrink from superior honour on account of its dangers, nor after 30 years of active service ought I to condemn myself without an effort.

I am well aware that now, every word I utter and every step I take will be canvassed & perhaps twisted to my disadvantage. I know that there is a long settled disposition to oppose the measure of Government in Canada, & that the station of Governor there is not that quiet enjoyment of command to which I have been accustomed here. I know too that there are men who have gained honours deservedly, and yet lost them in not knowing how to wear them, while some have obtained the approbation of their King & Country, & yet have fallen a sacrifice to unmerited outcry & personal enemies. But these are the rocks & shoals in my destined voyage thro' life. I must go to my work willingly, fearing no dangers tho' I know them to be in my way. I must at starting assume a confidence in my march that may at least give me a chance of success, and of that satisfactory close in Canada which an unbiassed, impartial & straightforward discharge of my duties has obtained me here.

D[ALHOUSIE]

Epilogue

The end of the story is rather sad. Ramsay went to Harrow, as planned; Jim and Mr. Temple stayed on in Canada for a couple of years, and then Jim went to Oxford and Ramsay into the army and then to India with his father.

In India they all fell victim to ill health and returned as invalids. Ramsay's condition is described as a rheumatism; he lost the sight of one eye, became terribly crippled and emaciated, and the handsome fair-haired young man of twenty died in pain before he was thirty.

Lord Dalhousie died not long after – blind, infirm, a sad shadow of the man who had in Halifax been so handsome, so energetic and healthy. India killed him, as it did so many others.

Little Jim thus became the tenth Earl, and to India he went too, eventually, as Governor-General; he also suffered in health for most of the years he spent there. His much-loved wife died of fever on the ship going home to England. It was a tale told all too often.

Notes

MAY 1816

Lady D.: Throughout the Journal, Lord Dalhousie refers to his wife affectionately as Lady D. She was Miss Christian Broun (1786-1839), daughter of Charles Broun of Coalstoun in East Lothian, not far from Edinburgh. She was some fifteen years younger than her husband; she died only a few months after him, on the 22nd of January, 1839, while sitting in conversation in the house of her old friend Dean Ramsay of Edinburgh.

The Duke of York: Frederick, second son of George III (1763-1827), and Commander-in-Chief of the Army.

Earl Bathurst: Henry, third Earl (1762-1834), at the time Secretary of War and the Colonies.

Sir Gordon Drummond (1771-1854): Born in Quebec City, son of Colin Drummond, Paymaster General of the forces in Lower Canada. Served in the Napoleonic wars, returned to Canada in 1813 as second in command to Sir George Prevost. His vigorous execution of the war against the United States turned the tide of events in favour of the British. He captured Niagara, commanded the land forces in the combined operation against Oswego and won the fiercely contested victory at Lundy's Lane. In 1815 he succeeded Prevost as Commander in Chief and Administrator of the Canadas.

JUNE 1816

D. Castle: Dalhousie Castle, then in a rural area some miles from Edinburgh, today on the fringes of the city. It is perhaps the oldest castle in continuous use in Scotland, and in 1816 was already well over 400 years old. In recent years Dalhousie Castle has been variously a school, a hotel and a restaurant serving mediaeval dinners. The present Earl of Dalhousie lives elsewhere.

The Prince Regent: George Augustus Frederick, Prince of Wales and later King George IV (1762-1830), eldest son of George III and Queen Charlotte. George III was old and ailing and in the last years of his mental illness, and the Prince of Wales happily grasped the reins of power as Prince Regent.

Lord Melville: Robert Saunders Dundas, second Viscount Melville

VIII

(1771-1851). Educated at Edinburgh High School with Lord Dalhousie. Melville was First Lord of the Admiralty.

Sir John Coape Sherbrooke (1764-1830): Professional soldier and colonial administrator. After years of active service in almost every quarter of the globe, he was appointed Lieutenant-Governor of Nova Scotia in 1811, succeeding Sir George Prevost. He capably conducted Nova Scotia through the War of 1812 and was then posted to the Canadas. He left Halifax in June 1816, and Major-General Smyth acted as Administrator until Lord Dalhousie arrived in October.

John Smith: Lord Dalhousie's agent or factor who administered the estate, renting the farms, and so on. Smith proved to be too young and inexperienced for the job.

13TH SEPTEMBER

Lady Louis: Wife of Sir John Louis, captain of the *Forth*.

20TH SEPTEMBER

Admiral Sir David Milne: Of Edinburgh. Born 1763, entered the Royal Navy in 1779. Had a long, active career in the Napoleonic Wars. In 1816 he was appointed Commander in Chief of the North American Station, with *Leander* as his flagship, but his departure was delayed so that he could take part in the expedition that year against the pirate stronghold of Algiers. The heavy British bombardment lasted only eight hours, but it ended the cruel trade in Christian slaves that had terrorized the Mediterranean for centuries. The *Leander* required major repairs after the battle, and it was 1817 before the Admiral reached Halifax.

30TH SEPTEMBER

Major Couper: Aide-de-camp to Lord Dalhousie. As Captain George Couper, 92nd Highlanders, he had served with Dalhousie in the Peninsular Wars. After the War of 1812 he rejoined Dalhousie's staff and subsequently served on the staff of Sir James Kempt, Dalhousie's successor in Nova Scotia. He turns up again in Canada as Military Secretary to Lord Durham in 1838. He seems to have spent much time with Jim, the Dalhousies' youngest son, who travelled with them, for when Jim grew up to become Governor General of India, he referred to Couper (by then Sir George Couper, Bart.) as "my oldest friend."

19TH SEPTEMBER

Sambro Head: Guards the outer approaches to Halifax Harbour. There has been a lighthouse at Sambro since 1759.

24TH OCTOBER

George's Island: At that time this small green island in the harbour was an important part of the fortifications of Halifax.

General Smyth: Lieutenant-General George Strachey Smyth, Governor of New Brunswick from 1817 to 1823. He was said to be more a military man than an administrator, with a soldier's strong views on questions of authority and prerogative, and his term of office was stormy. But the military administrators in early Canada do not seem to have conformed to any stereotype; the authoritarian Smyth was interested in improving both education and agriculture.

Taking my seat in Parliament: Under the 1707 Treaty of Union between Scotland and England, sixteen Scottish peers were elected to represent the rest of the Scottish peerage in the House of Lords in Westminster, and from 1796 to 1815 Dalhousie was a representative peer. This system has lapsed and now all Scottish peers have seats in the House of Lords.

Chief Justice Blowers: Sampson Salter Blowers (1743-1843), Chief Justice of Nova Scotia from 1797 to 1833. The son of Lieut. Blowers who died at the seige of Louisburg, Justice Blowers was born in Boston, and, a Harvard man, had a successful career in Boston and New York before coming to Halifax as a Loyalist. He was appointed Attorney-General of the new Nova Scotia, as reconstituted after 1784 (when the huge land-mass that had been Nova Scotia was split into three provinces, New Brunswick, Nova Scotia and Cape Breton). He was elected Speaker of the House of Assembly in 1785, a post he vacated after he was appointed to the Legislative Council in 1788. He became Chief Justice in 1797.

Government House: Still the residence of the Lieutenant-Governor and one of the architectural pleasures of Halifax. Built in the Adam style, faced with sandstone from the quarry at Wallace in Nova Scotia, it was completed in 1805. The architect was Isaac Hildreth, a Yorkshireman.

11TH NOVEMBER

Point Pleasant: A park at the tip of the peninsula on which Halifax stands, it looks out to the harbour entrance and the open Atlantic. It is nearly 200 acres in extent, with paths skirting the shore and wandering through the woods. Queen Victoria leased the park to the citizens of Halifax for 999 years.

24TH NOVEMBER

St. Paul's Church: Built in 1750, the year after Halifax was founded. It was the first Protestant church in British North America and is today the oldest building in the city. Of white frame, modelled on St. Peter's Vere Street, Marylebone, London, built by James Gibbs in 1721.

Dr. John Inglis (1777-1850): The son of Dr. Charles Inglis (1734-1816), the first Bishop of Nova Scotia. Charles Inglis had been Rector of Trinity Church in New York, had lost his house and all his possessions and seen his church burnt in the American War of Independence. He came to Nova Scotia in 1787. Father and son were King's men and Tories. Dr. John Inglis became the third Bishop of Nova Scotia in 1825.

1ST DECEMBER

Michael Wallace: Provincial Treasurer, also a strong Tory.

15TH DECEMBER

The Scotch Kirk: Originally known as Mather's church and used by all dissenters, it eventually, according to T.B. Akins, historian of early Halifax, "fell into the hands of the Presbyterians" and became St. Matthew's Church and the property of the Church of Scotland. Today it flourishes in a new location and is the property of the United Church of Canada.

26TH JANUARY, 1817

Sparrow: One of Dalhousie's aides. He left Halifax in the following June, promoted to Lieutenant-Colonel, for service in Jamaica.

Judge Wilkins: Lewis Morris Wilkins, a Judge on the Pictou circuit, M.L.A., Speaker in 1806. Came from a Loyalist family.

1ST FEBRUARY

York Redoubt: A fort on the shore of Halifax harbour.

11TH FEBRUARY

Mount Uniacke: Built by Richard John Uniacke (1753-1830), who was born in Dublin and studied for the Bar in Dublin and London. He came to Nova Scotia in 1776, before the Loyalist migration, and, like many others, deeply resented Colonial Office policy of rewarding Loyalists at the expense of older settlers. His appointment as Attorney-General did not come to him until 1797, when the Loyalist Sampson Blowers was made Chief Justice. Uniacke did much for the slowly growing province; he campaigned for colonial advancement and for aid from Britain, and as early as 1806 he had begun to think of legislative union of the Maritime Provinces and eventually of the Canadas. The house he built at Mount Uniacke must have been the most beautiful of its time in Nova Scotia. Until 1949 the Uniacke family owned it; it is now part of the Nova Scotia Museum complex.

12TH FEBRUARY

Horton, Cornwallis, Cape Blowmedown and the Bason of Minas: Horton, first known as Mud Creek, was renamed Wolfville about 1850. Kentville, the neighbouring town, was first called Horton's Corners. Early maps show Cornwallis as a community, but it was a township as well. In this thickly settled part of the Annapolis Valley, with towns and villages running together, it is difficult today to pinpoint a community that might have been the Corwallis of the old maps. Cape Blowmedown is now Blomidon, a majestic promontory 670 feet high that extends into the Minas Basin. The origin of the name is uncertain. Blowmedown is sometimes used by Lord Dalhousie, whose spelling of place names was erratic; he tries several versions. But his spelling of Bason was customary at the time. The township was the unit of settlement; typically, it was ten miles square, or, if on navigable water, twelve miles in depth with a nine-mile water frontage.

King's College, Dr. Porter and Dr. Cochrane: Dr. William Cochrane, a graduate of Trinity College, Dublin, had originally been the President of King's College at Windsor (founded by Bishop Charles Inglis in 1788). However, new statutes required that the president be a graduate of Oxford, Cambridge or King's itself. Dr. Cochrane was replaced by Dr. Charles Porter, an Oxford man, an appointment that gave good reason for rancour and bitterness.

15TH FEBRUARY

Mr. Robie: Simon Bradstreet Robie (1770-1858). Lawyer, politician, M.L.A., Speaker of the House of Assembly.

4TH MARCH

General Ainslie: George Robert Ainslie (1776-1839). Scots-born, entered the British Army, served in campaigns in Flanders and Holland. His particular interest was in old coins, and he published an important numismatic study, *Anglo-French Coinage.*

Fort Cumberland: On the border between New Brunswick and Nova Scotia, now again called Fort Beauséjour and a National Historic Park.

18TH APRIL

The insult offered to the Regent: After Waterloo and the end of the wars, Britain suffered a catastrophic depression. Bad debts and bankruptcy flourished, and hundreds of factories closed. In such a deluge of ruin, it was an added disaster that the summer of 1816 (the first without war in fourteen years) should prove the worst in living memory. Crops all over Britain failed. After a winter of bitter starvation, riots and mass demonstrations broke out in many places, with much political tension. Compared to the rioting the insult to the Prince Regent was minor: driving to Westminster through a mocking crowd to open Parliament, the glass of his coach was broken in two places, either by stones or bullets.

10TH JULY

Moose Island: The Treaty of Ghent after the War of 1812 restored peace and (in part) the 1783 boundary between New Brunswick and Maine. A commission was set up to define that boundary more accurately, together with the ownership of Moose Island, in Passamaquoddy Bay.

17TH JULY

Sir George Prevost: After an energetic army career in the Napoleonic wars, he was appointed Lieutenant-Governor of Nova Scotia in 1808. In 1811 he was transferred to Quebec, where he proved to be particularly successful in creating harmony with the French Canadians. But as Commander in Chief of the British forces in Canada during the War of 1812, Prevost was personally responsible for two humiliating episodes: the withdrawal after the successful attack on Sackett's Harbour and the disastrous defeat at Plattsburg. He was recalled to England but died a week before he was to be courtmartialled.

29TH JULY

The Packet Signal: There was an excellent view of the harbour approaches from Citadel Hill (Fort George) in the centre of the city. A system had been devised to signal what type of vessel had been sighted from the hill. Mail was brought by Packets.

31ST AUGUST

Des Barres' Charts: Colonel Joseph Frederick Wallet Des Barres (1721-1824), cartographer and rugged individualist. He was born in Switzerland of Huguenot stock, educated at Basel and at the Royal Military College, Woolwich. When in 1784 Cape Breton was separated from the mainland of Nova Scotia, Des Barres was made the first Lieutenant-Governor. He was an impetuous spender and his duties as governor ruined him financially. He also dreamed of becoming a landed proprietor in the English style, and obtained grants for large tracts of land along the Northumberland Straits. To this area he brought Protestant settlers from Montbeliard, a small independent Protestant duchy near Alsace. Today there are hundreds of people in the shore communities, with names such as Tattrie, Langille and Patriquin, who are descendants of the Des Barres settlers. His dream of establishing his own duchy was fraught with endless litigation and financial problems, and his domestic life was eccentric and caused a good deal of gossip. But his professional life was beyond criticism: he was probably the best-qualified military engineer in North America. From 1763 to 1773 he, with a group of assistants, surveyed the coast of Nova Scotia and Cape Breton, and his superb collection of charts, plans and views was published as *The Atlantic Neptune*. It is still astonishingly accurate. Des Barres retired to Halifax in 1813 and died in 1824 at the age of 103.

10TH SEPTEMBER

Mr. Mortimer: Edward Mortimer (1767-1819). The most important businessman in Pictou and indeed in the eastern part of the province. He arrived penniless from Scotland and prospered in the timber business, fisheries and general trade with the West Indies. He built a fine stone house in Pictou in the late Georgian style. He was a strong supporter of Thomas McCulloch both as a member of the Assembly and in his efforts to launch Pictou Academy and keep it going. Mortimer was elected as member for Pictou in 1799.

Judge Halliburton: Sir Brenton Halliburton (1775-1860). A distinguished member of a Loyalist family, he came to Nova Scotia in

1783. He studied law in England, was admitted to the Nova Scotia Bar in 1803, appointed Chief Justice in 1833 and knighted in 1859.

Judge Wiswall: Peleg Wiswall, another Loyalist judge.

11TH SEPTEMBER

Coal Mines at the East River: Coal had been discovered in 1798. Dr. James McGregor, the minister, took out a government licence to dig coal on his own property and regularly got out his winter's supply. By 1817 coal in the Pictou area was being used commercially in large quantities.

14TH SEPTEMBER

Father Burke: The first Catholic Bishop in Halifax, widely liked and respected throughout the province. He arrived from Montreal in 1801, full of zeal, and found the Irish population in great need of education. The anti-Catholic laws had not yet been repealed and Catholics were forbidden to have their own schools. Though Burke was not officially able to open a school, he seems to have taught clandestinely in his own house, while the governor tolerantly turned a blind eye to this infraction of the law. An act to emancipate Catholics was passed in 1829.

17TH SEPTEMBER

Pictou in 1775: Mr. Uniacke's memory may be faulty here. Robert Patterson and James McCabe arrived in Pictou in 1767, along with four other families. More important was the landing in 1773 of the first emigrant ship from Scotland, the *Hector*. By 1775 there were about 50 families settled in the area. It is true, however, that there were no roads.

Mr. Archibald of Truro: S.G.W. Archibald (1777-1846). One of the most successful lawyers of his day. His family came to Nova Scotia before the Loyalist migration in 1783; they were therefore classed as Pre-Revolutionary Loyalists, a matter of great pride. He was continuously a member of the Assembly from 1806 to 1834, and during that time was Speaker, Solicitor-General and Attorney General.

19TH SEPTEMBER

Souiac River: This is the Stewiacke River. At least one old map gives this spelling, as do early land deeds.

28TH SEPTEMBER

The Chesapeake blacks at Preston: There were three major migrations of blacks to Nova Scotia in the late eighteenth and early nineteenth century: the Black Loyalists in 1783, after the American War of Independence, the Maroons from Jamaica in 1796 and the refugee blacks from the War of 1812. Dalhousie is referring here to a group of refugees brought to Halifax after the British expedition to Chesapeake Bay in 1814, when they seized the city of Washington and burned public buildings. Hundreds of plantation slaves made their way to the British ships and begged to be given their freedom. They were brought to Halifax and granted small plots of land in Preston, already a black settlement. Dalhousie persuaded an unwilling Lord Bathurst to extend the period during which they would be given rations and other help, but he was never very optimistic about their being self-supporting in the near future.

8TH OCTOBER

Clermont: The seat of the late Bishop Charles Inglis, was on the outskirts of the town of Aylesford. Bishop Inglis died at Clermont in 1816.

1ST DECEMBER

120 Scotchmen and St. Andrew: This would have been a meeting of the North British Society, founded in 1768 and still in existence.

6TH DECEMBER

The Castine duties: In September 1814, Sir John Sherbrooke led an expedition to the Maine coast and captured several communities, including the fort at Castine. These American outports had been trading secretly with Britain. After Sherbrooke's invasion the trade was carried on openly and the British collected customs duties at Castine. By the end of the war some £10,000 had been amassed, and this fund was turned over to Dalhousie to use for the benefit of the colony.

10TH JANUARY 1818

The death of Princess Charlotte: She was the daughter of the Prince Regent (the future George IV) by his estranged wife Princess Caroline. Her grandparents, George III and Queen Charlotte, had fifteen children, but Princess Charlotte was their sole legitimate heir and the only heir to the throne. Of their six daughters, only three married, and rather late in life. None had had children. The sons,

Charlotte's uncles, had sired many children, but none then living was legitimate. So her death in childbirth was indeed a serious blow. As a result the Duke of Kent was forced into marriage "for the succession," and fathered Victoria.

1ST MAY

Admiralty Instance Court: The Court of Vice-Admiralty, Maritime causes and contracts.

17TH MAY

Duke of Richmond: Charles Lennox (1764-1819), Governor General of the Canadas, 1818-19. He had been Lord Lieutenant of Ireland 1807-13, where he lived in such regal state that he could not afford afterwards to live at Goodwood, his estate in England, and in 1813 he moved to Brussels, where living was cheaper. It was his Duchess who gave the famous ball the night before the battle of Waterloo. He was a professional soldier and had served with Wellington in several of his campaigns. The Canadians were highly flattered to have a governor of the rank and distinction of the Duke of Richmond.

7TH JULY

Mr. Prescott: Charles Ramage Prescott (1772-1859). Owner of the Prescott House, one of the finest examples of Georgian domestic architecture in Nova Scotia. The foundations for the house were laid in 1799. Prescott's parents came to Nova Scotia before the Loyalist migration of 1783 and flourished there. Prescott himself became a prosperous merchant, but he owes his fame to his work in horticulture and his contribution to the development of the Nova Scotia apple industry. Dalhousie had noted the poor quality of apples in the Annapolis Valley. Preston generously supplied grafting stock to farmers and, thanks to him, Nova Scotians have ever since enjoyed such apples as Gravensteins, Blenheims, Alexanders, Golden Pippins, Baldwins, Greenings and Sweet Boughs.

1ST AUGUST

Lt. Ross of the Nova Scotia Fencibles: Lieut. William Ross' farm, Rosebank, is today a glowing example of good mid-nineteenth-century husbandry and farming practice, for it is a farm museum operated by the Nova Scotia Museum.

18TH AUGUST

The good old Queen: Charlotte, wife of George III, mother of the Prince Regent, who was to become George IV.

3RD SEPTEMBER

Jeffery's maps: Thomas Jeffery, map engraver, carried on his trade at St. Martin's Lane in London. He was appointed Geographer to the Prince of Wales, later George III. He specialized in North American maps. Died 1771.

10TH SEPTEMBER

Mr. Kavanagh's in St. Peter's: Laurence Kavanagh (1764-1830), the first Catholic to be elected to the House of Assembly. He was elected in 1820 but he did not take his seat until 1823, after permission had been received from King George IV. The reason for the delay was that all Members were required to take an oath against transubstantiation, and Kavanagh refused to take the oath. A procedure was finally worked out that made it possible for Kavanagh (and other elected Catholics) to take their seats without abjuring their faith. Thus Catholic Emancipation came about in Nova Scotia six years earlier than in Britain.

3RD NOVEMBER

Judge Stewart: A Loyalist from the southern United States, educated at Edinburgh University.

Howe our Postmaster: John Howe (1754-1835), a Loyalist, born in Boston. He was a printer and publisher and became publisher of the *Nova Scotia Gazette.* He set a new standard of printing in the Maritimes and was appointed Deputy Postmaster-General in 1803. He was the father of Joseph Howe, journalist and politician.

Mr. Gourlay, disturber of Upper Canada: Robert Gourlay was a Scottish reformer, a complex and exasperating visionary whose irrational and impractical proposals probably delayed the land reforms Upper Canada so urgently needed. Bad judgment in his pursuit of justice got him into trouble with the authorities in Britain. He came to Canada in 1817 with the hope of retrieving his fortunes, but became involved in a struggle with the ruling oligarchy. Perhaps his worst offence was to organize a convention that was seen as dangerously close to the sort of mass demonstration which had resulted in the attack on the Prince Regent in 1817. In Ontario he was harassed, imprisoned and finally deported. It would be easy for those who supported his causes to lament Gourlay's methods, and easy for those who distrusted him to see him as mad. See also Dalhousie's references to Gourlay and Spa Field on 13 July, 1819.

Bouchette: Colonel Joseph Bouchette (1774-1841), Surveyor-General of Quebec. He surveyed the country along the St. Croix River to ascertain where the boundary between New Brunswick and Maine should run.

1ST DECEMBER

Agricola: John Young (1773-1837). Born near Falkirk, educated at Glasgow University, emigrated to Nova Scotia about 1815. In 1818 he contributed to the *Acadian Recorder* a number of articles pointing out the backward state of agriculture in the province, and in 1822 these articles were published in book form as the *Letters of Agricola*. As a result of the articles in the *Acadian Recorder,* a provincial Board of Agriculture was created in 1818 and Young was appointed Secretary in the following year. From 1825 until 1837 he sat as Member for Sydney in the Assembly.

15TH DECEMBER

Garrison Library: This Library still exists, a facility available to the personnel of Maritime Command. It is now called the Cambridge Library.

21ST JUNE 1819

The red Indian tribe: These were the Beothucks, the aboriginal inhabitants of Newfoundland, now extinct; the last member of the tribe died in 1829. There is evidence today to suggest that the Beothucks died as much from tuberculosis as from genocide.

1ST JULY

Castle St. Louis: The Château St. Louis, the Governor's residence at Quebec.

3RD JULY

The steamboat Malsham: We tend to forget that Fulton's *Clermont,* the first commercial paddle-steamer, was launched as early as 1807. John Molson the brewer and hotel-keeper had his first steamship, the *Accommodation,* running between Quebec and Montreal in 1809.

5TH JULY

Sir Peregrine Maitland (1777-1854): Of high moral character but imbued with such excessively conservative ideas that he was unsuitable as a colonial administrator. His persecution of the Reformers in Upper Canada was such that he was removed from office in 1828. In compensation he was named Lieutenant-Governor of Nova Scotia.

Robert Gourlay: A meeting at Spa Field in London at the end of 1816 was turned into a riot by men wearing the revolutionary tricolour. One man was killed. It was not long since the horrors of the French Revolution, and for a man to call himself a democrat was tantamount to declaring himself a revolutionary. Maitland had dealt with Gourlay by getting an act passed by the Legislature banning "seditious meetings."

18TH JULY

Paymaster Scott: Brother of Sir Walter Scott, the anonymous author of the Waverley Novels. Sir Walter acquiesced in rumours attributing the novels to others, especially to his brother Thomas, then in Canada.

23RD JULY

Futtering: A fine Scots verb meaning to bungle.

26TH JULY

Sir John Johnson (1742-1830): Second baronet, a Loyalist. Only son of Sir William Johnson and his white wife, Catherine Weisenberg. (By his Indian wife, Molly Brant, William had at least eight children.) In 1774 Sir John inherited his father's estates in the Mohawk Valley, but in 1776, because of his Loyalist sympathies, he fled to Canada. He took a prominent part in the border forays that marked the latter stages of the revolutionary war. In 1782 he became Superintendent-General of Indian Affairs of British North America.

29TH JULY

Bishop Mountain (1749-1825): Jacob Mountain, first Anglican Bishop of Quebec.

30TH OCTOBER

Mr. Wilson, farmer: Mr. Wilson's troubles are precisely those which caused so much popular unrest in Britain in 1816 and 1817.

12TH APRIL 1820

Thistlewood & several Radicals: The Spa Field riot of 1816 had developed into an attempted assault on the Tower of London, led by one Arthur Thistlewood. Thistlewood and his group had plotted to assassinate the whole of the Cabinet, including the Prime Minister; the ministerial heads were to be exhibited to the mob and borne on pikes to the Mansion House, the official residence of the Lord Mayor, where Thistlewood was to be proclaimed President of a Provisional Government.

REFERENCES

		YEAR
SIR JOHN JOHNSON	140, 147, 148	1819
BANK OF MONTREAL	105	1818
BEGINS COLLEGE AT HALIFAX	110	1819
x QUEBEC	119, 120	"
MONTREAL	123, 124	"
JOHN MOLSON & MANSION HOUSE HOTEL	124	"
JOEL STONE & GANANOQUE	127, 128	"
COMMENTS ON VARIOUS GOVERNORS	129, 130	"
YORK (TORONTO)	131	"
NIAGARA FALLS	134, 135	"
x QUEBEC CITY	151	"
DO (BATTLEFIELD)	152	"
FREDERICTON	71	1817